William Shakespeare (bapt. 26 April 1564 – 23 April 1616) was an English poet, playwright and actor, widely regarded as the greatest writer in the English language and the world's greatest dramatist. He is often called England's national poet and the "Bard of Avon". His extant works, including collaborations, consist of approximately 39 plays, 154 sonnets, two long narrative poems, and a few other verses, some of uncertain authorship. His plays have been translated into every major living language and are performed more often than those of any other playwright. Shakespeare was born and raised in Stratford-upon-Avon, Warwickshire. At the age of 18, he married Anne Hathaway, with whom he had three children: Susanna and twins Hamnet and Judith. Sometime between 1585 and 1592, he began a successful career in London as an actor, writer, and part-owner of a playing company called the Lord Chamberlain's Men, later known as the King's Men. At age 49 (around 1613), he appears to have retired to Stratford, where he died three years later. (Source: Wikipedia)

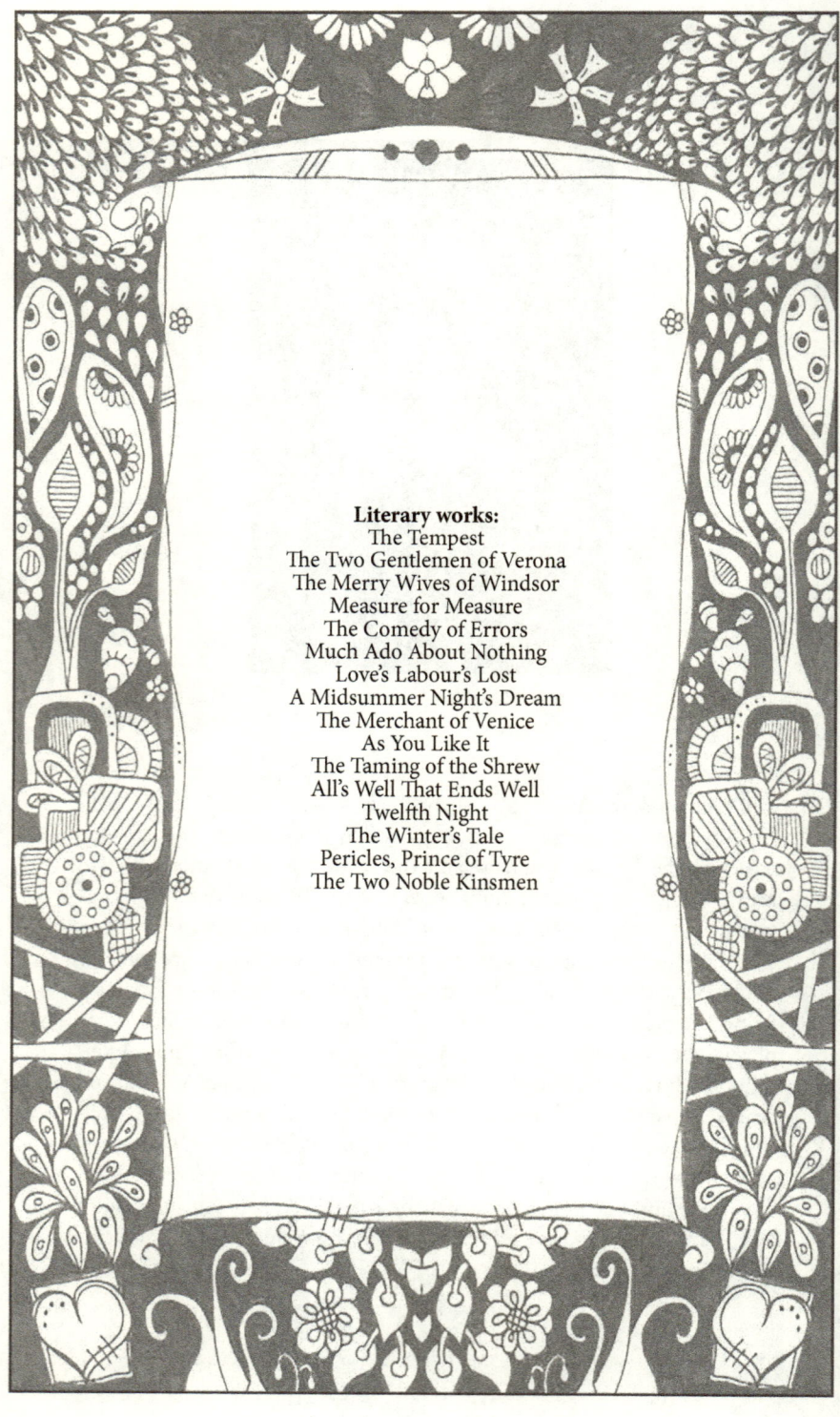

Literary works:
The Tempest
The Two Gentlemen of Verona
The Merry Wives of Windsor
Measure for Measure
The Comedy of Errors
Much Ado About Nothing
Love's Labour's Lost
A Midsummer Night's Dream
The Merchant of Venice
As You Like It
The Taming of the Shrew
All's Well That Ends Well
Twelfth Night
The Winter's Tale
Pericles, Prince of Tyre
The Two Noble Kinsmen

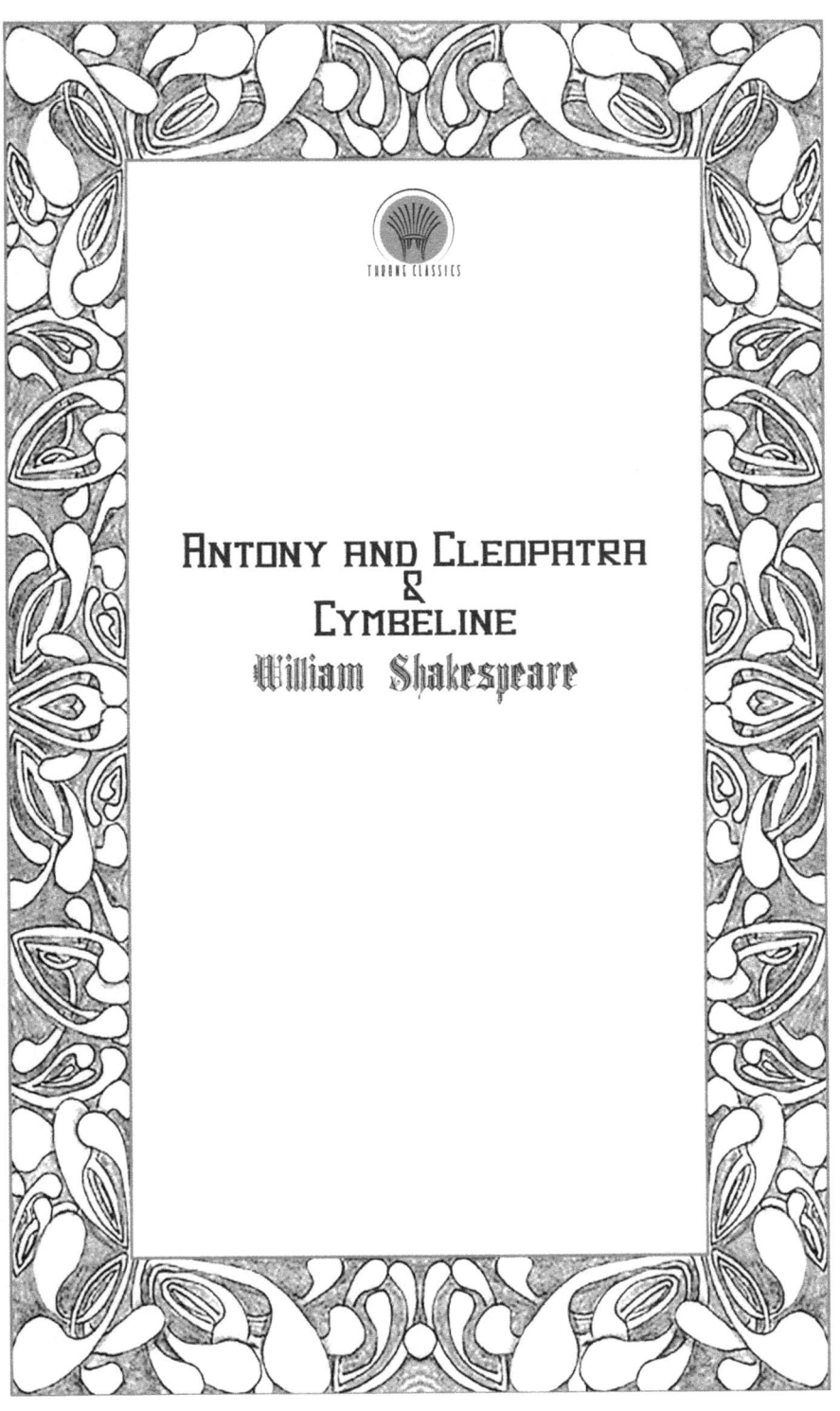

THRONG CLASSICS

Antony and Cleopatra
&
Cymbeline

William Shakespeare

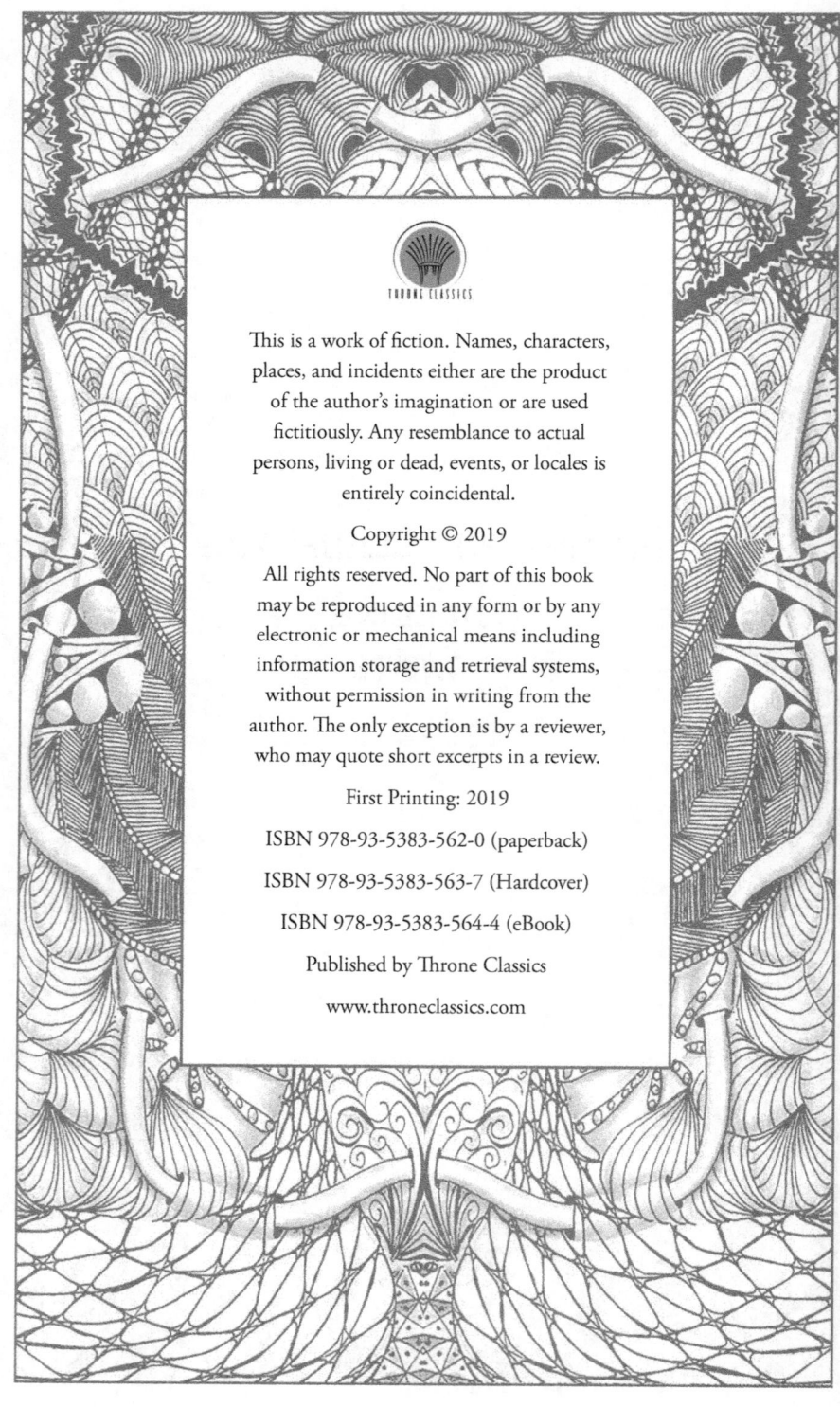

First Printing: 2019

ISBN 978-93-5383-562-0 (paperback)

ISBN 978-93-5383-563-7 (Hardcover)

ISBN 978-93-5383-564-4 (eBook)

Published by Throne Classics

www.throneclassics.com

Contents

Antony and Cleopatra
&
Cymbeline

ANTONY AND CLEOPATRA

PERSONS REPRESENTED.

M.ANTONY, Triumvir

OCTAVIUS CAESAR, Triumvir

M. AEMIL. LEPIDUS, Triumvir

SEXTUS POMPEIUS Triumvir

DOMITIUS ENOBARBUS, friend to Antony

VENTIDIUS, friend to Antony

EROS, friend to Antony

SCARUS, friend to Antony

DERCETAS, friend to Antony

DEMETRIUS, friend to Antony

PHILO, friend to Antony

MAECENAS, friend to Caesar

AGRIPPA, friend to Caesar

DOLABELLA, friend to Caesar

PROCULEIUS, friend to Caesar

THYREUS, friend to Caesar

GALLUS, friend to Caesar

MENAS, friend to Pompey

MENECRATES, friend to Pompey

VARRIUS, friend to Pompey

TAURUS, Lieutenant-General to Caesar

CANIDIUS, Lieutenant-General to Antony

SILIUS, an Officer in Ventidius's army

EUPHRONIUS, an Ambassador from Antony to Caesar

ALEXAS, attendant on Cleopatra

MARDIAN, attendant on Cleopatra

SELEUCUS, attendant on Cleopatra

DIOMEDES, attendant on Cleopatra

A SOOTHSAYER

A CLOWN

CLEOPATRA, Queen of Egypt

OCTAVIA, sister to Caesar and wife to Antony

CHARMIAN, Attendant on Cleopatra

IRAS, Attendant on Cleopatra

Officers, Soldiers, Messengers, and other Attendants

ACT I.

SCENE I. Alexandria. A Room in CLEOPATRA'S palace.

[Enter DEMETRIUS and PHILO.]

PHILO.

Nay, but this dotage of our general's

O'erflows the measure: those his goodly eyes,

That o'er the files and musters of the war

Have glow'd like plated Mars, now bend, now turn,

The office and devotion of their view

Upon a tawny front: his captain's heart,

Which in the scuffles of great fights hath burst

The buckles on his breast, reneges all temper,

And is become the bellows and the fan

To cool a gipsy's lust.

[Flourish within.]

Look where they come:

Take but good note, and you shall see in him

The triple pillar of the world transform'd

Into a strumpet's fool: behold and see.

[Enter ANTONY and CLEOPATRA, with their trains; Eunuchs fanning her.]

CLEOPATRA.

If it be love indeed, tell me how much.

ANTONY.

There's beggary in the love that can be reckon'd.

CLEOPATRA.

I'll set a bourn how far to be belov'd.

ANTONY.

Then must thou needs find out new heaven, new earth.

[Enter an Attendant.]

ATTENDANT.

News, my good lord, from Rome.

ANTONY.

Grates me:—the sum.

CLEOPATRA.

Nay, hear them, Antony:

Fulvia perchance is angry; or who knows

If the scarce-bearded Caesar have not sent

His powerful mandate to you: 'Do this or this;

Take in that kingdom and enfranchise that;

Perform't, or else we damn thee.'

ANTONY.

How, my love!

CLEOPATRA.

Perchance! Nay, and most like:—

You must not stay here longer,—your dismission

Is come from Caesar; therefore hear it, Antony. —

Where's Fulvia's process?—Caesar's I would say?—Both?—

Call in the messengers.—As I am Egypt's queen,

Thou blushest, Antony; and that blood of thine

Is Caesar's homager: else so thy cheek pays shame

When shrill-tongu'd Fulvia scolds.—The messengers!

ANTONY.

Let Rome in Tiber melt, and the wide arch

Of the rang'd empire fall! Here is my space.

Kingdoms are clay: our dungy earth alike

Feeds beast as man: the nobleness of life

Is to do thus [Embracing]; when such a mutual pair

And such a twain can do't, in which I bind,

On pain of punishment, the world to weet

We stand up peerless.

CLEOPATRA.

Excellent falsehood!

Why did he marry Fulvia, and not love her?—

I'll seem the fool I am not; Antony

Will be himself.

ANTONY.

But stirr'd by Cleopatra.—

Now, for the love of Love and her soft hours,

Let's not confound the time with conference harsh:

There's not a minute of our lives should stretch

Without some pleasure now:—what sport to-night?

CLEOPATRA.

Hear the ambassadors.

ANTONY.

Fie, wrangling queen!

Whom everything becomes,—to chide, to laugh,

To weep; whose every passion fully strives

To make itself in thee fair and admir'd!

No messenger; but thine, and all alone

To-night we'll wander through the streets and note

The qualities of people. Come, my queen;

Last night you did desire it:—speak not to us.

   [Exeunt ANTONY and CLEOPATRA, with their Train.]

DEMETRIUS.

Is Caesar with Antonius priz'd so slight?

PHILO.

Sir, sometimes when he is not Antony,

He comes too short of that great property

Which still should go with Antony.

DEMETRIUS.

I am full sorry

That he approves the common liar, who

Thus speaks of him at Rome: but I will hope

Of better deeds to-morrow. Rest you happy!

[Exeunt.]

SCENE II. Alexandria. Another Room in CLEOPATRA'S palace.

[Enter CHARMIAN, IRAS, ALEXAS, and a Soothsayer.]

CHARMIAN. Lord Alexas, sweet Alexas, most anything Alexas, almost most absolute Alexas, where's the soothsayer that you praised so to the queen? O that I knew this husband, which you say must charge his horns with garlands!

ALEXAS.

Soothsayer,—

SOOTHSAYER.

Your will?

CHARMIAN.

Is this the man?—Is't you, sir, that know things?

SOOTHSAYER.

In nature's infinite book of secrecy

A little I can read.

ALEXAS.

Show him your hand.

[Enter ENOBARBUS.]

ENOBARBUS.

Bring in the banquet quickly; wine enough

Cleopatra's health to drink.

CHARMIAN.

Good, sir, give me good fortune.

SOOTHSAYER.

I make not, but foresee.

CHARMIAN.

Pray, then, foresee me one.

SOOTHSAYER.

You shall be yet far fairer than you are.

CHARMIAN.

He means in flesh.

IRAS.

No, you shall paint when you are old.

CHARMIAN.

Wrinkles forbid!

ALEXAS.

Vex not his prescience; be attentive.

CHARMIAN.

Hush!

SOOTHSAYER.

You shall be more beloving than beloved.

CHARMIAN.

I had rather heat my liver with drinking.

ALEXAS.

Nay, hear him.

CHARMIAN. Good now, some excellent fortune! Let me be married to three kings in a forenoon, and widow them all: let me have a child at fifty, to whom Herod of Jewry may do homage: find me to marry me with Octavius Caesar, and companion me with my mistress.

SOOTHSAYER.

You shall outlive the lady whom you serve.

CHARMIAN.

O, excellent! I love long life better than figs.

SOOTHSAYER.

You have seen and prov'd a fairer former fortune

Than that which is to approach.

CHARMIAN. Then belike my children shall have no names:—pr'ythee, how many boys and wenches must I have?

SOOTHSAYER.

If every of your wishes had a womb,

And fertile every wish, a million.

CHARMIAN.

Out, fool! I forgive thee for a witch.

ALEXAS.

You think none but your sheets are privy to your wishes.

CHARMIAN.

Nay, come, tell Iras hers.

ALEXAS.

We'll know all our fortunes.

ENOBARBUS. Mine, and most of our fortunes, to-night, shall be—

drunk to bed.

IRAS.

There's a palm presages chastity, if nothing else.

CHARMIAN.

E'en as the o'erflowing Nilus presageth famine.

IRAS.

Go, you wild bedfellow, you cannot soothsay.

CHARMIAN. Nay, if an oily palm be not a fruitful prognostication, I cannot scratch mine ear.—Pr'ythee, tell her but worky-day fortune.

SOOTHSAYER.

Your fortunes are alike.

IRAS.

But how, but how? give me particulars.

SOOTHSAYER.

I have said.

IRAS.

Am I not an inch of fortune better than she?

CHARMIAN. Well, if you were but an inch of fortune better than I, where would you choose it?

IRAS.

Not in my husband's nose.

CHARMIAN. Our worser thoughts heavens mend!—Alexas,—come, his fortune! his fortune!—O, let him marry a woman that cannot go, sweet Isis, I beseech thee! And let her die too, and give him a worse! and let worse follow worse, till the worst of all follow him laughing to his grave, fiftyfold a cuckold! Good Isis, hear me this prayer, though thou deny me a matter of more weight; good Isis, I beseech thee!

IRAS. Amen. Dear goddess, hear that prayer of the people! for, as it is a heartbreaking to see a handsome man loose-wived, so it is a deadly sorrow to behold a foul knave uncuckolded: therefore, dear Isis, keep decorum, and fortune him accordingly!

CHARMIAN.

Amen.

ALEXAS. Lo now, if it lay in their hands to make me a cuckold, they would make themselves whores but they'd do't!

ENOBARBUS.

Hush! Here comes Antony.

CHARMIAN.

Not he; the queen.

[Enter CLEOPATRA.]

CLEOPATRA.

Saw you my lord?

ENOBARBUS.

No, lady.

CLEOPATRA.

Was he not here?

CHARMIAN.

No, madam.

CLEOPATRA.

He was dispos'd to mirth; but on the sudden

A Roman thought hath struck him.—Enobarbus,—

ENOBARBUS.

Madam?

CLEOPATRA.

Seek him, and bring him hither.—Where's Alexas?

ALEXAS.

Here, at your service.—My lord approaches.

CLEOPATRA.

We will not look upon him: go with us.

[Exeunt CLEOPATRA, ENOBARBUS, CHAR., IRAS, ALEX., and
Soothsayer.]

[Enter ANTONY, with a MESSENGER and Attendants.]

MESSENGER.

Fulvia thy wife first came into the field.

ANTONY.

Against my brother Lucius.

MESSENGER.

Ay:

But soon that war had end, and the time's state

Made friends of them, jointing their force 'gainst Caesar;

Whose better issue in the war, from Italy

Upon the first encounter, drave them.

ANTONY.

Well, what worst?

MESSENGER.

The nature of bad news infects the teller.

ANTONY.

When it concerns the fool or coward.—On:—

Things that are past are done with me.—'Tis thus;

Who tells me true, though in his tale lie death,

I hear him as he flatter'd.

MESSENGER.

Labienus,—

This is stiff news,—hath, with his Parthian force,

Extended Asia from Euphrates;

His conquering banner shook from Syria

To Lydia and to Ionia;

Whilst,—

ANTONY.

Antony, thou wouldst say,—

MESSENGER.

O, my lord!

ANTONY.

Speak to me home, mince not the general tongue:

Name Cleopatra as she is call'd in Rome;

Rail thou in Fulvia's phrase; and taunt my faults

With such full licence as both truth and malice

Have power to utter. O, then we bring forth weeds

When our quick minds lie still; and our ills told us

Is as our earing. Fare thee well awhile.

MESSENGER.

At your noble pleasure.

[Exit.]

ANTONY.

From Sicyon, ho, the news! Speak there!

FIRST ATTENDANT.

The man from Sicyon—is there such an one?

SECOND ATTENDANT.

He stays upon your will.

ANTONY.

Let him appear.—

These strong Egyptian fetters I must break,

Or lose myself in dotage.—

[Enter another MESSENGER.]

What are you?

SECOND MESSENGER.

Fulvia thy wife is dead.

ANTONY.

Where died she?

SECOND MESSENGER.

In Sicyon:

Her length of sickness, with what else more serious

Importeth thee to know, this bears. [Gives a letter.]

ANTONY.

Forbear me.

[Exit MESSENGER.]

There's a great spirit gone! Thus did I desire it:

What our contempts doth often hurl from us,

We wish it ours again; the present pleasure,

By revolution lowering, does become

The opposite of itself: she's good, being gone;

The hand could pluck her back that shov'd her on.

I must from this enchanting queen break off:

Ten thousand harms, more than the ills I know,

My idleness doth hatch—ho, Enobarbus!

[Re-enter ENOBARBUS.]

ENOBARBUS.

What's your pleasure, sir?

ANTONY.

I must with haste from hence.

ENOBARBUS. Why, then we kill all our women: we see how mortal an unkindness is to them; if they suffer our departure, death's the word.

ANTONY.

I must be gone.

ENOBARBUS. Under a compelling occasion, let women die: it were pity to cast them away for nothing; though, between them and a great cause they should be esteemed nothing. Cleopatra, catching but the least noise of this, dies instantly; I have seen her die twenty times upon far poorer moment: I do think there is mettle in death, which commits some loving act upon her, she hath such a celerity in dying.

ANTONY.

She is cunning past man's thought.

ENOBARBUS. Alack, sir, no: her passions are made of nothing but the finest part of pure love: we cannot call her winds and waters, sighs and tears; they are greater storms and tempests than almanacs can report: this cannot be cunning in her; if it be, she makes a shower of rain as well as Jove.

ANTONY.

Would I had never seen her!

ENOBARBUS. O sir, you had then left unseen a wonderful piece of work; which not to have been blest withal would have discredited your travel.

ANTONY.

Fulvia is dead.

ENOBARBUS.

Sir?

ANTONY.

Fulvia is dead.

ENOBARBUS.

Fulvia?

ANTONY.

Dead.

ENOBARBUS. Why, sir, give the gods a thankful sacrifice. When it pleaseth their deities to take the wife of a man from him, it shows to man the tailors of the earth; comforting therein that when old robes are worn out there are members to make new. If there were no more women but Fulvia, then had you indeed a cut, and the case to be lamented: this grief is crown'd with consolation; your old smock brings forth a new petticoat:—and, indeed, the tears live in an onion that should water this sorrow.

ANTONY.

The business she hath broached in the state

Cannot endure my absence.

ENOBARBUS. And the business you have broached here cannot be without you; especially that of Cleopatra's, which wholly depends on your abode.

ANTONY.

No more light answers. Let our officers

Have notice what we purpose. I shall break

The cause of our expedience to the queen,

And get her leave to part. For not alone

The death of Fulvia, with more urgent touches,

Do strongly speak to us; but the letters too

Of many our contriving friends in Rome

Petition us at home: Sextus Pompeius

Hath given the dare to Caesar, and commands

The empire of the sea; our slippery people,—

Whose love is never link'd to the deserver

Till his deserts are past,—begin to throw

Pompey the Great, and all his dignities,

Upon his son; who, high in name and power,

Higher than both in blood and life, stands up

For the main soldier: whose quality, going on,

The sides o' the world may danger: much is breeding

Which, like the courser's hair, hath yet but life

And not a serpent's poison. Say, our pleasure

To such whose place is under us, requires

Our quick remove from hence.

ENOBARBUS.

I shall do't.

[Exeunt.]

SCENE III. Alexandria. A Room in CLEOPATRA'S palace.

[Enter CLEOPATRA, CHARMIAN, IRAS, and ALEXAS.]

CLEOPATRA.

Where is he?

CHARMIAN.

I did not see him since.

CLEOPATRA.

See where he is, who's with him, what he does:—

I did not send you:—if you find him sad,

Say I am dancing; if in mirth, report

That I am sudden sick: quick, and return.

[Exit ALEXAS.]

CHARMIAN.

Madam, methinks, if you did love him dearly,

You do not hold the method to enforce

The like from him.

CLEOPATRA.

What should I do, I do not?

CHARMIAN.

In each thing give him way; cross him in nothing.

CLEOPATRA.

Thou teachest like a fool,—the way to lose him.

CHARMIAN.

Tempt him not so too far; I wish, forbear;

In time we hate that which we often fear.

But here comes Antony.

[Enter ANTONY.]

CLEOPATRA.

I am sick and sullen.

ANTONY.

I am sorry to give breathing to my purpose,—

CLEOPATRA.

Help me away, dear Charmian; I shall fall;

It cannot be thus long, the sides of nature

Will not sustain it.

ANTONY.

Now, my dearest queen,—

CLEOPATRA.

Pray you, stand farther from me.

ANTONY.

What's the matter?

CLEOPATRA.

I know by that same eye there's some good news.

What says the married woman?—You may go.

Would she had never given you leave to come!

Let her not say 'tis I that keep you here,—

I have no power upon you; hers you are.

ANTONY.

The gods best know,—

CLEOPATRA.

O, never was there queen

So mightily betray'd! Yet at the first

I saw the treasons planted.

ANTONY.

Cleopatra,—

CLEOPATRA.

Why should I think you can be mine and true,

Though you in swearing shake the throned gods,

Who have been false to Fulvia? Riotous madness,

To be entangled with those mouth-made vows,

Which break themselves in swearing!

ANTONY.

Most sweet queen,—

CLEOPATRA.

Nay, pray you, seek no colour for your going,

But bid farewell, and go: when you su'd staying,

Then was the time for words: no going then;—

Eternity was in our lips and eyes,

Bliss in our brows' bent; none our parts so poor

But was a race of heaven: they are so still,

Or thou, the greatest soldier of the world,

Art turn'd the greatest liar.

ANTONY.

How now, lady!

CLEOPATRA.

I would I had thy inches; thou shouldst know

There were a heart in Egypt.

ANTONY.

Hear me, queen:

The strong necessity of time commands

Our services awhile; but my full heart

Remains in use with you. Our Italy

Shines o'er with civil swords: Sextus Pompeius

Makes his approaches to the port of Rome;

Equality of two domestic powers

Breed scrupulous faction: the hated, grown to strength,

Are newly grown to love: the condemn'd Pompey,

Rich in his father's honour, creeps apace

Into the hearts of such as have not thriv'd

Upon the present state, whose numbers threaten;

And quietness, grown sick of rest, would purge

By any desperate change. My more particular,

And that which most with you should safe my going,

Is Fulvia's death.

CLEOPATRA.

Though age from folly could not give me freedom,

It does from childishness:—can Fulvia die?

ANTONY.

She's dead, my queen.

Look here, and, at thy sovereign leisure, read

The garboils she awak'd;at the last, best.

See when and where she died.

CLEOPATRA.

O most false love!

Where be the sacred vials thou shouldst fill

With sorrowful water? Now I see, I see,

In Fulvia's death how mine receiv'd shall be.

ANTONY.

Quarrel no more, but be prepar'd to know

The purposes I bear; which are, or cease,

As you shall give theadvice. By the fire

That quickens Nilus' slime, I go from hence

Thy soldier, servant, making peace or war

As thou affect'st.

CLEOPATRA.

Cut my lace, Charmian, come;—

But let it be: I am quickly ill and well,

So Antony loves.

ANTONY.

My precious queen, forbear;

And give true evidence to his love, which stands

An honourable trial.

CLEOPATRA.

So Fulvia told me.

I pr'ythee, turn aside and weep for her;

Then bid adieu to me, and say the tears

Belong to Egypt: good now, play one scene

Of excellent dissembling; and let it look

Like perfect honour.

ANTONY.

You'll heat my blood: no more.

CLEOPATRA.

You can do better yet; but this is meetly.

ANTONY.

Now, by my sword,—

CLEOPATRA.

And target.—Still he mends;

But this is not the best:—look, pr'ythee, Charmian,

How this Herculean Roman does become

The carriage of his chafe.

ANTONY.

I'll leave you, lady.

CLEOPATRA.

Courteous lord, one word.

Sir, you and I must part,—but that's not it;

Sir, you and I have lov'd,—but there's not it;

That you know well: something it is I would,—

O, my oblivion is a very Antony,

And I am all forgotten.

ANTONY.

But that your royalty

Holds idleness your subject, I should take you

For idleness itself.

CLEOPATRA.

'Tis sweating labour

To bear such idleness so near the heart

As Cleopatra this. But, sir, forgive me;

Since my becomings kill me, when they do not

Eye well to you: your honour calls you hence;

Therefore be deaf to my unpitied folly,

And all the gods go with you! upon your sword

Sit laurel victory! and smooth success

Be strew'd before your feet!

ANTONY.

Let us go. Come;

Our separation so abides, and flies,

That thou, residing here, goes yet with me,

And I, hence fleeting, here remain with thee.

Away!

[Exeunt.]

SCENE IV. Rome. An Apartment in CAESAR'S House.

[Enter OCTAVIUS CAESAR, LEPIDUS, and Attendants.]

CAESAR.

You may see, Lepidus, and henceforth know,

It is not Caesar's natural vice to hate

Our great competitor. From Alexandria

This is the news:—he fishes, drinks, and wastes

The lamps of night in revel: is not more manlike

Than Cleopatra;, nor the queen of Ptolemy

More womanly than he: hardly gave audience, or

Vouchsaf'd to think he had partners: you shall find there

A man who is the abstract of all faults

That all men follow.

LEPIDUS.

I must not think there are

Evils enow to darken all his goodness:

His faults in him seem as the spots of heaven,

More fiery by night's blackness; hereditary

Rather than purchas'd; what he cannot change

Than what he chooses.

CAESAR.

You are too indulgent. Let's grant it is not

Amiss to tumble on the bed of Ptolemy;

To give a kingdom for a mirth; to sit

And keep the turn of tippling with a slave;

To reel the streets at noon, and stand the buffet

With knaves that smell of sweat: say this becomes him,—

As his composure must be rare indeed

Whom these things cannot blemish,—yet must Antony

No way excuse his foils when we do bear

So great weight in his lightness. If he fill'd

His vacancy with his voluptuousness,

Full surfeits and the dryness of his bones

Call on him for't: but to confound such time

That drums him from his sport, and speaks as loud

As his own state and ours,—'tis to be chid

As we rate boys, who, being mature in knowledge,

Pawn their experience to their present pleasure,

And so rebel to judgment.

[Enter a Messenger.]

LEPIDUS.

Here's more news.

MESSENGER.

Thy biddings have been done; and every hour,

Most noble Caesar, shalt thou have report

How 'tis abroad. Pompey is strong at sea;

And it appears he is belov'd of those

That only have fear'd Caesar: to the ports

The discontents repair, and men's reports

Give him much wrong'd.

CAESAR.

I should have known no less:

It hath been taught us from the primal state

That he which is was wish'd until he were;

And the ebb'd man, ne'er lov'd till ne'er worth love,

Comes dear'd by being lack'd. This common body,

Like to a vagabond flag upon the stream,

Goes to and back, lackeying the varying tide,

To rot itself with motion.

MESSENGER.

Caesar, I bring thee word

Menecrates and Menas, famous pirates,

Make the sea serve them, which they ear and wound

With keels of every kind: many hot inroads

They make in Italy; the borders maritime

Lack blood to think on't, and flush youth revolt:

No vessel can peep forth but 'tis as soon

Taken as seen; for Pompey's name strikes more

Than could his war resisted.

CAESAR.

Antony,

Leave thy lascivious wassails. When thou once

Was beaten from Modena, where thou slew'st

Hirtius and Pansa, consuls, at thy heel

Did famine follow; whom thou fought'st against,

Though daintily brought up, with patience more

Than savages could suffer: thou didst drink

The stale of horses, and the gilded puddle

Which beasts would cough at: thy palate then did deign

The roughest berry on the rudest hedge;

Yea, like the stag when snow the pasture sheets,

The barks of trees thou browsed'st; on the Alps

It is reported thou didst eat strange flesh,

Which some did die to look on: and all this,—

It wounds thine honour that I speak it now,—

Was borne so like a soldier that thy cheek

So much as lank'd not.

LEPIDUS.

'Tis pity of him.

CAESAR.

Let his shames quickly

Drive him to Rome; 'tis time we twain

Did show ourselves i' thefield; and to that end

Assemble we immediate council: Pompey

Thrives in our idleness.

LEPIDUS.

To-morrow, Caesar,

I shall be furnish'd to inform you rightly

Both what by sea and land I can be able

To front this present time.

CAESAR.

Till which encounter

It is my business too. Farewell.

LEPIDUS.

Farewell, my lord: what you shall know meantime

Of stirs abroad, I shall beseech you, sir,

To let me be partaker.

CAESAR.

Doubt not, sir;

I knew it for my bond.

[Exeunt.]

SCENE V. Alexandria. A Room in the Palace.

[Enter CLEOPATRA, CHARMIAN, IRAS, and MARDIAN.]

CLEOPATRA.

Charmian,—

CHARMIAN.

Madam?

CLEOPATRA.

Ha, ha!—

Give me to drink mandragora.

CHARMIAN.

Why, madam?

CLEOPATRA.

That I might sleep out this great gap of time

My Antony is away.

CHARMIAN.

You think of him too much.

CLEOPATRA.

O, 'tis treason!

CHARMIAN.

Madam, I trust, not so.

CLEOPATRA.

Thou, eunuch Mardian!

MARDIAN.

What's your highness' pleasure?

CLEOPATRA.

Not now to hear thee sing; I take no pleasure

In aught an eunuch has; 'tis well for thee

That, being unseminar'd, thy freer thoughts

May not fly forth of Egypt. Hast thou affections?

MARDIAN.

Yes, gracious madam.

CLEOPATRA.

Indeed!

MARDIAN.

Not in deed, madam; for I can do nothing

But what indeed is honest to be done:

Yet have I fierce affections, and think

What Venus did with Mars.

CLEOPATRA.

O Charmian,

Where think'st thou he is now? Stands he or sits he?

Or does he walk? or is he on his horse?

O happy horse, to bear the weight of Antony!

Do bravely, horse! for wott'st thou whom thou mov'st?

The demi-Atlas of this earth, the arm

And burgonet of men.—He's speaking now,

Or murmuring 'Where's my serpent of old Nile?'

For so he calls me.—Now I feed myself

With most delicious poison:—think on me,

That am with Phoebus' amorous pinches black,

And wrinkled deep in time? Broad-fronted Caesar,

When thou wast here above the ground I was

A morsel for a monarch: and great Pompey

Would stand and make his eyes grow in my brow;

There would he anchor his aspect and die

With looking on his life.

[Enter ALEXAS.]

ALEXAS.

Sovereign of Egypt, hail!

CLEOPATRA.

How much unlike art thou Mark Antony!

Yet, coming from him, that great medicine hath

With his tinct gilded thee.—

How goes it with my brave Mark Antony?

ALEXAS.

Last thing he did, dear queen,

He kiss'd,—the last of many doubled kisses,—

This orient pearl: his speech sticks in my heart.

CLEOPATRA.

Mine ear must pluck it thence.

ALEXAS.

'Good friend,' quoth he

'Say, the firm Roman to great Egypt sends

This treasure of an oyster; at whose foot,

To mend the petty present, I will piece

Her opulent throne with kingdoms; all the east,

Say thou, shall call her mistress.' So he nodded,

And soberly did mount an arm-girt steed,

Who neigh'd so high that what I would have spoke

Was beastly dumb'd by him.

CLEOPATRA.

What, was he sad or merry?

ALEXAS.

Like to the time o' the year between the extremes

Of hot and cold, he was nor sad nor merry.

CLEOPATRA.

O well-divided disposition!—Note him,

Note him, good Charmian; 'tis the man; but note him:

He was not sad,—for he would shine on those

That make their looks by his; he was not merry,—

Which seem'd to tell them his remembrance lay

In Egypt with his joy; but between both:

O heavenly mingle!—Be'st thou sad or merry,

The violence of either thee becomes,

So does it no man else.—Mett'st thou my posts?

ALEXAS.

Ay, madam, twenty several messengers.

Why do you send so thick?

CLEOPATRA.

Who's born that day

When I forget to send to Antony

Shall die a beggar.—Ink and paper, Charmian.—

Welcome, my good Alexas.—Did I, Charmian,

Ever love Caesar so?

CHARMIAN.

O that brave Caesar!

CLEOPATRA.

Be chok'd with such another emphasis!

Say 'the brave Antony.'

CHARMIAN.

The valiant Caesar!

CLEOPATRA.

By Isis, I will give thee bloody teeth

If thou with Caesar paragon again

My man of men.

CHARMIAN.

By your most gracious pardon,

I sing but after you.

CLEOPATRA.

My salad days,

When I was green in judgment:—cold in blood,

To say as I said then!—But come, away;

Get me ink and paper: he shall have every day

A several greeting,

Or I'll unpeople Egypt.

[Exeunt.]

ACT II.

SCENE I. Messina. A Room in POMPEY'S house.

[Enter POMPEY, MENECRATES, and MENAS.]

POMPEY.

If the great gods be just, they shall assist

The deeds of justest men.

MENECRATES.

Know, worthy Pompey,

That what they do delay they not deny.

POMPEY.

Whiles we are suitors to their throne, decays

The thing we sue for.

MENECRATES.

We, ignorant of ourselves,

Beg often our own harms, which the wise powers

Deny us for our good; so find we profit

By losing of our prayers.

POMPEY.

I shall do well;

The people love me, and the sea is mine;

My powers are crescent, and my auguring hope

Says it will come to the full. Mark Antony

In Egypt sits at dinner, and will make

No wars without doors: Caesar gets money where

He loses hearts: Lepidus flatters both,

Of both is flatter'd; but he neither loves

Nor either cares for him.

MENAS.

Caesar and Lepidus

Are in the field: a mighty strength they carry.

POMPEY.

Where have you this? 'tis false.

MENAS.

From Silvius, sir.

POMPEY.

He dreams: I know they are in Rome together,

Looking for Antony. But all the charms of love,

Salt Cleopatra, soften thy wan'd lip!

Let witchcraft join with beauty, lust with both!

Tie up the libertine in a field of feasts,

Keep his brain fuming; Epicurean cooks

Sharpen with cloyless sauce his appetite;

That sleep and feeding may prorogue his honour

Even till a Lethe'd dullness.

[Enter VARRIUS.]

How now, Varrius!

VARRIUS.

This is most certain that I shall deliver:—

Mark Antony is every hour in Rome

Expected: since he went from Egypt 'tis

A space for further travel.

POMPEY.

I could have given less matter

A better ear.—Menas, I did not think

This amorous surfeiter would have donn'd his helm

For such a petty war; his soldiership

Is twice the other twain: but let us rear

The higher our opinion, that our stirring

Can from the lap of Egypt's widow pluck

The ne'er lust-wearied Antony.

MENAS.

I cannot hope

Caesar and Antony shall well greet together:

His wife that's dead did trespasses to Caesar;

His brother warr'd upon him; although, I think,

Not mov'd by Antony.

POMPEY.

I know not, Menas,

How lesser enmities may give way to greater.

Were't not that we stand up against them all,

'Twere pregnant they should square between themselves;

For they have entertained cause enough

To draw their swords: but how the fear of us

May cement their divisions, and bind up

The petty difference, we yet not know.

Be't as our gods will have't! It only stands

Our lives upon to use our strongest hands.

Come, Menas.

[Exeunt.]

SCENE II. Rome. A Room in the House of LEPIDUS.

[Enter ENOBARBUS and LEPIDUS.]

LEPIDUS.

Good Enobarbus, 'tis a worthy deed,

And shall become you well, to entreat your captain

To soft and gentle speech.

ENOBARBUS.

I shall entreat him

To answer like himself: if Caesar move him,

Let Antony look over Caesar's head,

And speak as loud as Mars. By Jupiter,

Were I the wearer of Antonius' beard,

I would not shave't to-day.

LEPIDUS.

'Tis not a time

For private stomaching.

ENOBARBUS.

Every time

Serves for the matter that is then born in't.

LEPIDUS.

But small to greater matters must give way.

ENOBARBUS.

Not if the small come first.

LEPIDUS.

Your speech is passion:

But, pray you, stir no embers up. Here comes

The noble Antony.

[Enter ANTONY and VENTIDIUS.]

ENOBARBUS.

And yonder, Caesar.

[Enter CAESAR, MAECENAS, and AGRIPPA.]

ANTONY.

If we compose well here, to Parthia;

Hark, Ventidius.

CAESAR.

I do not know,

Maecenas; ask Agrippa.

LEPIDUS.

Noble friends,

That which combin'd us was most great, and let not

A leaner action rend us. What's amiss,

May it be gently heard: when we debate

Our trivial difference loud, we do commit

Murder in healing wounds: then, noble partners,—

The rather for I earnestly beseech,—

Touch you the sourest points with sweetest terms,

Nor curstness grow to the matter.

ANTONY.

'Tis spoken well.

Were we before our armies, and to fight,

I should do thus.

CAESAR.

Welcome to Rome.

ANTONY.

Thank you.

CAESAR.

Sit.

ANTONY.

Sit, sir.

CAESAR.

Nay, then.

ANTONY.

I learn you take things ill which are not so,

Or being, concern you not.

CAESAR.

I must be laugh'd at

If, or for nothing or a little, I

Should say myself offended, and with you

Chiefly i' the world; more laugh'd at that I should

Once name you derogately, when to sound your name

It not concern'd me.

ANTONY.

My being in Egypt, Caesar,

What was't to you?

CAESAR.

No more than my residing here at Rome

Might be to you in Egypt: yet, if you there

Did practise on my state, your being in Egypt

Might be my question.

ANTONY.

How intend you practis'd?

CAESAR.

You may be pleas'd to catch at mine intent

By what did here befall me. Your wife and brother

Made wars upon me; and their contestation

Was theme for you, you were the word of war.

ANTONY.

You do mistake your business; my brother never

Did urge me in his act: I did inquire it;

And have my learning from some true reports

That drew their swords with you. Did he not rather

Discredit my authority with yours;

And make the wars alike against my stomach,

Having alike your cause? Of this my letters

Before did satisfy you. If you'll patch a quarrel

As matter whole you have not to make it with,

It must not be with this.

CAESAR.

You praise yourself

By laying defects of judgment to me; but

You patch'd up your excuses.

ANTONY.

Not so, not so;

I know you could not lack, I am certain on't,

Very necessity of this thought, that I,

Your partner in the cause 'gainst which he fought,

Could not with graceful eyes attend those wars

Which 'fronted mine own peace. As for my wife,

I would you had her spirit in such another:

The third o' theworld is yours; which with a snaffle

You may pace easy, but not such a wife.

ENOBARBUS.

Would we had all such wives, that the men

Might go to wars with the women.

ANTONY.

So much uncurbable, her garboils, Caesar,

Made out of her impatience,—which not wanted

Shrewdness of policy too,—I grieving grant

Did you too much disquiet: for that you must

But say I could not help it.

CAESAR.

I wrote to you

When rioting in Alexandria; you

Did pocket up my letters, and with taunts

Did gibe my missive out of audience.

ANTONY.

Sir,

He fell upon me ere admitted: then

Three kings I had newly feasted, and did want

Of what I was i' the morning: but next day

I told him of myself; which was as much

As to have ask'd him pardon. Let this fellow

Be nothing of our strife; if we contend,

Out of our question wipe him.

CAESAR.

You have broken

The article of your oath; which you shall never

Have tongue to charge me with.

LEPIDUS.

Soft, Caesar!

ANTONY.

No; Lepidus, let him speak.

The honour is sacred which he talks on now,

Supposing that I lack'd it.—But on, Caesar;

The article of my oath.

CAESAR.

To lend me arms and aid when I requir'd them;

The which you both denied.

ANTONY.

Neglected, rather;

And then when poison'd hours had bound me up

From mine own knowledge. As nearly as I may,

I'll play the penitent to you: but mine honesty

Shall not make poor my greatness, nor my power

Work without it. Truth is, that Fulvia,

To have me out of Egypt, made wars here;

For which myself, the ignorant motive, do

So far ask pardon as befits mine honour

To stoop in such a case.

LEPIDUS.

'Tis noble spoken.

MAECENAS.

If it might please you to enforce no further

The griefs between ye: to forget them quite

Were to remember that the present need

Speaks to atone you.

LEPIDUS.

Worthily spoken, Maecenas.

ENOBARBUS. Or, if you borrow one another's love for the instant, you may, when you hear no more words of Pompey, return it again: you shall have time to wrangle in when you have nothing else to do.

ANTONY.

Thou art a soldier only: speak no more.

ENOBARBUS.

That truth should be silent I had almost forgot.

ANTONY.

You wrong this presence; therefore speak no more.

ENOBARBUS.

Go to, then; your considerate stone!

CAESAR.

I do not much dislike the matter, but

The manner of his speech; for't cannot be

We shall remain in friendship, our conditions

So differing in their acts. Yet if I knew

What hoop should hold us stanch, from edge to edge

O' the world, I would pursue it.

AGRIPPA.

Give me leave, Caesar,—

CAESAR.

Speak, Agrippa.

AGRIPPA.

Thou hast a sister by the mother's side,

Admir'd Octavia: great Mark Antony

Is now a widower.

CAESAR.

Say not so, Agrippa:

If Cleopatra heard you, your reproof

Were well deserv'd of rashness.

ANTONY.

I am not married, Caesar: let me hear

Agrippa further speak.

AGRIPPA.

To hold you in perpetual amity,

To make you brothers, and to knit your hearts

With an unslipping knot, take Antony

Octavia to his wife; whose beauty claims

No worse a husband than the best of men;

Whose virtue and whose general graces speak

That which none else can utter. By this marriage

All little jealousies, which now seem great,

And all great fears, which now import their dangers,

Would then be nothing: truths would be tales,

Where now half tales be truths: her love to both

Would each to other, and all loves to both,

Draw after her. Pardon what I have spoke;

For 'tis a studied, not a present thought,

By duty ruminated.

ANTONY.

Will Caesar speak?

CAESAR.

Not till he hears how Antony is touch'd

With what is spoke already.

ANTONY.

What power is in Agrippa,

If I would say 'Agrippa, be it so,'

To make this good?

CAESAR.

The power of Caesar, and

His power unto Octavia.

ANTONY.

May I never

To this good purpose, that so fairly shows,

Dream of impediment!—Let me have thy hand:

Further this act of grace; and from this hour

The heart of brothers govern in our loves

And sway our great designs!

CAESAR.

There is my hand.

A sister I bequeath you, whom no brother

Did ever love so dearly: let her live

To join our kingdoms and our hearts; and never

Fly off our loves again!

LEPIDUS.

Happily, amen!

ANTONY.

I did not think to draw my sword 'gainst Pompey;

For he hath laid strange courtesies and great

Of late upon me. I must thank him only,

Lest my remembrance suffer ill report;

At heel of that, defy him.

LEPIDUS.

Time calls upon's:

Of us must Pompey presently be sought,

Or else he seeks out us.

ANTONY.

Where lies he?

CAESAR.

About the Mount Misenum.

ANTONY.

What is his strength

By land?

CAESAR.

Great and increasing; but by sea

He is an absolute master.

ANTONY.

So is the fame.

Would we had spoke together! Haste we for it:

Yet, ere we put ourselves in arms, despatch we

The business we have talk'd of.

CAESAR.

With most gladness;

And do invite you to my sister's view,

Whither straight I'll lead you.

ANTONY.

Let us, Lepidus,

Not lack your company.

LEPIDUS.

Noble Antony,

Not sickness should detain me.

[Flourish. Exeunt CAESAR, ANTONY, and LEPIDUS.]

MAECENAS.

Welcome from Egypt, sir.

ENOBARBUS.

Half the heart of Caesar, worthy Maecenas!—my honourable friend,

Agrippa!—

AGRIPPA.

Good Enobarbus!

MAECENAS. We have cause to be glad that matters are so well digested. You stay'd well by it in Egypt.

ENOBARBUS. Ay, sir; we did sleep day out of countenance, and made the night light with drinking.

MAECENAS. Eight wild boars roasted whole at a breakfast, and but twelve persons there. Is this true?

ENOBARBUS. This was but as a fly by an eagle: we had much more monstrous matter of feast, which worthily deserved noting.

MAECENAS.

She's a most triumphant lady, if report be square to her.

ENOBARBUS. When she first met Mark Antony she pursed up his heart, upon the river of Cydnus.

AGRIPPA.

There she appeared indeed; or my reporter devised well for her.

ENOBARBUS.

I will tell you.

The barge she sat in, like a burnish'd throne,

Burn'd on the water: the poop was beaten gold;

Purple the sails, and so perfumed that

The winds were love-sick with them; the oars were silver,

Which to the tune of flutes kept stroke, and made

The water which they beat to follow faster,

As amorous of their strokes. For her own person,

It beggar'd all description: she did lie

In her pavilion,—cloth-of-gold of tissue,—

O'er-picturing that Venus where we see

The fancy out-work nature: on each side her

Stood pretty dimpled boys, like smiling Cupids,

With divers-colour'd fans, whose wind did seem

To glow the delicate cheeks which they did cool,

And what they undid did.

AGRIPPA.

O, rare for Antony!

ENOBARBUS.

Her gentlewomen, like the Nereids,

So many mermaids, tended her i' the eyes,

And made their bends adornings: at the helm

A seeming mermaid steers: the silken tackle

Swell with the touches of those flower-soft hands

That yarely frame the office. From the barge

A strange invisible perfume hits the sense

Of the adjacent wharfs. The city cast

Her people out upon her; and Antony,

Enthron'd i' the market-place, did sit alone,

Whistling to the air; which, but for vacancy,

Had gone to gaze on Cleopatra too,

And made a gap in nature.

AGRIPPA.

Rare Egyptian!

ENOBARBUS.

Upon her landing, Antony sent to her,

Invited her to supper: she replied

It should be better he became her guest;

Which she entreated: our courteous Antony,

Whom ne'er the word of 'No' woman heard speak,

Being barber'd ten times o'er, goes to the feast,

And, for his ordinary, pays his heart

For what his eyes eat only.

AGRIPPA.

Royal wench!

She made great Caesar lay his sword to bed:

He ploughed her, and she cropp'd.

ENOBARBUS.

I saw her once

Hop forty paces through the public street;

And, having lost her breath, she spoke and panted,

That she did make defect perfection,

And, breathless, power breathe forth.

MAECENAS.

Now Antony must leave her utterly.

ENOBARBUS.

Never; he will not:

Age cannot wither her, nor custom stale

Her infinite variety: other women cloy

The appetites they feed; but she makes hungry

Where most she satisfies: for vilest things

Become themselves in her; that the holy priests

Bless her when she is riggish.

MAECENAS.

If beauty, wisdom, modesty, can settle

The heart of Antony, Octavia is

A blessed lottery to him.

AGRIPPA.

Let us go.—

Good Enobarbus, make yourself my guest

Whilst you abide here.

ENOBARBUS.

Humbly, sir, I thank you.

[Exeunt.]

SCENE III. Rome. A Room in CAESAR'S House.

[Enter CAESAR, ANTONY, OCTAVIA between them, and Attendants.]

ANTONY.

The world and my great office will sometimes

Divide me from your bosom.

OCTAVIA.

All which time

Before the gods my knee shall bow my prayers

To them for you.

ANTONY.

Good night, sir.—My Octavia,

Read not my blemishes in the world's report:

I have not kept my square; but that to come

Shall all be done by the rule. Good night, dear lady.—

OCTAVIA.

Good night, sir.

CAESAR.

Good night.

[Exeunt CAESAR and OCTAVIA.]

[Enter SOOTHSAYER.]

ANTONY.

Now, sirrah, you do wish yourself in Egypt?

SOOTHSAYER.

Would I had never come from thence, nor you

Thither!

ANTONY.

If you can, your reason.

SOOTHSAYER.

I see it in my motion, have it not in my tongue; but yet

Hie you to Egypt again.

ANTONY.

Say to me,

Whose fortunes shall rise higher, Caesar's or mine?

SOOTHSAYER.

Caesar's.

Therefore, O Antony, stay not by his side:

Thy demon, that thy spirit which keeps thee, is

Noble, courageous, high, unmatchable,

Where Caesar's is not; but near him thy angel

Becomes a fear, as being o'erpower'd: therefore

Make space enough between you.

ANTONY.

Speak this no more.

SOOTHSAYER.

To none but thee; no more but when to thee.

If thou dost play with him at any game,

Thou art sure to lose; and of that natural luck

He beats thee 'gainst the odds: thy lustre thickens

When he shines by: I say again, thy spirit

Is all afraid to govern thee near him;

But, he away, 'tis noble.

ANTONY.

Get thee gone:

Say to Ventidius I would speak with him:—

[Exit SOOTHSAYER.]

He shall to Parthia.—Be it art or hap,

He hath spoken true: the very dice obey him;—

And in our sports my better cunning faints

Under his chance: if we draw lots, he speeds;

His cocks do win the battle still of mine,

When it is all to nought; and his quails ever

Beat mine, inhoop'd, at odds. I will to Egypt:

And though I make this marriage for my peace,

I' the East my pleasure lies.

[Enter VENTIDIUS.]

O, come, Ventidius,

You must to Parthia: your commission's ready;

Follow me and receive it.

[Exeunt.]

SCENE IV. Rome. A street.

[Enter LEPIDUS, MAECENAS, and AGRIPPA.]

LEPIDUS.

Trouble yourselves no further: pray you, hasten

Your generals after.

AGRIPPA.

Sir, Mark Antony

Will e'en but kiss Octavia, and we'll follow.

LEPIDUS.

Till I shall see you in your soldier's dress,

Which will become you both, farewell.

MAECENAS.

We shall,

As I conceive the journey, be at the mount

Before you, Lepidus.

LEPIDUS.

Your way is shorter;

My purposes do draw me much about.

You'll win two days upon me.

BOTH.

Sir, good success!

LEPIDUS.

Farewell.

[Exeunt.]

SCENE V. Alexandria. A Room in the Palace.

[Enter CLEOPATRA, CHARMIAN, IRAS, ALEXAS, and Attendants.]

CLEOPATRA.

Give me some music,—music, moody food

Of us that trade in love.

ALL.

The music, ho!

[Enter MARDIAN.]

CLEOPATRA.

Let it alone; let's to billiards:

Come, Charmian.

CHARMIAN.

My arm is sore; best play with Mardian.

CLEOPATRA.

As well a woman with an eunuch play'd

As with a woman.—Come, you'll play with me, sir?

MARDIAN.

As well as I can, madam.

CLEOPATRA.

And when good will is show'd, though't come too short,

The actor may plead pardon. I'll none now:—

Give me mine angle,—we'll to the river. There,

My music playing far off, I will betray

Tawny-finn'd fishes; my bended hook shall pierce

Their slimy jaws; and as I draw them up

I'll think them every one an Antony,

And say 'Ah ha! You're caught.'

CHARMIAN.

'Twas merry when

You wager'd on your angling; when your diver

Did hang a salt fish on his hook, which he

With fervency drew up.

CLEOPATRA.

That time?—O times!—

I laughed him out of patience; and that night

I laugh'd him into patience: and next morn,

Ere the ninth hour, I drunk him to his bed;

Then put my tires and mantles on him, whilst

I wore his sword Philippan.

[Enter a MESSENGER.]

O! from Italy!—

Ram thou thy fruitful tidings in mine ears,

That long time have been barren.

MESSENGER.

Madam, madam,—

CLEOPATRA.

Antony's dead!—

If thou say so, villain, thou kill'st thy mistress;

But well and free,

If thou so yield him, there is gold, and here

My bluest veins to kiss,—a hand that kings

Have lipp'd, and trembled kissing.

MESSENGER.

First, madam, he's well.

CLEOPATRA.

Why, there's more gold.

But, sirrah, mark, we use

To say the dead are well: bring it to that,

The gold I give thee will I melt and pour

Down thy ill-uttering throat.

MESSENGER.

Good madam, hear me.

CLEOPATRA.

Well, go to, I will;

But there's no goodness in thy face: if Antony

Be free and healthful,—why so tart a favour

To trumpet such good tidings! If not well,

Thou shouldst come like a fury crown'd with snakes,

Not like a formal man.

MESSENGER.

Will't please you hear me?

CLEOPATRA.

I have a mind to strike thee ere thou speak'st:

Yet, if thou say Antony lives, is well,

Or friends with Caesar, or not captive to him,

I'll set thee in a shower of gold, and hail

Rich pearls upon thee.

MESSENGER.

Madam, he's well.

CLEOPATRA.

Well said.

MESSENGER.

And friends with Caesar.

CLEOPATRA.

Th'art an honest man.

MESSENGER.

Caesar and he are greater friends than ever.

CLEOPATRA.

Make thee a fortune from me.

MESSENGER.

But yet, madam,—

CLEOPATRA.

I do not like 'but yet', it does allay

The good precedence; fie upon 'but yet'!

'But yet' is as a gaoler to bring forth

Some monstrous malefactor. Pr'ythee, friend,

Pour out the pack of matter to mine ear,

The good and bad together: he's friends with Caesar;

In state of health, thou say'st; and, thou say'st, free.

MESSENGER.

Free, madam! no; I made no such report:

He's bound unto Octavia.

CLEOPATRA.

For what good turn?

MESSENGER.

For the best turn i' the bed.

CLEOPATRA.

I am pale, Charmian.

MESSENGER.

Madam, he's married to Octavia.

CLEOPATRA.

The most infectious pestilence upon thee!

[Strikes him down.]

MESSENGER.

Good madam, patience.

CLEOPATRA.

What say you?—Hence,

[Strikes him again.]

Horrible villain! or I'll spurn thine eyes

Like balls before me; I'll unhair thy head:

[She hales him up and down.]

Thou shalt be whipp'd with wire and stew'd in brine,

Smarting in ling'ring pickle.

MESSENGER.

Gracious madam,

I that do bring the news made not the match.

CLEOPATRA.

Say 'tis not so, a province I will give thee,

And make thy fortunes proud: the blow thou hadst

Shall make thy peace for moving me to rage;

And I will boot thee with what gift beside

Thy modesty can beg.

MESSENGER.

He's married, madam.

CLEOPATRA.

Rogue, thou hast liv'd too long.

[Draws a dagger.]

MESSENGER.

Nay, then I'll run.—

What mean you, madam? I have made no fault.

[Exit.]

CHARMIAN.

Good madam, keep yourself within yourself:

The man is innocent.

CLEOPATRA.

Some innocents scape not the thunderbolt.—

Melt Egypt into Nile! and kindly creatures

Turn all to serpents!—Call the slave again:—

Though I am mad, I will not bite him:—call!

CHARMIAN.

He is afear'd to come.

CLEOPATRA.

I will not hurt him.

[Exit CHARMIAN.]

These hands do lack nobility, that they strike

A meaner than myself; since I myself

Have given myself the cause.

[Re-enter CHARMIAN and Messenger.]

Come hither, sir.

Though it be honest, it is never good

To bring bad news: give to a gracious message

An host of tongues; but let ill tidings tell

Themselves when they be felt.

MESSENGER.

I have done my duty.

CLEOPATRA.

Is he married?

I cannot hate thee worser than I do

If thou again say 'Yes.'

MESSENGER.

He's married, madam.

CLEOPATRA.

The gods confound thee! dost thou hold there still!

MESSENGER.

Should I lie, madam?

CLEOPATRA.

O, I would thou didst,

So half my Egypt were submerg'd, and made

A cistern for scal'd snakes! Go, get thee hence:

Hadst thou Narcissus in thy face, to me

Thou wouldst appear most ugly. He is married?

MESSENGER.

I crave your highness' pardon.

CLEOPATRA.

He is married?

MESSENGER.

Take no offence that I would not offend you:

To punish me for what you make me do

Seems much unequal: he's married to Octavia.

CLEOPATRA.

O, that his fault should make a knave of thee

That art not what tho'rt sure of!—Get thee hence:

The merchandise which thou hast brought from Rome

Are all too dear for me: lie they upon thy hand,

And be undone by 'em!

[Exit Messenger.]

CHARMIAN.

Good your highness, patience.

CLEOPATRA.

In praising Antony I have disprais'd Caesar.

CHARMIAN.

Many times, madam.

CLEOPATRA.

I am paid for't now.

Lead me from hence;

I faint:—O Iras, Charmian!—'tis no matter.—

Go to the fellow, good Alexas; bid him

Report the feature of Octavia, her years,

Her inclination; let him not leave out

The colour of her hair:—bring me word quickly.

[Exit ALEXAS.]

Let him for ever go:—let him not, Charmian—

Though he be painted one way like a Gorgon,

T'other way he's a Mars.—[To MARDIAN] Bid you Alexas

Bring me word how tall she is.—Pity me, Charmian,

But do not speak to me.—Lead me to my chamber.

[Exeunt.]

SCENE VI. Near Misenum.

[Flourish. Enter POMPEY and MENAS at one side, with drum and trumpet; at the other, CAESAR, ANTONY, LEPIDUS, ENOBARBUS, MAECENAS, with Soldiers marching.]

POMPEY.

Your hostages I have, so have you mine;

And we shall talk before we fight.

CAESAR.

Most meet

That first we come to words; and therefore have we

Our written purposes before us sent;

Which, if thou hast consider'd, let us know

If 'twill tie up thy discontented sword,

And carry back to Sicily much tall youth

That else must perish here.

POMPEY.

To you all three,

The senators alone of this great world,

Chief factors for the gods,—I do not know

Wherefore my father should revengers want,

Having a son and friends; since Julius Caesar,

Who at Philippi the good Brutus ghosted,

There saw you labouring for him. What was't

That mov'd pale Cassius to conspire; and what

Made the all-honour'd, honest Roman, Brutus,

With the arm'd rest, courtiers of beauteous freedom,

To drench the Capitol, but that they would

Have one man but a man? And that is it

Hath made me rig my navy; at whose burden

The anger'd ocean foams; with which I meant

To scourge the ingratitude that despiteful Rome

Cast on my noble father.

CAESAR.

Take your time.

ANTONY.

Thou canst not fear us, Pompey, with thy sails;

We'll speak with thee at sea: at land thou know'st

How much we do o'er-count thee.

POMPEY.

At land, indeed,

Thou dost o'er-count me of my father's house:

But, since the cuckoo builds not for himself,

Remain in't as thou mayst.

LEPIDUS.

Be pleas'd to tell us,—

For this is from the present,—how you take

The offers we have sent you.

CAESAR.

There's the point.

ANTONY.

Which do not be entreated to, but weigh

What it is worth embrac'd.

CAESAR.

And what may follow,

To try a larger fortune.

POMPEY.

You have made me offer

Of Sicily, Sardinia; and I must

Rid all the sea of pirates; then to send

Measures of wheat to Rome; this 'greed upon,

To part with unhack'd edges and bear back

Our targes undinted.

CAESAR, ANTONY, and LEPIDUS.

That's our offer.

POMPEY.

Know, then,

I came before you here a man prepar'd

To take this offer: but Mark Antony

Put me to some impatience:—though I lose

The praise of it by telling, you must know,

When Caesar and your brother were at blows,

Your mother came to Sicily, and did find

Her welcome friendly.

ANTONY.

I have heard it, Pompey,

And am well studied for a liberal thanks

Which I do owe you.

POMPEY.

Let me have your hand:

I did not think, sir, to have met you here.

ANTONY.

The beds i' the East are soft; and, thanks to you,

That call'd me, timelier than my purpose, hither;

For I have gained by it.

CAESAR.

Since I saw you last

There is a change upon you.

POMPEY.

Well, I know not

What counts harsh fortune casts upon my face;

But in my bosom shall she never come

To make my heart her vassal.

LEPIDUS.

Well met here.

POMPEY.

I hope so, Lepidus.—Thus we are agreed:

I crave our composition may be written,

And seal'd between us.

CAESAR.

That's the next to do.

POMPEY.

We'll feast each other ere we part; and let's

Draw lots who shall begin.

ANTONY.

That will I, Pompey.

POMPEY.

No, Antony, take the lot: but, first

Or last, your fine Egyptian cookery

Shall have the fame. I have heard that Julius Caesar

Grew fat with feasting there.

ANTONY.

You have heard much.

POMPEY.

I have fair meanings, sir.

ANTONY.

And fair words to them.

POMPEY.

Then so much have I heard;

And I have heard Apollodorus carried,—

ENOBARBUS.

No more of that:—he did so.

POMPEY.

What, I pray you?

ENOBARBUS.

A certain queen to Caesar in a mattress.

POMPEY.

I know thee now: how far'st thou, soldier?

ENOBARBUS.

Well;

And well am like to do; for I perceive

Four feasts are toward.

POMPEY.

Let me shake thy hand;

I never hated thee: I have seen thee fight,

When I have envied thy behaviour.

ENOBARBUS.

Sir,

I never lov'd you much; but I ha' prais'd ye

When you have well deserv'd ten times as much

As I have said you did.

POMPEY.

Enjoy thy plainness;

It nothing ill becomes thee.—

Aboard my galley I invite you all:

Will you lead, lords?

CAESAR, ANTONY, and LEPIDUS.

Show's the way, sir.

POMPEY.

Come.

[Exeunt all but ENOBARBUS and MENAS.]

MENAS.

[Aside.] Thy father, Pompey, would ne'er have made this treaty.—

You and I have known, sir.

ENOBARBUS.

At sea, I think.

MENAS.

We have, sir.

ENOBARBUS.

You have done well by water.

MENAS.

And you by land.

ENOBARBUS. I will praise any man that will praise me; though it cannot be denied what I have done by land.

MENAS.

Nor what I have done by water.

ENOBARBUS. Yes, something you can deny for your own safety: you have been a great thief by sea.

MENAS.

And you by land.

ENOBARBUS. There I deny my land service. But give me your hand, Menas: if our eyes had authority, here they might take two thieves kissing.

MENAS.

All men's faces are true, whatsome'er their hands are.

ENOBARBUS.

But there is never a fair woman has a true face.

MENAS.

No slander; they steal hearts.

ENOBARBUS.

We came hither to fight with you.

MENAS. For my part, I am sorry it is turn'd to a drinking. Pompey doth this day laugh away his fortune.

ENOBARBUS.

If he do, sure he cannot weep it back again.

MENAS. You have said, sir. We look'd not for Mark Antony here: pray you, is he married to Cleopatra?

ENOBARBUS.

Caesar's sister is called Octavia.

MENAS.

True, sir; she was the wife of Caius Marcellus.

ENOBARBUS.

But she is now the wife of Marcus Antonius.

MENAS.

Pray you, sir?

ENOBARBUS.

'Tis true.

MENAS.

Then is Caesar and he for ever knit together.

ENOBARBUS.

If I were bound to divine of this unity, I would not prophesy so.

MENAS. I think the policy of that purpose made more in the marriage than the love of the parties.

ENOBARBUS. I think so too. But you shall find the band that seems to tie their friendship together will be the very strangler of their amity: Octavia is of a holy, cold, and still conversation.

MENAS.

Who would not have his wife so?

ENOBARBUS. Not he that himself is not so; which is Mark Antony. He will to his Egyptian dish again: then shall the sighs of Octavia blow the fire up in Caesar; and, as I said before, that which is the strength of their amity shall prove the immediate author of their variance. Antony will use his affection where it is: he married but his occasion here.

MENAS. And thus it may be. Come, sir, will you aboard? I have a health for you.

ENOBARBUS.

I shall take it, sir: we have used our throats in Egypt.

MENAS.

Come, let's away.

[Exeunt.]

SCENE VII. On board POMPEY'S Galley, lying near Misenum.

[Music. Enter two or three SERVANTS with a banquet.]

FIRST SERVANT. Here they'll be, man. Some o' their plants are ill-rooted already; the least wind i' the world will blow them down.

SECOND SERVANT.

Lepidus is high-coloured.

FIRST SERVANT.

They have made him drink alms-drink.

SECOND SERVANT. As they pinch one another by the disposition, he cries out 'no more'; reconciles them to his entreaty and himself to the drink.

FIRST SERVANT.

But it raises the greater war between him and his discretion.

SECOND SERVANT. Why, this it is to have a name in great men's fellowship: I had as lief have a reed that will do me no service as a partizan I could not heave.

FIRST SERVANT. To be called into a huge sphere, and not to be seen to move in't, are the holes where eyes should be, which pitifully disaster the cheeks.

[A sennet sounded. Enter CAESAR, ANTONY, LEPIDUS, POMPEY, AGRIPPA, MAECENAS, ENOBARBUS, MENAS, with other Captains.]

ANTONY.

[To CAESAR.] Thus do they, sir: they take the flow o' the Nile

By certain scales i' the pyramid; they know

By the height, the lowness, or the mean, if dearth

Or foison follow: the higher Nilus swells

The more it promises; as it ebbs, the seedsman

Upon the slime and ooze scatters his grain,

And shortly comes to harvest.

LEPIDUS.

You've strange serpents there.

ANTONY.

Ay, Lepidus.

LEPIDUS. Your serpent of Egypt is bred now of your mud by the operation of your sun: so is your crocodile.

ANTONY.

They are so.

POMPEY.

Sit —and some wine!—A health to Lepidus!

LEPIDUS.

I am not so well as I should be, but I'll ne'er out.

ENOBARBUS.

Not till you have slept; I fear me you'll be in till then.

LEPIDUS. Nay, certainly, I have heard the Ptolemies' pyramises are very goodly things; without contradiction I have heard that.

MENAS.

[Aside to POMPEY.] Pompey, a word.

POMPEY.

[Aside to MENAS.] Say in mine ear: what is't?

MENAS.

[Aside to POMPEY.] Forsake thy seat, I do beseech thee, captain,

And hear me speak a word.

POMPEY.

[Aside to MENAS.] Forbear me till ano.n—

This wine for Lepidus!

LEPIDUS.

What manner o' thing is your crocodile?

ANTONY. It is shaped, sir, like itself; and it is as broad as it hath breadth: it is just so high as it is, and moves with it own organs: it lives by that which nourisheth it, and the elements once out of it, it transmigrates.

LEPIDUS.

What colour is it of?

ANTONY.

Of its own colour too.

LEPIDUS.

'Tis a strange serpent.

ANTONY.

'Tis so. And the tears of it are wet.

CAESAR.

Will this description satisfy him?

ANTONY.

With the health that Pompey gives him, else he is a very epicure.

POMPEY.

[Aside to MENAS.] Go, hang, sir, hang! Tell me of that! away!

Do as I bid you.—Where's this cup I call'd for?

MENAS.

[Aside to POMPEY.] If for the sake of merit thou wilt hear me,

Rise from thy stool.

POMPEY.

[Aside to MENAS.] I think thou'rt mad.

[Rises and walks aside.]

The matter?

MENAS.

I have ever held my cap off to thy fortunes.

POMPEY.

Thou hast serv'd me with much faith.

What's else to say?—

Be jolly, lords.

ANTONY.

These quicksands, Lepidus,

Keep off them, for you sink.

MENAS.

Wilt thou be lord of all the world?

POMPEY.

What say'st thou?

MENAS.

Wilt thou be lord of the whole world?

That's twice.

POMPEY.

How should that be?

MENAS.

But entertain it,

And though you think me poor, I am the man

Will give thee all the world.

POMPEY.

Hast thou drunk well?

MENAS.

No, Pompey, I have kept me from the cup.

Thou art, if thou dar'st be, the earthly Jove:

Whate'er the ocean pales or sky inclips

Is thine, if thou wilt have't.

POMPEY.

Show me which way.

MENAS.

These three world-sharers, these competitors,

Are in thy vessel: let me cut the cable;

And when we are put off, fall to their throats:

All then is thine.

POMPEY.

Ah, this thou shouldst have done,

And not have spoke on't! In me 'tis villainy:

In thee't had been good service. Thou must know

'Tis not my profit that does lead mine honour:

Mine honour it. Repent that e'er thy tongue

Hath so betray'd thine act: being done unknown,

I should have found it afterwards well done;

But must condemn it now. Desist, and drink.

MENAS.

[Aside.] For this,

I'll never follow thy pall'd fortunes more.

Who seeks, and will not take when once 'tis offer'd,

Shall never find it more.

POMPEY.

This health to Lepidus!

ANTONY.

Bear him ashore. I'll pledge it for him, Pompey.

ENOBARBUS.

Here's to thee, Menas!

MENAS.

Enobarbus, welcome!

POMPEY.

Fill till the cup be hid.

ENOBARBUS.

There's a strong fellow, Menas.

[Pointing to the servant who carries off LEPIDUS.]

MENAS.

Why?

ENOBARBUS.

'A bears the third part of the world, man; see'st not?

MENAS.

The third part, then, is drunk; would it were all,

That it might go on wheels!

ENOBARBUS.

Drink thou; increase the reels.

MENAS.

Come.

POMPEY.

This is not yet an Alexandrian feast.

ANTONY.

It ripens towards it.—Strike the vessels, ho!—

Here is to Caesar!

CAESAR.

I could well forbear't.

It's monstrous labour when I wash my brain

And it grows fouler.

ANTONY.

Be a child o' the time.

CAESAR.

Possess it, I'll make answer:

But I had rather fast from all four days

Than drink so much in one.

ENOBARBUS.

[To ANTONY.] Ha, my brave emperor!

Shall we dance now the Egyptian Bacchanals

And celebrate our drink?

POMPEY.

Let's ha't, good soldier.

ANTONY.

Come, let's all take hands,

Till that the conquering wine hath steep'd our sense

In soft and delicate Lethe.

ENOBARBUS.

All take hands.—

Make battery to our ears with the loud music:—

The while I'll place you: then the boy shall sing;

The holding every man shall bear as loud

As his strong sides can volley.

[Music plays. ENOBARBUS places them hand in hand.]

SONG.

Come, thou monarch of the vine,

Plumpy Bacchus with pink eyne!

In thy fats our cares be drown'd,

With thy grapes our hairs be crown'd:

Cup us, till the world go round,

Cup us, till the world go round!

CAESAR.

What would you more?—Pompey, good night. Good brother,

Let me request you off: our graver business

Frowns at this levity.—Gentle lords, let's part;

You see we have burnt our cheeks: strong Enobarb

Is weaker than the wine; and mine own tongue

Splits what it speaks: the wild disguise hath almost

Antick'd us all. What needs more words. Good night.—

Good Antony, your hand.

POMPEY.

I'll try you on the shore.

ANTONY.

And shall, sir: give's your hand.

POMPEY.

O Antony,

You have my father's house,—but, what? we are friends.

Come, down into the boat.

ENOBARBUS.

Take heed you fall not.

       [Exeunt POMPEY, CAESAR, ANTONY, and Attendants.]

Menas, I'll not on shore.

MENAS.

No, to my cabin.—

These drums!—these trumpets, flutes! what!—

Let Neptune hear we bid a loud farewell

To these great fellows: sound and be hang'd, sound out!

[A flourish of trumpets, with drums.]

ENOBARBUS.

Hoo! says 'a.—There's my cap.

MENAS.

Hoo!—noble captain, come.

[Exeunt.]

ACT III.

SCENE I. A plain in Syria.

[Enter VENTIDIUS, in triumph, with SILIUS and other Romans, Officers and Soldiers; the dead body of PACORUS borne in front.]

VENTIDIUS.

Now, darting Parthia, art thou struck; and now

Pleas'd fortune does of Marcus Crassus' death

Make me revenger.—Bear the king's son's body

Before our army.—Thy Pacorus, Orodes,

Pays this for Marcus Crassus.

SILIUS.

Noble Ventidius,

Whilst yet with Parthian blood thy sword is warm

The fugitive Parthians follow; spur through Media,

Mesopotamia, and the shelters whither

The routed fly: so thy grand captain Antony

Shall set thee on triumphant chariots, and

Put garlands on thy head.

VENTIDIUS.

O Silius, Silius,

I have done enough: a lower place, note well,

May make too great an act; for learn this, Silius,—

Better to leave undone, than by our deed

Acquire too high a fame when him we serve's away.

Caesar and Antony have ever won

More in their officer, than person: Sossius,

One of my place in Syria, his lieutenant,

For quick accumulation of renown,

Which he achiev'd by the minute, lost his favour.

Who does i' the wars more than his captain can

Becomes his captain's captain; and ambition,

The soldier's virtue, rather makes choice of loss

Than gain which darkens him.

I could do more to do Antonius good,

But 'twould offend him; and in his offence

Should my performance perish.

SILIUS.

Thou hast, Ventidius, that

Without the which a soldier and his sword

Grants scarce distinction. Thou wilt write to Antony?

VENTIDIUS.

I'll humbly signify what in his name,

That magical word of war, we have effected;

How, with his banners, and his well-paid ranks,

The ne'er-yet-beaten horse of Parthia

We have jaded out o' the field.

SILIUS.

Where is he now?

VENTIDIUS.

He purposeth to Athens: whither, with what haste

The weight we must convey with's will permit,

We shall appear before him.—On, there; pass along!

[Exeunt.]

SCENE II. Rome. An Ante-chamber in CAESAR'S house.

[Enter AGRIPPA and ENOBARBUS, meeting.]

AGRIPPA.

What, are the brothers parted?

ENOBARBUS.

They have despatch'd with Pompey; he is gone;

The other three are sealing. Octavia weeps

To part from Rome: Caesar is sad; and Lepidus,

Since Pompey's feast, as Menas says, is troubled

With the green sickness.

AGRIPPA.

'Tis a noble Lepidus.

ENOBARBUS.

A very fine one: O, how he loves Caesar!

AGRIPPA.

Nay, but how dearly he adores Mark Antony!

ENOBARBUS.

Caesar? Why he's the Jupiter of men.

AGRIPPA.

What's Antony? The god of Jupiter.

ENOBARBUS.

Spake you of Caesar? How! the nonpareil!

AGRIPPA.

O, Antony! O thou Arabian bird!

ENOBARBUS.

Would you praise Caesar, say 'Caesar'—go no further.

AGRIPPA.

Indeed, he plied them both with excellent praises.

ENOBARBUS.

But he loves Caesar best;—yet he loves Antony:

Hoo! hearts, tongues, figures, scribes, bards, poets, cannot

Think, speak, cast, write, sing, number—hoo!—

His love to Antony. But as for Caesar,

Kneel down, kneel down, and wonder.

AGRIPPA.

Both he loves.

ENOBARBUS.

They are his shards, and he their beetle.

[Trumpets within.]

So,—

This is to horse.—Adieu, noble Agrippa.

AGRIPPA.

Good fortune, worthy soldier; and farewell.

[Enter CAESAR, ANTONY, LEPIDUS, and OCTAVIA.]

ANTONY.

No further, sir.

CAESAR.

You take from me a great part of myself;

Use me well in't.—Sister, prove such a wife

As my thoughts make thee, and as my furthest band

Shall pass on thy approof.—Most noble Antony,

Let not the piece of virtue which is set

Betwixt us as the cement of our love,

To keep it builded, be the ram to batter

The fortress of it; for better might we

Have lov'd without this mean if on both parts

This be not cherish'd.

ANTONY.

Make me not offended

In your distrust.

CAESAR.

I have said.

ANTONY.

You shall not find,

Though you be therein curious, the least cause

For what you seem to fear: so, the gods keep you,

And make the hearts of Romans serve your ends!

We will here part.

CAESAR.

Farewell, my dearest sister, fare thee well:

The elements be kind to thee, and make

Thy spirits all of comfort! Fare thee well.

OCTAVIA.

My noble brother!—

ANTONY.

The April's in her eyes: it is love's spring,

And these the showers to bring it on.—Be cheerful.

OCTAVIA.

Sir, look well to my husband's house; and—

CAESAR.

What,

Octavia?

OCTAVIA.

I'll tell you in your ear.

ANTONY.

Her tongue will not obey her heart, nor can

Her heart inform her tongue,—the swan's down feather,

That stands upon the swell at the full of tide,

And neither way inclines.

ENOBARBUS.

[Aside to AGRIPPA.] Will Caesar weep?

AGRIPPA.

[Aside to ENOBARBUS.] He has a cloud in's face.

ENOBARBUS.

[Aside to AGRIPPA.] He were the worse for that, were he a horse;

So is he, being a man.

AGRIPPA.

[Aside to ENOBARBUS.] Why, Enobarbus,

When Antony found Julius Caesar dead,

He cried almost to roaring; and he wept

When at Philippi he found Brutus slain.

ENOBARBUS.

[Aside to AGRIPPA.] That year, indeed, he was troubled with a

rheum;

What willingly he did confound he wail'd:

Believe't till I weep too.

CAESAR.

No, sweet Octavia,

You shall hear from me still; the time shall not

Out-go my thinking on you.

ANTONY.

Come, sir, come;

I'll wrestle with you in my strength of love:

Look, here I have you; thus I let you go,

And give you to the gods.

CAESAR.

Adieu; be happy!

LEPIDUS.

Let all the number of the stars give light

To thy fair way!

CAESAR.

Farewell, farewell!

[Kisses OCTAVIA.]

ANTONY.

Farewell!

[Trumpets sound within. Exeunt.]

SCENE III. Alexandria. A Room in the Palace.

[Enter CLEOPATRA, CHARMIAN, IRAS, and ALEXAS.]

CLEOPATRA.

Where is the fellow?

ALEXAS.

Half afear'd to come.

CLEOPATRA.

Go to, go to.

[Enter a Messenger.]

Come hither, sir.

ALEXAS.

Good majesty,

Herod of Jewry dare not look upon you

But when you are well pleas'd.

CLEOPATRA.

That Herod's head

I'll have: but how? when Antony is gone,

Through whom I might command it?—Come thou near.

MESSENGER.

Most gracious majesty,—

CLEOPATRA.

Didst thou behold Octavia?

MESSENGER.

Ay, dread queen.

CLEOPATRA.

Where?

MESSENGER.

Madam, in Rome

I look'd her in the face, and saw her led

Between her brother and Mark Antony.

CLEOPATRA.

Is she as tall as me?

MESSENGER.

She is not, madam.

CLEOPATRA.

Didst hear her speak? is she shrill-tongu'd or low?

MESSENGER.

Madam, I heard her speak: she is low-voic'd.

CLEOPATRA.

That's not so good:—he cannot like her long.

CHARMIAN.

Like her! O Isis! 'tis impossible.

CLEOPATRA.

I think so, Charmian: dull of tongue and dwarfish!—

What majesty is in her gait? Remember,

If e'er thou look'dst on majesty.

MESSENGER.

She creeps,—

Her motion and her station are as one;

She shows a body rather than a life,

A statue than a breather.

CLEOPATRA.

Is this certain?

MESSENGER.

Or I have no observance.

CHARMIAN.

Three in Egypt

Cannot make better note.

CLEOPATRA.

He's very knowing;

I do perceive't:—there's nothing in her yet:—

The fellow has good judgment.

CHARMIAN.

Excellent.

CLEOPATRA.

Guess at her years, I pr'ythee.

MESSENGER.

Madam,

She was a widow.

CLEOPATRA.

Widow!—Charmian, hark!

MESSENGER.

And I do think she's thirty.

CLEOPATRA.

Bear'st thou her face in mind? is't long or round?

MESSENGER.

Round even to faultiness.

CLEOPATRA.

For the most part, too, they are foolish that are so.—

Her hair, what colour?

MESSENGER.

Brown, madam: and her forehead

As low as she would wish it.

CLEOPATRA.

There's gold for thee.

Thou must not take my former sharpness ill:—

I will employ thee back again; I find thee

Most fit for business:—go make thee ready;

Our letters are prepar'd.

[Exit Messenger.]

CHARMIAN.

A proper man.

CLEOPATRA.

Indeed, he is so: I repent me much

That so I harried him. Why, methinks, by him,

This creature's no such thing.

CHARMIAN.

Nothing, madam.

CLEOPATRA.

The man hath seen some majesty, and should know.

CHARMIAN.

Hath he seen majesty? Isis else defend,

And serving you so long!

CLEOPATRA.

I have one thing more to ask him yet, good Charmian:

But 'tis no matter; thou shalt bring him to me

Where I will write. All may be well enough.

CHARMIAN.

I warrant you, madam.

[Exeunt.]

SCENE IV. Athens. A Room in ANTONY'S House.

[Enter ANTONY and OCTAVIA.]

ANTONY.

Nay, nay, Octavia, not only that,—

That were excusable, that and thousands more

Of semblable import—but he hath wag'd

New wars 'gainst Pompey; made his will, and read it

To public ear:

Spoke scandy of me: when perforce he could not

But pay me terms of honour, cold and sickly

He vented them:most narrow measure lent me;

When the best hint was given him, he not took't,

Or did it from his teeth.

OCTAVIA.

O my good lord,

Believe not all; or if you must believe,

Stomach not all. A more unhappy lady,

If this division chance, ne'er stood between,

Praying for both parts:

Sure the good gods will mock me presently

When I shall pray 'O, bless my lord and husband!'

Undo that prayer by crying out as loud

'O, bless my brother!' Husband win, win brother,

Prays and destroys the prayer; no mid-way

'Twixt these extremes at all.

ANTONY.

Gentle Octavia,

Let your best love draw to that point which seeks

Best to preserve it: if I lose mine honour,

I lose myself: better I were not yours

Than yours so branchless. But, as you requested,

Yourself shall go between's: the meantime, lady,

I'll raise the preparation of a war

Shall stain your brother: make your soonest haste;

So your desires are yours.

OCTAVIA.

Thanks to my lord.

The Jove of power make me, most weak, most weak,

Your reconciler! Wars 'twixt you twain would be

As if the world should cleave, and that slain men

Should solder up the rift.

ANTONY.

When it appears to you where this begins,

Turn your displeasure that way; for our faults

Can never be so equal that your love

Can equally move with them. Provide your going;

Choose your own company, and command what cost

Your heart has mind to.

[Exeunt.]

SCENE V. Athens. Another Room in ANTONY'S House.

[Enter ENOBARBUS and EROS, meeting.]

ENOBARBUS.

How now, friend Eros!

EROS.

There's strange news come, sir.

ENOBARBUS.

What, man?

EROS.

Caesar and Lepidus have made wars upon Pompey.

ENOBARBUS.

This is old: what is the success?

EROS. Caesar, having made use of him in the wars 'gainst Pompey, presently denied him rivality; would not let him partake in the glory of the action: and not resting here, accuses him of letters he had formerly wrote to Pompey; upon his own appeal, seizes him: so the poor third is up, till death enlarge his confine.

ENOBARBUS.

Then, world, thou hast a pair of chaps, no more;

And throw between them all the food thou hast,

They'll grind the one the other. Where's Antony?

EROS.

He's walking in the garden—thus; and spurns

The rush that lies before him; cries 'Fool Lepidus!'

And threats the throat of that his officer

That murder'd Pompey.

ENOBARBUS.

Our great navy's rigg'd.

EROS.

For Italy and Caesar. More, Domitius;

My lord desires you presently: my news

I might have told hereafter.

ENOBARBUS.

'Twill be naught;

But let it be.—Bring me to Antony.

EROS.

Come, sir.

[Exeunt.]

SCENE VI. Rome. A Room in CAESAR'S House.

[Enter CAESAR, AGRIPPA, and MAECENAS.]

CAESAR.

Contemning Rome, he has done all this, and more,

In Alexandria. Here's the manner of't:—

I' the market-place, on a tribunal silver'd,

Cleopatra and himself in chairs of gold

Were publicly enthron'd: at the feet sat

Caesarion, whom they call my father's son,

And all the unlawful issue that their lust

Since then hath made between them. Unto her

He gave the 'stablishment of Egypt; made her

Of lower Syria, Cyprus, Lydia,

Absolute queen.

MAECENAS.

This in the public eye?

CAESAR.

I' the common show-place, where they exercise.

His sons he there proclaim'd the kings of kings:

Great Media, Parthia, and Armenia,

He gave to Alexander; to Ptolemy he assign'd

Syria, Cilicia, and Phoenicia: she

In the habiliments of the goddess Isis

That day appear'd; and oft before gave audience,

As 'tis reported, so.

MAECENAS.

Let Rome be thus

Inform'd.

AGRIPPA.

Who, queasy with his insolence

Already, will their good thoughts call from him.

CAESAR.

The people knows it: and have now receiv'd

His accusations.

AGRIPPA.

Who does he accuse?

CAESAR.

Caesar: and that, having in Sicily

Sextus Pompeius spoil'd, we had not rated him

His part o' the isle: then does he say he lent me

Some shipping, unrestor'd: lastly, he frets

That Lepidus of the triumvirate

Should be depos'd; and, being, that we detain

All his revenue.

AGRIPPA.

Sir, this should be answer'd.

CAESAR.

'Tis done already, and messenger gone.

I have told him Lepidus was grown too cruel;

That he his high authority abus'd,

And did deserve his change: for what I have conquer'd

I grant him part; but then, in his Armenia

And other of his conquer'd kingdoms, I

Demand the like.

MAECENAS.

He'll never yield to that.

CAESAR.

Nor must not then be yielded to in this.

[Enter OCTAVIA, with her train.]

OCTAVIA.

Hail, Caesar, and my lord! hail, most dear Caesar!

CAESAR.

That ever I should call thee castaway!

OCTAVIA.

You have not call'd me so, nor have you cause.

CAESAR.

Why have you stol'n upon us thus? You come not

Like Caesar's sister: the wife of Antony

Should have an army for an usher, and

The neighs of horse to tell of her approach

Long ere she did appear; the trees by the way

Should have borne men; and expectation fainted,

Longing for what it had not; nay, the dust

Should have ascended to the roof of heaven,

Rais'd by your populous troops: but you are come

A market-maid to Rome; and have prevented

The ostentation of our love, which left unshown

Is often left unlov'd; we should have met you

By sea and land; supplying every stage

With an augmented greeting.

OCTAVIA.

Good my lord,

To come thus was I not constrain'd, but did it

On my free will. My lord, Mark Antony,

Hearing that you prepar'd for war, acquainted

My grieved ear withal: whereon I begg'd

His pardon for return.

CAESAR.

Which soon he granted,

Being an obstruct 'tween his lust and him.

OCTAVIA.

Do not say so, my lord.

CAESAR.

I have eyes upon him,

And his affairs come to me on the wind.

Where is he now?

OCTAVIA.

My lord, in Athens.

CAESAR.

No, my most wronged sister; Cleopatra

Hath nodded him to her. He hath given his empire

Up to a whore; who now are levying

The kings o' theearth for war: he hath assembled

Bocchus, the king of Libya; Archelaus

Of Cappadocia; Philadelphos, king

Of Paphlagonia; the Thracian king, Adallas;

King Manchus of Arabia; King of Pont;

Herod of Jewry; Mithridates, king

Of Comagene; Polemon and Amyntas,

The kings of Mede and Lycaonia, with

More larger list of sceptres.

OCTAVIA.

Ay me, most wretched,

That have my heart parted betwixt two friends,

That do afflict each other!

CAESAR.

Welcome hither:

Your letters did withhold our breaking forth,

Till we perceiv'd both how you were wrong led

And we in negligent danger. Cheer your heart:

Be you not troubled with the time, which drives

O'er your content these strong necessities;

But let determin'd things to destiny

Hold unbewail'd their way. Welcome to Rome;

Nothing more dear to me. You are abus'd

Beyond the mark of thought: and the high gods,

To do you justice, make their ministers

Of us and those that love you. Best of comfort;

And ever welcome to us.

AGRIPPA.

Welcome, lady.

MAECENAS.

Welcome, dear madam.

Each heart in Rome does love and pity you:

Only theadulterous Antony, most large

In his abominations, turns you off,

And gives his potent regiment to a trull

That noises it against us.

OCTAVIA.

Is it so, sir?

CAESAR.

Most certain. Sister, welcome: pray you

Be ever known to patience: my dear'st sister!

[Exeunt.]

SCENE VII. ANTONY'S Camp near the Promontory of Actium.

[Enter CLEOPATRA and ENOBARBUS.]

CLEOPATRA.

I will be even with thee, doubt it not.

ENOBARBUS.

But why, why, why?

CLEOPATRA.

Thou hast forspoke my being in these wars,

And say'st it is not fit.

ENOBARBUS.

Well, is it, is it?

CLEOPATRA.

If not denounc'd against us, why should not we

Be there in person?

ENOBARBUS.

[Aside.] Well, I could reply:—

If we should serve with horse and mares together

The horse were merely lost; the mares would bear

A soldier and his horse.

CLEOPATRA.

What is't you say?

ENOBARBUS.

Your presence needs must puzzle Antony;

Take from his heart, take from his brain, from's time,

What should not then be spar'd. He is already

Traduc'd for levity: and 'tis said in Rome

That Photinus an eunuch and your maids

Manage this war.

CLEOPATRA.

Sink Rome, and their tongues rot

That speak against us! A charge we bear i' the war,

And, as the president of my kingdom, will

Appear there for a man. Speak not against it;

I will not stay behind.

ENOBARBUS.

Nay, I have done.

Here comes the emperor.

[Enter ANTONY and CANIDIUS.]

ANTONY.

Is it not strange, Canidius,

That from Tarentum and Brundusium

He could so quickly cut the Ionian sea,

And take in Toryne?—You have heard on't, sweet?

CLEOPATRA.

Celerity is never more admir'd

Than by the negligent.

ANTONY.

A good rebuke,

Which might have well becom'd the best of men

To taunt at slackness.—Canidius, we

Will fight with him by sea.

CLEOPATRA.

By sea! what else?

CANIDIUS.

Why will my lord do so?

ANTONY.

For that he dares us to't.

ENOBARBUS.

So hath my lord dar'd him to single fight.

CANIDIUS.

Ay, and to wage this battle at Pharsalia,

Where Caesar fought with Pompey. But these offers,

Which serve not for his vantage, he shakes off;

And so should you.

ENOBARBUS.

Your ships are not well mann'd:

Your mariners are muleteers, reapers, people

Ingross'd by swift impress; in Caesar's fleet

Are those that often have 'gainst Pompey fought:

Their ships are yare; yours heavy: no disgrace

Shall fall you for refusing him at sea,

Being prepar'd for land.

ANTONY.

By sea, by sea.

ENOBARBUS.

Most worthy sir, you therein throw away

The absolute soldiership you have by land;

Distract your army, which doth most consist

Of war-mark'd footmen; leave unexecuted

Your own renowned knowledge; quite forgo

The way which promises assurance; and

Give up yourself merely to chance and hazard

From firm security.

ANTONY.

I'll fight at sea.

CLEOPATRA.

I have sixty sails, Caesar none better.

ANTONY.

Our overplus of shipping will we burn;

And, with the rest full-mann'd, from the head of Actium

Beat the approaching Caesar. But if we fail,

We then can do't at land.

133

[Enter a Messenger.]

Thy business?

MESSENGER.

The news is true, my lord: he is descried;

Caesar has taken Toryne.

ANTONY.

Can he be there in person? 'tis impossible—

Strange that his power should be.—Canidius,

Our nineteen legions thou shalt hold by land,

And our twelve thousand horse.—We'll to our ship:

Away, my Thetis!

[Enter a SOLDIER.]

How now, worthy soldier?

SOLDIER.

O noble emperor, do not fight by sea;

Trust not to rotten planks: do you misdoubt

This sword and these my wounds? Let the Egyptians

And the Phoenicians go a-ducking: we

Have us'd to conquer standing on the earth

And fighting foot to foot.

ANTONY.

Well, well:—away.

[Exeunt ANTONY, CLEOPATRA, and ENOBARBUS.]

SOLDIER.

By Hercules, I think I am i' the right.

CANIDIUS.

Soldier, thou art: but his whole action grows

Not in the power on't: so our leader's led,

And we are women's men.

SOLDIER.

You keep by land

The legions and the horse whole, do you not?

CANIDIUS.

Marcus Octavius, Marcus Justeius,

Publicola, and Caelius are for sea:

But we keep whole by land. This speed of Caesar's

Carries beyond belief.

SOLDIER.

While he was yet in Rome

His power went out in such distractions as

Beguil'd all spies.

CANIDIUS.

Who's his lieutenant, hear you?

SOLDIER.

They say one Taurus.

CANIDIUS.

Well I know the man.

[Enter a Messenger.]

MESSENGER.

The Emperor calls Canidius.

CANIDIUS.

With news the time's with labour; and throes forth

Each minute some.

[Exeunt.]

SCENE VIII. A plain near Actium.

[Enter CAESAR, TAURUS, Officers, and others.]

CAESAR.

Taurus,—

TAURUS.

My lord?

CAESAR.

Strike not by land; keep whole; provoke not battle

Till we have done at sea. Do not exceed

The prescript of this scroll: our fortune lies

Upon this jump.

[Exeunt.]

SCENE IX. Another part of the Plain.

[Enter ANTONY and ENOBARBUS.]

ANTONY.

Set we our squadrons on yon side o' the hill,

In eye of Caesar's battle; from which place

We may the number of the ships behold,

And so proceed accordingly.

[Exeunt.]

SCENE X. Another part of the Plain.

[Enter CANIDIUS, marching with his land Army one way; and
TAURUS, the Lieutenant of CAESAR, with his Army, the other way.
After their going in, is heard the noise of a sea-fight.]

[Alarum. Enter ENOBARBUS.]

ENOBARBUS.

Naught, naught, all naught! I can behold no longer:

The Antoniad, the Egyptian admiral,

With all their sixty, fly and turn the rudder:

To see't mine eyes are blasted.

[Enter SCARUS.]

SCARUS.

Gods and goddesses,

All the whole synod of them!

ENOBARBUS.

What's thy passion?

SCARUS.

The greater cantle of the world is lost

With very ignorance; we have kiss'd away

Kingdoms and provinces.

ENOBARBUS.

How appears the fight?

SCARUS.

On our side like the token'd pestilence,

Where death is sure. Yon ribaudred nag of Egypt,—

Whom leprosy o'ertake!—i' the midst o' the fight,

When vantage like a pair of twins appear'd,

Both as the same, or rather ours the elder,—

The breese upon her, like a cow in June,—

Hoists sails and flies.

ENOBARBUS.

That I beheld:

Mine eyes did sicken at the sight, and could not

Endure a further view.

SCARUS.

She once being loof'd,

The noble ruin of her magic, Antony,

Claps on his sea-wing, and, like a doting mallard,

Leaving the fight in height, flies after her:

I never saw an action of such shame;

Experience, manhood, honour, ne'er before

Did violate so itself.

ENOBARBUS.

Alack, alack!

[Enter CANIDIUS.]

CANIDIUS.

Our fortune on the sea is out of breath,

And sinks most lamentably. Had our general

Been what he knew himself, it had gone well:

O, he has given example for our flight

Most grossly by his own!

ENOBARBUS.

Ay, are you thereabouts?

Why, then, good night indeed.

CANIDIUS.

Toward Peloponnesus are they fled.

SCARUS.

'Tis easy to't; and there I will attend

What further comes.

CANIDIUS.

To Caesar will I render

My legions and my horse; six kings already

Show me the way of yielding.

ENOBARBUS.

I'll yet follow

The wounded chance of Antony, though my reason

Sits in the wind against me.

[Exeunt.]

SCENE XI. Alexandria. A Room in the Palace.

[Enter ANTONY and attendants.]

ANTONY.

Hark! the land bids me tread no more upon't;—

It is asham'd to bear me.—Friends, come hither:

I am so lated in the world that I

Have lost my way for ever:—I have a ship

Laden with gold; take that; divide it; fly,

And make your peace with Caesar.

ALL.

Fly! Not we.

ANTONY.

I have fled myself, and have instructed cowards

To run and show their shoulders.—Friends, be gone;

I have myself resolv'd upon a course

Which has no need of you; be gone;

My treasure's in the harbour, take it.—O,

I follow'd that I blush to look upon:

My very hairs do mutiny; for the white

Reprove the brown for rashness, and they them

For fear and doting.—Friends, be gone: you shall

Have letters from me to some friends that will

Sweep your way for you. Pray you, look not sad,

Nor make replies of loathness: take the hint

Which my despair proclaims; let that be left

Which leaves itself: to the sea-side straightway:

I will possess you of that ship and treasure.

Leave me, I pray, a little: pray you now:—

Nay, do so; for indeed I have lost command,

Therefore I pray you:—I'll see you by and by.

[Sits down.]

[Enter CLEOPATRA, led by CHARMIAN and IRAS, EROS following.]

EROS.

Nay, gentle madam, to him!—comfort him.

IRAS.

Do, most dear queen.

CHARMIAN.

Do! why, what else?

CLEOPATRA.

Let me sit down. O Juno!

ANTONY.

No, no, no, no, no.

EROS.

See you here, sir?

ANTONY.

O, fie, fie, fie!

143

CHARMIAN.

Madam,—

IRAS.

Madam, O good empress,—

EROS.

Sir, sir,—

ANTONY.

Yes, my lord, yes;—he at Philippi kept

His sword e'en like a dancer; while I struck

The lean and wrinkled Cassius; and 'twas I

That the mad Brutus ended; he alone

Dealt on lieutenantry, and no practice had

In the brave squares of war: yet now—no matter.

CLEOPATRA.

Ah, stand by.

EROS.

The queen, my lord, the queen!

IRAS.

Go to him, madam, speak to him:

He is unqualitied with very shame.

CLEOPATRA.

Well then,—sustain me.—O!

EROS.

Most noble sir, arise; the queen approaches:

Her head's declin'd, and death will seize her, but

Your comfort makes the rescue.

ANTONY.

I have offended reputation,—

A most unnoble swerving.

EROS.

Sir, the queen.

ANTONY.

O, whither hast thou led me, Egypt? See

How I convey my shame out of thine eyes

By looking back, what I have left behind

'Stroy'd in dishonour.

CLEOPATRA.

O my lord, my lord,

Forgive my fearful sails! I little thought

You would have follow'd.

ANTONY.

Egypt, thou knew'st too well

My heart was to thy rudder tied by the strings,

And thou shouldst tow me after: o'er my spirit

Thy full supremacy thou knew'st, and that

Thy beck might from the bidding of the gods

Command me.

CLEOPATRA.

O, my pardon!

ANTONY.

Now I must

To the young man send humble treaties, dodge

And palter in the shifts of lowness; who

With half the bulk o' the world play'd as I pleas'd,

Making and marring fortunes. You did know

How much you were my conqueror; and that

My sword, made weak by my affection, would

Obey it on all cause.

CLEOPATRA.

Pardon, pardon!

ANTONY.

Fall not a tear, I say; one of them rates

All that is won and lost: give me a kiss;

Even this repays me.—We sent our schoolmaster;

Is he come back?—Love, I am full of lead.—

Some wine, within there, and our viands!—Fortune knows

We scorn her most when most she offers blows.

[Exeunt.]

SCENE XII. CAESAR'S camp in Egypt.

[Enter CAESAR, DOLABELLA, THYREUS, with others.]

CAESAR.

Let him appear that's come from Antony.—

Know you him?

DOLABELLA.

Caesar, 'tis his schoolmaster:

An argument that he is pluck'd, when hither

He sends so poor a pinion of his wing,

Which had superfluous kings for messengers

Not many moons gone by.

[Enter EUPHRONIUS.]

CAESAR.

Approach, and speak.

EUPHRONIUS.

Such as I am, I come from Antony:

I was of late as petty to his ends

As is the morn-dew on the myrtle leaf

To his grand sea.

CAESAR.

Be't so: declare thine office.

EUPHRONIUS.

Lord of his fortunes he salutes thee, and

Requires to live in Egypt: which not granted,

He lessens his requests; and to thee sues

To let him breathe between the heavens and earth,

A private man in Athens: this for him.

Next, Cleopatra does confess thy greatness;

Submits her to thy might, and of thee craves

The circle of the Ptolemies for her heirs,

Now hazarded to thy grace.

CAESAR.

For Antony,

I have no ears to his request. The queen

Of audience nor desire shall fail; so she

From Egypt drive her all-disgraced friend,

Or take his life there: this if she perform,

She shall not sue unheard. So to them both.

EUPHRONIUS.

Fortune pursue thee!

CAESAR.

Bring him through the bands.

[Exit EUPHRONIUS.]

[To THYREUS.] To try thy eloquence, now 'tis time. Despatch;

From Antony win Cleopatra. Promise,

And in our name, what she requires; add more,

From thine invention, offers: women are not

In their best fortunes strong; but want will perjure

The ne'er-touch'd vestal: try thy cunning, Thyreus;

Make thine own edict for thy pains, which we

Will answer as a law.

THYREUS.

Caesar, I go.

CAESAR.

Observe how Antony becomes his flaw,

And what thou think'st his very action speaks

In every power that moves.

THYREUS.

Caesar, I shall.

[Exeunt.]

SCENE XIII. Alexandria. A Room in the Palace.

[Enter CLEOPATRA, ENOBARBUS, CHARMIAN, and IRAS.]

CLEOPATRA.

What shall we do, Enobarbus?

ENOBARBUS.

Think, and die.

CLEOPATRA.

Is Antony or we in fault for this?

ENOBARBUS.

Antony only, that would make his will

Lord of his reason. What though you fled

From that great face of war, whose several ranges

Frighted each other? why should he follow?

The itch of his affection should not then

Have nick'd his captainship; at such a point,

When half to half the world oppos'd, he being

The mered question; 'twas a shame no less

Than was his loss, to course your flying flags

And leave his navy gazing.

CLEOPATRA.

Pr'ythee, peace.

[Enter ANTONY, with EUPHRONIUS.]

ANTONY.

Is that his answer?

EUPHRONIUS.

Ay, my lord.

ANTONY.

The queen shall then have courtesy, so she

Will yield us up.

EUPHRONIUS.

He says so.

ANTONY.

Let her know't.—

To the boy Caesar send this grizzled head,

And he will fill thy wishes to the brim

With principalities.

CLEOPATRA.

That head, my lord?

ANTONY.

To him again: tell him he wears the rose

Of youth upon him; from which the world should note

Something particular: his coins, ships, legions,

May be a coward's; whose ministers would prevail

Under the service of a child as soon

As i' the command of Caesar: I dare him therefore

To lay his gay comparisons apart,

And answer me declin'd, sword against sword,

Ourselves alone. I'll write it: follow me.

[Exeunt ANTONY and EUPHRONIUS.]

EUPHRONIUS.

Yes, like enough high-battled Caesar will

Unstate his happiness, and be stag'd to the show

Against a sworder.—I see men's judgments are

A parcel of their fortunes; and things outward

Do draw the inward quality after them,

To suffer all alike. That he should dream,

Knowing all measures, the full Caesar will

Answer his emptiness!—Caesar, thou hast subdu'd

His judgment too.

[Enter an Attendant.]

ATTENDANT.

A messenger from Caesar.

CLEOPATRA.

What, no more ceremony?—See, my women!—

Against the blown rose may they stop their nose

That kneel'd unto the buds.—Admit him, sir.

[Exit Attendant.]

ENOBARBUS.

[Aside.] Mine honesty and I begin to square.

The loyalty well held to fools does make

Our faith mere folly:—yet he that can endure

To follow with allegiance a fallen lord

Does conquer him that did his master conquer,

And earns a place i' the story.

[Enter THYREUS.]

CLEOPATRA.

Caesar's will?

THYREUS.

Hear it apart.

CLEOPATRA.

None but friends: say boldly.

THYREUS.

So, haply, are they friends to Antony.

ENOBARBUS.

He needs as many, sir, as Caesar has;

Or needs not us. If Caesar please, our master

Will leap to be his friend: for us, you know

Whose he is we are, and that is Caesar's.

THYREUS.

So.—

Thus then, thou most renown'd: Caesar entreats

Not to consider in what case thou stand'st

Further than he is Caesar.

CLEOPATRA.

Go on: right royal.

THYREUS.

He knows that you embrace not Antony

As you did love, but as you fear'd him.

CLEOPATRA. O!

THYREUS.

The scars upon your honour, therefore, he

Does pity, as constrained blemishes,

Not as deserv'd.

CLEOPATRA.

He is a god, and knows

What is most right: mine honour was not yielded,

But conquer'd merely.

ENOBARBUS.

[Aside.] To be sure of that,

I will ask Antony.—Sir, sir, thou art so leaky

That we must leave thee to thy sinking, for

Thy dearest quit thee.

[Exit.]

THYREUS.

Shall I say to Caesar

What you require of him? for he partly begs

To be desir'd to give. It much would please him

That of his fortunes you should make a staff

To lean upon: but it would warm his spirits

To hear from me you had left Antony,

And put yourself under his shroud, who is

The universal landlord.

CLEOPATRA.

What's your name?

THYREUS.

My name is Thyreus.

CLEOPATRA.

Most kind messenger,

Say to great Caesar this:—in deputation

I kiss his conquring hand: tell him I am prompt

To lay my crown at's feet, and there to kneel:

Tell him, from his all-obeying breath I hear

The doom of Egypt.

THYREUS.

'Tis your noblest course.

Wisdom and fortune combating together,

If that the former dare but what it can,

No chance may shake it. Give me grace to lay

My duty on your hand.

CLEOPATRA.

Your Caesar's father

Oft, when he hath mus'd of taking kingdoms in,

Bestow'd his lips on that unworthy place,

As it rain'd kisses.

[Re-enter ANTONY and ENOBARBUS.]

ANTONY.

Favours, by Jove that thunders!—

What art thou, fellow?

THYREUS.

One that but performs

The bidding of the fullest man, and worthiest

To have command obey'd.

ENOBARBUS.

[Aside.] You will be whipp'd.

ANTONY.

Approach there.—Ah, you kite!—Now, gods and devils!

Authority melts from me: of late, when I cried 'Ho!'

Like boys unto a muss, kings would start forth

And cry 'Your will?' Have you no ears? I am

Antony yet.

[Enter Attendants.]

Take hence this Jack and whip him.

ENOBARBUS.

'Tis better playing with a lion's whelp

Than with an old one dying.

ANTONY.

Moon and stars!

Whip him.—Were't twenty of the greatest tributaries

That do acknowledge Caesar, should I find them

So saucy with the hand of she here,—what's her name

Since she was Cleopatra?—Whip him, fellows,

Till like a boy you see him cringe his face,

And whine aloud for mercy: take him hence.

THYMUS.

Mark Antony,—

ANTONY.

Tug him away: being whipp'd,

Bring him again.—This Jack of Caesar's shall

Bear us an errand to him.—

                [Exeunt Attendants with THYREUS.]

You were half blasted ere I knew you.—Ha!

Have I my pillow left unpress'd in Rome,

Forborne the getting of a lawful race,

And by a gem of women, to be abus'd

By one that looks on feeders?

CLEOPATRA.

Good my lord,—

ANTONY.

You have been a boggler ever:—

But when we in our viciousness grow hard,—

O misery on't!—the wise gods seal our eyes;

In our own filth drop our clear judgments: make us

Adore our errors; laugh at's while we strut

To our confusion.

CLEOPATRA.

O, is't come to this?

ANTONY.

I found you as a morsel cold upon

Dead Caesar's trencher; nay, you were a fragment

Of Cneius Pompey's; besides what hotter hours,

Unregist'red in vulgar fame, you have

Luxuriously pick'd out:—for I am sure,

Though you can guess what temperance should be,

You know not what it is.

CLEOPATRA.

Wherefore is this?

ANTONY.

To let a fellow that will take rewards,

And say 'God quit you!' be familiar with

My playfellow, your hand; this kingly seal

And plighter of high hearts!—O that I were

Upon the hill of Basan, to outroar

The horned herd! for I have savage cause;

And to proclaim it civilly were like

A halter'd neck which does the hangman thank

For being yare about him.

[Re-enter Attendants with THYREUS.]

Is he whipp'd?

FIRST ATTENDANT.

Soundly, my lord.

ANTONY.

Cried he? and begg'd he pardon?

FIRST ATTENDANT.

He did ask favour.

ANTONY.

If that thy father live, let him repent

Thou wast not made his daughter; and be thou sorry

To follow Caesar in his triumph, since

Thou hast been whipp'd for following him: henceforth

The white hand of a lady fever thee,

Shake thou to look on't.—Get thee back to Caesar;

Tell him thy entertainment: look thou say

He makes me angry with him; for he seems

Proud and disdainful, harping on what I am,

Not what he knew I was: he makes me angry;

And at this time most easy 'tis to do't,

When my good stars, that were my former guides,

Have empty left their orbs, and shot their fires

Into the abysm of hell. If he mislike

My speech and what is done, tell him he has

Hipparchus, my enfranched bondman, whom

He may at pleasure, whip, or hang, or torture,

As he shall like, to quit me: urge it thou:

Hence with thy stripes, be gone.

[Exit THYREUS.]

CLEOPATRA.

Have you done yet?

ANTONY.

Alack, our terrene moon

Is now eclips'd, and it portends alone

The fall of Antony!

CLEOPATRA.

I must stay his time.

ANTONY.

To flatter Caesar, would you mingle eyes

With one that ties his points?

CLEOPATRA.

Not know me yet?

ANTONY.

160

Cold-hearted toward me?

CLEOPATRA.

Ah, dear, if I be so,

From my cold heart let heaven engender hail,

And poison it in the source; and the first stone

Drop in my neck: as it determines, so

Dissolve my life! The next Caesarion smite!

Till, by degrees, the memory of my womb,

Together with my brave Egyptians all,

By the discandying of this pelleted storm,

Lie graveless,—till the flies and gnats of Nile

Have buried them for prey!

ANTONY.

I am satisfied.

Caesar sits down in Alexandria; where

I will oppose his fate. Our force by land

Hath nobly held: our sever'd navy to

Have knit again, and fleet, threat'ning most sea-like.

Where hast thou been, my heart?—Dost thou hear, lady?

If from the field I shall return once more

To kiss these lips, I will appear in blood:

I and my sword will earn our chronicle:

There's hope in't yet.

CLEOPATRA.

That's my brave lord!

ANTONY.

I will be treble-sinew'd, hearted, breath'd,

And fight maliciously: for when mine hours

Were nice and lucky, men did ransom lives

Of me for jests; but now I'll set my teeth,

And send to darkness all that stop me.—Come,

Let's have one other gaudy night: call to me

All my sad captains; fill our bowls; once more

Let's mock the midnight bell.

CLEOPATRA.

It is my birthday.

I had thought t'have held it poor; but since my lord

Is Antony again I will be Cleopatra.

ANTONY.

We will yet do well.

CLEOPATRA.

Call all his noble captains to my lord.

ANTONY.

Do so; we'll speak to them: and to-night I'll force

The wine peep through their scars.—Come on, my queen;

There's sap in't yet. The next time I do fight

I'll make death love me; for I will contend

Even with his pestilent scythe.

[Exeunt all but ENOBARBUS.]

ENOBARBUS.

Now he'll outstare the lightning. To be furious

Is to be frighted out of fear; and in that mood

The dove will peck the estridge; and I see still

A diminution in our captain's brain

Restores his heart: when valour preys on reason,

It eats the sword it fights with. I will seek

Some way to leave him.

[Exit.]

ACT IV.

SCENE I. CAESAR'S Camp at Alexandria.

[Enter CAESAR reading a letter; AGRIPPA, MAECENAS, and others.]

CAESAR.

He calls me boy; and chides as he had power

To beat me out of Egypt; my messenger

He hath whip'd with rods; dares me to personal combat,

Caesar to Antony:—let the old ruffian know

I have many other ways to die; meantime

Laugh at his challenge.

MAECENAS.

Caesar must think

When one so great begins to rage, he's hunted

Even to falling. Give him no breath, but now

Make boot of his distraction:—never anger

Made good guard for itself.

CAESAR.

Let our best heads

Know that to-morrow the last of many battles

We mean to fight.—Within our files there are

Of those that serv'd Mark Antony but late,

Enough to fetch him in. See it done:

And feast the army; we have store to do't,

And they have earn'd the waste. Poor Antony!

[Exeunt.]

SCENE II. Alexandria. A Room in the Palace.

[Enter ANTONY, CLEOPATRA, ENOBARBUS, CHARMIAN, IRAS, ALEXAS, and others.]

ANTONY.

He will not fight with me, Domitius?

ENOBARBUS.

No.

ANTONY.

Why should he not?

ENOBARBUS.

He thinks, being twenty times of better fortune,

He is twenty men to one.

ANTONY.

To-morrow, soldier,

By sea and land I'll fight; or I will live,

Or bathe my dying honour in the blood

Shall make it live again. Woo't thou fight well?

ENOBARBUS.

I'll strike, and cry 'Take all.'

ANTONY.

Well said; come on.—

Call forth my household servants: let's to-night

Be bounteous at our meal.—

[Enter Servants.]

Give me thy hand,

Thou has been rightly honest;—so hast thou;—

Thou,—and thou,—and thou;—you have serv'd me well,

And kings have been your fellows.

CLEOPATRA.

[Aside to ENOBARBUS.] What means this?

ENOBARBUS.

[Aside to CLEOPATRA.] 'Tis one of those odd tricks which sorrow

shoots

Out of the mind.

ANTONY.

And thou art honest too.

I wish I could be made so many men,

And all of you clapp'd up together in

An Antony, that I might do you service

So good as you have done.

SERVANT.

The gods forbid!

ANTONY.

Well, my good fellows, wait on me to-night:

Scant not my cups; and make as much of me

As when mine empire was your fellow too,

And suffer'd my command.

CLEOPATRA.

[Aside to ENOBARBUS.] What does he mean?

ENOBARBUS.

[Aside to CLEOPATRA.] To make his followers weep.

ANTONY.

Tend me to-night;

May be it is the period of your duty:

Haply you shall not see me more; or if,

A mangled shadow: perchance to-morrow

You'll serve another master. I look on you

As one that takes his leave. Mine honest friends,

I turn you not away; but, like a master

Married to your good service, stay till death:

Tend me to-night two hours, I ask no more,

And the gods yield you for't!

ENOBARBUS.

What mean you, sir,

To give them this discomfort? Look, they weep;

And I, an ass, am onion-ey'd: for shame,

Transform us not to women.

ANTONY.

Ho, ho, ho!

Now the witch take me, if I meant it thus!

Grace grow where those drops fall! My hearty friends,

You take me in too dolorous a sense;

For I spake to you for your comfort,—did desire you

To burn this night with torches: know, my hearts,

I hope well of to-morrow; and will lead you

Where rather I'll expect victorious life

Than death and honour. Let's to supper; come,

And drown consideration.

[Exeunt.]

SCENE III. Alexandria. Before the Palace.

[Enter two Soldiers to their guard.]

FIRST SOLDIER.

Brother, good night: to-morrow is the day.

SECOND SOLDIER.

It will determine one way: fare you well.

Heard you of nothing strange about the streets?

FIRST SOLDIER.

Nothing. What news?

SECOND SOLDIER.

Belike 'tis but a rumour. Good night to you.

FIRST SOLDIER.

Well, sir, good night.

[Enter two other Soldiers.]

SECOND SOLDIER.

Soldiers, have careful watch.

THIRD SOLDIER.

And you. Good night, good night.

[The first two place themselves at their posts.]

FOURTH SOLDIER.

Here we: [The third and fourth take their posts.] and if
to-morrow

Our navy thrive, I have an absolute hope

Our landmen will stand up.

THIRD SOLDIER.

'Tis a brave army,

And full of purpose.

[Music as of hautboys under the stage.]

FOURTH SOLDIER.

Peace, what noise?

FIRST SOLDIER.

List, list!

SECOND SOLDIER.

Hark!

FIRST SOLDIER.

Music i' the air.

THIRD SOLDIER.

Under the earth.

FOURTH SOLDIER.

It signs well, does it not?

THIRD SOLDIER.

No.

FIRST SOLDIER.

Peace, I say!

What should this mean?

SECOND SOLDIER.

'Tis the god Hercules, whom Antony lov'd,

Now leaves him.

FIRST SOLDIER.

Walk; let's see if other watchmen

Do hear what we do.

[They advance to another post.]

SECOND SOLDIER.

How now, masters!

SOLDIERS.

[Speaking together.] How now!

How now! Do you hear this?

FIRST SOLDIER.

Ay; is't not strange?

THIRD SOLDIER.

Do you hear, masters? do you hear?

FIRST SOLDIER.

Follow the noise so far as we have quarter;

Let's see how it will give off.

SOLDIERS.

[Speaking together.] Content. 'Tis strange.

[Exeunt.]

SCENE IV. Alexandria. A Room in the Palace.

[Enter ANTONY and CLEOPATRA, CHARMIAN, IRAS, and others attending.]

ANTONY.

Eros! mine armour, Eros!

CLEOPATRA.

Sleep a little.

ANTONY.

No, my chuck.—Eros! Come, mine armour, Eros!

[Enter EROS with armour.]

Come, good fellow, put mine iron on.—

If fortune be not ours to-day, it is

Because we brave her.—Come.

CLEOPATRA.

Nay, I'll help too.

What's this for?

ANTONY.

Ah, let be, let be! Thou art

The armourer of my heart. False, false; this, this.

CLEOPATRA.

Sooth, la, I'll help: thus it must be.

ANTONY.

Well, well;

We shall thrive now.—Seest thou, my good fellow?

Go put on thy defences.

EROS.

Briefly, sir.

CLEOPATRA.

Is not this buckled well?

ANTONY.

Rarely, rarely;

He that unbuckles this, till we do please

To daff't for our repose, shall hear a storm.—

Thou fumblest, Eros, and my queen's a squire

More tight at this than thou: despatch.—O love,

That thou couldst see my wars to-day, and knew'st

The royal occupation! Thou shouldst see

A workman in't.—

[Enter an Officer, armed.]

Good-morrow to thee; welcome:

Thou look'st like him that knows a warlike charge:

To business that we love we rise betime,

And go to't with delight.

OFFICER.

A thousand, sir,

Early though't be, have on their riveted trim,

And at the port expect you.

[Shout. Flourish of trumpets within.]

[Enter other Officers and Soldiers.]

SECOND OFFICER.

The morn is fair.—Good morrow, general.

ALL.

Good morrow, general.

ANTONY.

'Tis well blown, lads:

This morning, like the spirit of a youth

That means to be of note, begins betimes.—

So, so; come, give me that: this way; well said.—

Fare thee well, dame, whate'er becomes of me:

[Kisses her.]

This is a soldier's kiss: rebukeable,

And worthy shameful check it were, to stand

On more mechanic compliment; I'll leave thee

Now like a man of steel.—You that will fight,

Follow me close; I'll bring you to't. Adieu.

[Exeunt ANTONY, EROS, Officers and Soldiers.]

CHARMIAN.

Please you, retire to your chamber.

CLEOPATRA.

Lead me.

He goes forth gallantly. That he and Caesar might

Determine this great war in single fight!

Then, Antony,—but now—Well, on.

[Exeunt.]

SCENE V. ANTONY'S camp near Alexandria.

[Trumpets sound within. Enter ANTONY and EROS; a SOLDIER meeting them.]

SOLDIER.

The gods make this a happy day to Antony!

ANTONY.

Would thou and those thy scars had once prevail'd

To make me fight at land!

SOLDIER.

Hadst thou done so,

The kings that have revolted, and the soldier

That has this morning left thee, would have still

Follow'd thy heels.

ANTONY.

Who's gone this morning?

SOLDIER.

Who.

One ever near thee. Call for Enobarbus,

He shall not hear thee; or from Caesar's camp

Say 'I am none of thine.'

ANTONY.

What say'st thou?

SOLDIER.

Sir,

He is with Caesar.

EROS.

Sir, his chests and treasure

He has not with him.

ANTONY.

Is he gone?

SOLDIER.

Most certain.

ANTONY.

Go, Eros, send his treasure after; do it;

Detain no jot, I charge thee; write to him—

I will subscribe,—gentle adieus and greetings;

Say that I wish he never find more cause

To change a master.—O, my fortunes have

Corrupted honest men!—Eros, despatch.

[Exeunt.]

SCENE VI. Alexandria. CAESAR'S camp.

[Flourish. Enter AGRIPPA, CAESAR, with DOLABELLA and ENOBARBUS.]

CAESAR.

Go forth, Agrippa, and begin the fight:

Our will is Antony be took alive;

Make it so known.

AGRIPPA.

Caesar, I shall.

[Exit.]

CAESAR.

The time of universal peace is near:

Prove this a prosperous day, the three-nook'd world

Shall bear the olive freely.

[Enter a Messenger.]

MESSENGER.

Antony

Is come into the field.

CAESAR.

Go charge Agrippa

Plant those that have revolted in the van,

That Antony may seem to spend his fury

Upon himself.

[Exeunt CAESAR and his Train.]

ENOBARBUS.

Alexas did revolt; and went to Jewry on

Affairs of Antony; there did dissuade

Great Herod to incline himself to Caesar

And leave his master Antony: for this pains

Casaer hath hang'd him. Canidius and the rest

That fell away, have entertainment, but

No honourable trust. I have done ill;

Of which I do accuse myself so sorely

That I will joy no more.

[Enter a SOLDIER of CAESAR'S.]

SOLDIER.

Enobarbus, Antony

Hath after thee sent all thy treasure, with

His bounty overplus: the messenger

Came on my guard, and at thy tent is now

Unloading of his mules.

ENOBARBUS.

I give it you.

SOLDIER.

Mock not, Enobarbus.

I tell you true: best you saf'd the bringer

Out of the host; I must attend mine office,

Or would have done't myself. Your emperor

Continues still a Jove.

[Exit.]

ENOBARBUS.

I am alone the villain of the earth,

And feel I am so most. O Antony,

Thou mine of bounty, how wouldst thou have paid

My better service, when my turpitude

Thou dost so crown with gold! This blows my heart:

If swift thought break it not, a swifter mean

Shall outstrike thought: but thought will do't, I feel.

I fight against thee!—No: I will go seek

Some ditch wherein to die; the foul'st best fits

My latter part of life.

[Exit.]

SCENE VII. Field of battle between the Camps.

[Alarum. Drums and trumpets. Enter AGRIPPA and others.]

AGRIPPA.

Retire, we have engag'd ourselves too far:

Caesar himself has work, and our oppression

Exceeds what we expected.

[Exeunt.]

[Alarum. Enter ANTONY, and SCARUS wounded.]

SCARUS.

O my brave emperor, this is fought indeed!

Had we done so at first, we had driven them home

With clouts about their heads.

ANTONY.

Thou bleed'st apace.

SCARUS.

I had a wound here that was like a T,

But now 'tis made an H.

ANTONY.

They do retire.

SCARUS.

We'll beat'em into bench-holes: I have yet

Room for six scotches more.

[Enter EROS.]

EROS.

They are beaten, sir; and our advantage serves

For a fair victory.

SCARUS.

Let us score their backs

And snatch 'em up, as we take hares, behind:

'Tis sport to maul a runner.

ANTONY.

I will reward thee

Once for thy sprightly comfort, and tenfold

For thy good valour. Come thee on.

SCARUS.

I'll halt after.

[Exeunt.]

SCENE VIII. Under the Walls of Alexandria.

[Alarum. Enter ANTONY, marching; SCARUS and Forces.]

ANTONY.

We have beat him to his camp. Run one before

And let the queen know of our gests.—To-morrow,

Before the sun shall see us, we'll spill the blood

That has to-day escap'd. I thank you all;

For doughty-handed are you, and have fought

Not as you serv'd the cause, but as't had been

Each man's like mine; you have shown all Hectors.

Enter the city, clip your wives, your friends,

Tell them your feats; whilst they with joyful tears

Wash the congealment from your wounds and kiss

The honour'd gashes whole.—[To SCARUS.] Give me thy hand;

[Enter CLEOPATRA, attended.]

To this great fairy I'll commend thy acts,

Make her thanks bless thee. O thou day o' the world,

Chain mine arm'd neck; leap thou, attire and all;

Through proof of harness to my heart, and there

Ride on the pants triumphing.

CLEOPATRA.

Lord of lords!

O infinite virtue, com'st thou smiling from

The world's great snare uncaught?

ANTONY.

Mine nightingale,

We have beat them to their beds. What, girl! though grey

Do something mingle with our younger brown, yet ha' we

A brain that nourishes our nerves, and can

Get goal for goal of youth. Behold this man;

Commend unto his lips thy favouring hand;—

Kiss it, my warrior: he hath fought to-day

As if a god, in hate of mankind, had

Destroyed in such a shape.

CLEOPATRA.

I'll give thee, friend,

An armour all of gold; it was a king's.

ANTONY.

He has deserv'd it, were it carbuncled

Like holy Phoebus' car.—Give me thy hand:

Through Alexandria make a jolly march;

Bear our hack'd targets like the men that owe them:

Had our great palace the capacity

To camp this host, we all would sup together,

And drink carouses to the next day's fate,

Which promises royal peril.—Trumpeters,

With brazen din blast you the city's ear;

Make mingle with our rattling tabourines;

That heaven and earth may strike their sounds together,

Applauding our approach.

[Exeunt.]

SCENE IX. CAESAR'S camp.

[Sentinels at their Post.]

FIRST SOLDIER.

If we be not reliev'd within this hour,

We must return to thecourt of guard: the night

Is shiny; and they say we shall embattle

By the second hour i' the morn.

SECOND SOLDIER.

This last day was

A shrewd one to's.

[Enter ENOBARBUS.]

ENOBARBUS.

O, bear me witness, night.—

THIRD SOLDIER.

What man is this?

SECOND SOLDIER.

Stand close and list him.

ENOBARBUS.

Be witness to me, O thou blessed moon,

When men revolted shall upon record

Bear hateful memory, poor Enobarbus did

Before thy face repent!—

FIRST SOLDIER.

Enobarbus!

THIRD SOLDIER.

Peace!

Hark further.

ENOBARBUS.

O sovereign mistress of true melancholy,

The poisonous damp of night disponge upon me,

That life, a very rebel to my will,

May hang no longer on me: throw my heart

Against the flint and hardness of my fault;

Which, being dried with grief, will break to powder,

And finish all foul thoughts. O Antony,

Nobler than my revolt is infamous,

Forgive me in thine own particular;

But let the world rank me in register

A master-leaver and a fugitive:

O Antony! O Antony!

[Dies.]

SECOND SOLDIER.

Let's speak to him.

FIRST SOLDIER.

Let's hear him, for the things he speaks

May concern Caesar.

THIRD SOLDIER.

Let's do so. But he sleeps.

FIRST SOLDIER.

Swoons rather; for so bad a prayer as his

Was never yet fore sleep.

SECOND SOLDIER.

Go we to him.

THIRD SOLDIER.

Awake, sir, awake; speak to us.

SECOND SOLDIER.

Hear you, sir?

FIRST SOLDIER.

The hand of death hath raught him.

[Drums afar off.]

Hark! the drums

Do merrily wake the sleepers. Let us bear him

To the court of guard; he is of note: our hour

Is fully out.

THIRD SOLDIER.

Come on, then;

He may recover yet.

[Exeunt with the body.]

SCENE X. Ground between the two Camps.

[Enter ANTONY and SCARUS, with Forces, marching.]

ANTONY.

Their preparation is to-day by sea;

We please them not by land.

SCARUS.

For both, my lord.

ANTONY.

I would they'd fight i' the fire or i' the air;

We'd fight there too. But this it is; our foot

Upon the hills adjoining to the city

Shall stay with us:—order for sea is given;

They have put forth the haven:—forward now,

Where their appointment we may best discover,

And look on their endeavour.

[Exeunt.]

SCENE XI. Another part of the Ground.

[**Enter CAESAR with his Forces, marching.**]

CAESAR.

But being charg'd, we will be still by land,

Which, as I take't, we shall; for his best force

Is forth to man his galleys. To the vales,

And hold our best advantage.

[Exeunt.]

SCENE XII. Another part of the Ground.

[Enter ANTONY and SCARUS.]

ANTONY.

Yet they are not join'd: where yond pine does stand

I shall discover all: I'll bring thee word

Straight how 'tis like to go.

[Exit.]

SCARUS.

Swallows have built

In Cleopatra's sails their nests: the augurers

Say they know not,—they cannot tell;—look grimly,

And dare not speak their knowledge. Antony

Is valiant and dejected; and, by starts,

His fretted fortunes give him hope and fear

Of what he has and has not.

[Alarum afar off, as at a sea-fight.]

[Re-enter ANTONY.]

ANTONY.

All is lost;

This foul Egyptian hath betrayed me:

My fleet hath yielded to the foe; and yonder

They cast their caps up, and carouse together

Like friends long lost.—Triple-turn'd whore! 'tis thou

Hast sold me to this novice; and my heart

Makes only wars on thee.—Bid them all fly;

For when I am reveng'd upon my charm,

I have done all.—Bid them all fly; begone.

[Exit SCARUS.]

O sun, thy uprise shall I see no more:

Fortune and Antony part here; even here

Do we shake hands.—All come to this!—The hearts

That spaniel'd me at heels, to whom I gave

Their wishes, do discandy, melt their sweets

On blossoming Caesar; and this pine is bark'd

That overtopp'd them all. Betray'd I am:

O this false soul of Egypt! this grave charm,

Whose eye beck'd forth my wars and call'd them home;

Whose bosom was my crownet, my chief end,—

Like a right gypsy, hath, at fast and loose,

Beguil'd me to the very heart of loss.—

What, Eros, Eros!

[Enter CLEOPATRA.]

Ah, thou spell! Avaunt!

CLEOPATRA.

Why is my lord enrag'd against his love?

ANTONY.

Vanish, or I shall give thee thy deserving,

And blemish Caesar's triumph. Let him take thee

And hoist thee up to the shouting plebeians:

Follow his chariot, like the greatest spot

Of all thy sex; most monster-like, be shown

For poor'st diminutives, for doits; and let

Patient Octavia plough thy visage up

With her prepared nails.

[Exit CLEOPATRA.]

'Tis well thou'rt gone,

If it be well to live; but better 'twere

Thou fell'st into my fury, for one death

Might have prevented many.—Eros, ho!—

The shirt of Nessus is upon me: teach me,

Alcides, thou mine ancestor, thy rage:

Let me lodge Lichas on the horns o' the moon;

And with those hands that grasp'd the heaviest club

Subdue my worthiest self. The witch shall die:

To the young Roman boy she hath sold me, and I fall

Under this plot:—she dies for't.—Eros, ho!

[Exit.]

SCENE XIII. Alexandria. A Room in the Palace.

[Enter CLEOPATRA, CHARMIAN, IRAS, and MARDIAN.]

CLEOPATRA.

Help me, my women! O, he is more mad

Than Telamon for his shield; the boar of Thessaly

Was never so emboss'd.

CHARMIAN.

To the monument!

There lock yourself, and send him word you are dead.

The soul and body rive not more in parting

Than greatness going off.

CLEOPATRA.

To the monument!—

Mardian, go tell him I have slain myself;

Say that the last I spoke was 'Antony',

And word it, pr'ythee, piteously: hence, Mardian;

And bring me how he takes my death.—

To the monument!

[Exeunt.]

SCENE XIV. Alexandria. Another Room.

[Enter ANTONY and EROS.]

ANTONY.

Eros, thou yet behold'st me?

EROS.

Ay, noble lord.

ANTONY.

Sometime we see a cloud that's dragonish;

A vapour sometime like a bear or lion,

A tower'd citadel, a pendant rock,

A forked mountain, or blue promontory

With trees upon't, that nod unto the world,

And mock our eyes with air: thou hast seen these signs;

They are black vesper's pageants.

EROS.

Ay, my lord.

ANTONY.

That which is now a horse, even with a thought

The rack dislimns; and makes it indistinct,

As water is in water.

EROS.

It does, my lord.

ANTONY.

My good knave Eros, now thy captain is

Even such a body: here I am Antony;

Yet cannot hold this visible shape, my knave.

I made these wars for Egypt; and the queen,—

Whose heart I thought I had, for she had mine;

Which, whilst it was mine, had annex'd unto't

A million moe, now lost,—she, Eros, has

Pack'd cards with Caesar, and false-play'd my glory

Unto an enemy's triumph.—

Nay, weep not, gentle Eros; there is left us

Ourselves to end ourselves.—

[Enter MARDIAN.]

O, thy vile lady!

She has robb'd me of my sword.

MARDIAN.

No, Antony;

My mistress lov'd thee, and her fortunes mingled

With thine entirely.

ANTONY.

Hence, saucy eunuch; peace!

She hath betray'd me, and shall die the death.

MARDIAN.

Death of one person can be paid but once,

And that she has discharg'd: what thou wouldst do

Is done unto thy hand: the last she spake

Was 'Antony! most noble Antony!'

Then in the midst a tearing groan did break

The name of Antony; it was divided

Between her heart and lips: she render'd life,

Thy name so buried in her.

ANTONY.

Dead then?

MARDIAN.

Dead.

ANTONY.

Unarm, Eros; the long day's task is done,

And we must sleep.—That thou depart'st hence safe

Does pay thy labour richly; go.

[Exit MARDIAN.]

Off, pluck off;—

The sevenfold shield of Ajax cannot keep

The battery from my heart. O, cleave, my sides!

Heart, once be stronger than thy continent,

Crack thy frail case!—Apace, Eros, apace.—

No more a soldier.—Bruised pieces, go;

You have been nobly borne.—From me awhile.—

[Exit EROS.]

I will o'ertake thee, Cleopatra, and

Weep for my pardon. So it must be, for now

All length is torture.—Since the torch is out,

Lie down, and stray no further:—now all labour

Mars what it does; yea, very force entangles

Itself with strength: seal then, and all is done.—

Eros!—I come, my queen.—Eros!—stay for me:

Where souls do couch on flowers, we'll hand in hand,

And with our sprightly port make the ghosts gaze:

Dido and her Aeneas shall want troops,

And all the haunt be ours.—Come, Eros, Eros!

[Re-enter EROS.]

EROS.

What would my lord?

ANTONY.

Since Cleopatra died,

I have liv'd in such dishonour that the gods

Detest my baseness. I, that with my sword

Quarter'd the world, and o'er green Neptune's back

With ships made cities, condemn myself to lack

The courage of a woman; less noble mind

Than she which by her death our Caesar tells

'I am conqueror of myself.' Thou art sworn, Eros,

That, when the exigent should come,—which now

Is come indeed—when I should see behind me

The inevitable prosecution of

Disgrace and horror, that, on my command,

Thou then wouldst kill me: do't; the time is come:

Thou strik'st not me; 'tis Caesar thou defeat'st.

Put colour in thy cheek.

EROS.

The gods withhold me!

Shall I do that which all the Parthian darts,

Though enemy, lost aim and could not?

ANTONY.

Eros,

Wouldst thou be window'd in great Rome and see

Thy master thus with pleach'd arms, bending down

His corrigible neck, his face subdu'd

To penetrative shame; whilst the wheel'd seat

Of fortunate Caesar, drawn before him, branded

His baseness that ensued?

EROS.

I would not see't.

ANTONY.

Come, then; for with a wound I must be cur'd.

Draw that thy honest sword, which thou hast worn

Most useful for thy country.

EROS.

O, sir, pardon me!

ANTONY.

When I did make thee free, swor'st thou not then

To do this when I bade thee? Do it at once;

Or thy precedent services are all

But accidents unpurpos'd. Draw, and come.

EROS.

Turn from me then that noble countenance,

Wherein the worship of the whole world lies.

ANTONY.

Lo thee!

[Turning from him.]

EROS.

My sword is drawn.

ANTONY.

Then let it do at once

The thing why thou hast drawn it.

EROS.

My dear master,

My captain and my emperor, let me say,

Before I strike this bloody stroke, farewell.

ANTONY.

'Tis said, man;—and farewell.

EROS.

Farewell, great chief. Shall I strike now?

ANTONY.

Now, Eros.

EROS.

Why, there then [falls on his sword]!—thus do I escape the

sorrow

Of Antony's death.

[Dies.]

ANTONY.

Thrice nobler than myself!

Thou teachest me, O valiant Eros, what

I should, and thou couldst not. My queen and Eros

Have, by their brave instruction, got upon me

A nobleness in record: but I will be

A bridegroom in my death, and run into't

As to a lover's bed. Come, then; and, Eros,

Thy master dies thy scholar: to do thus

[Falling on his sword.]

I learn'd of thee. How? not dead? not dead?—

The guard, ho!—O, despatch me!

[Enter DERCETAS and a guard.]

FIRST GUARD.

What's the noise?

ANTONY.

I have done my work ill, friends: O, make an end

Of what I have begun.

SECOND GUARD.

The star is fallen.

FIRST GUARD.

And time is at his period.

ALL.

Alas, and woe!

ANTONY.

Let him that loves me, strike me dead.

FIRST GUARD.

Not I.

SECOND GUARD.

Nor I.

THIRD GUARD.

Nor any one.

[Exeunt guard.]

DERCETAS.

Thy death and fortunes bid thy followers fly.

This sword but shown to Caesar, with this tidings,

Shall enter me with him.

[Enter DIOMEDES.]

DIOMEDES.

Where's Antony?

DERCETAS.

There, Diomed, there.

DIOMEDES.

Lives he?

Wilt thou not answer, man?

[Exit DERCETAS.]

ANTONY.

Art thou there, Diomed? Draw thy sword and give me

Sufficing strokes for death.

DIOMEDES.

Most absolute lord,

My mistress Cleopatra sent me to thee.

ANTONY.

When did she send thee?

DIOMEDES.

Now, my lord.

ANTONY.

Where is she?

DIOMEDES.

Lock'd in her monument. She had a prophesying fear

Of what hath come to pass: for when she saw,—

Which never shall be found,—you did suspect

She had dispos'd with Caesar, and that your rage

Would not be purg'd, she sent you word she was dead;

But, fearing since how it might work, hath sent

Me to proclaim the truth; and I am come,

I dread, too late.

ANTONY.

Too late, good Diomed.—Call my guard, I pr'ythee.

DIOMEDES.

What, ho! the emperor's guard! The guard, what ho!

Come, your lord calls!

[Enter some of the Guard.]

ANTONY.

Bear me, good friends, where Cleopatra bides;

'Tis the last service that I shall command you.

FIRST GUARD.

Woe, woe are we, sir, you may not live to wear

All your true followers out.

ALL.

Most heavy day!

ANTONY.

Nay, good my fellows, do not please sharp fate

To grace it with your sorrows: bid that welcome

Which comes to punish us, and we punish it,

Seeming to bear it lightly. Take me up:

I have led you oft: carry me now, good friends,

And have my thanks for all.

[Exeunt, bearing ANTONY.]

SCENE XV. Alexandria. A monument.

[Enter, above, CLEOPATRA, CHARMIAN and IRAS.]

CLEOPATRA.

O Charmian, I will never go from hence!

CHARMIAN.

Be comforted, dear madam.

CLEOPATRA.

No, I will not:

All strange and terrible events are welcome,

But comforts we despise; our size of sorrow,

Proportion'd to our cause, must be as great

As that which makes it.—

[Enter, below, DIOMEDES.]

How now! is he dead?

DIOMEDES.

His death's upon him, but not dead.

Look out o' the other side your monument;

His guard have brought him thither.

[Enter, below, ANTONY, borne by the Guard.]

CLEOPATRA.

O sun,

Burn the great sphere thou mov'st in!—darkling stand

The varying shore o' theworld.—O Antony,

Antony, Antony!—Help, Charmian; help, Iras, help,—

Help, friends below;—let's draw him hither.

ANTONY.

Peace!

Not Caesar's valour hath o'erthrown Antony,

But Antony's hath triumph'd on itself.

CLEOPATRA.

So it should be, that none but Antony

Should conquer Antony; but woe 'tis so!

ANTONY.

I am dying, Egypt, dying; only

I here importune death awhile, until

Of many thousand kisses the poor last

I lay upon thy lips.

CLEOPATRA.

I dare not, dear,—

Dear my lord, pardon,—I dare not,

Lest I be taken: not the imperious show

Of the full-fortun'd Caesar ever shall

Be brooch'd with me; if knife, drugs, serpents, have

Edge, sting, or operation, I am safe;

Your wife Octavia, with her modest eyes

And still conclusion, shall acquire no honour

Demuring upon me.—But come, come, Antony,—

Help me, my women,—we must draw thee up;

Assist, good friends.

ANTONY.

O, quick, or I am gone.

CLEOPATRA.

Here's sport indeed!—How heavy weighs my lord!

Our strength is all gone into heaviness;

That makes the weight: had I great Juno's power,

The strong-wing'd Mercury should fetch thee up,

And set thee by Jove's side. Yet come a little,—

Wishers were ever fools,—O come, come;

                        [They draw ANTONY up.]

And welcome, welcome! die where thou hast liv'd:

Quicken with kissing: had my lips that power,

Thus would I wear them out.

ALL.

A heavy sight!

ANTONY.

I am dying, Egypt, dying:

Give me some wine, and let me speak a little.

CLEOPATRA.

No, let me speak; and let me rail so high

That the false huswife Fortune break her wheel,

Provok'd by my offence.

ANTONY.

One word, sweet queen:

Of Caesar seek your honour, with your safety.—O!

CLEOPATRA.

They do not go together.

ANTONY.

Gentle, hear me:

None about Caesar trust but Proculeius.

CLEOPATRA.

My resolution and my hands I'll trust;

None about Caesar.

ANTONY.

The miserable change now at my end

Lament nor sorrow at: but please your thoughts

In feeding them with those my former fortunes

Wherein I liv'd, the greatest prince o' the world,

The noblest; and do now not basely die,

Not cowardly put off my helmet to

My countryman, a Roman by a Roman

Valiantly vanquish'd. Now my spirit is going:

I can no more.

CLEOPATRA.

Noblest of men, woo't die?

Hast thou no care of me? shall I abide

In this dull world, which in thy absence is

No better than a sty?—O, see, my women,

[Antony dies.]

The crown o' the earth doth melt.—My lord!—

O, wither'd is the garland of the war,

The soldier's pole is fallen: young boys and girls

Are level now with men: the odds is gone,

And there is nothing left remarkable

Beneath the visiting moon.

[Faints.]

CHARMIAN.

O, quietness, lady!

IRAS.

She is dead too, our sovereign.

CHARMIAN.

Lady!—

IRAS.

Madam!—

CHARMIAN.

O madam, madam, madam!—

IRAS.

Royal Egypt, Empress,—

CHARMIAN.

Peace, peace, Iras!

CLEOPATRA.

No more but e'en a woman, and commanded

By such poor passion as the maid that milks

And does the meanest chares.—It were for me

To throw my sceptre at the injurious gods;

To tell them that this world did equal theirs

Till they had stol'n our jewel. All's but naught;

Patience is sottish, and impatience does

Become a dog that's mad: then is it sin

To rush into the secret house of death

Ere death dare come to us?—How do you, women?

What, what! good cheer! Why, how now, Charmian!

My noble girls!—Ah, women, women, look,

Our lamp is spent, it's out!—Good sirs, take heart:—

We'll bury him; and then, what's brave, what's noble,

Let's do it after the high Roman fashion,

And make death proud to take us. Come, away:

This case of that huge spirit now is cold:

Ah, women, women!—Come; we have no friend

But resolution, and the briefest end.

[Exeunt; those above bearing off ANTONY'S body.]

ACT V.

SCENE I. CAESAR'S Camp before Alexandria.

[Enter CAESAR, AGRIPPA, DOLABELLA, MAECENAS, GALLUS, PROCULEIUS, and Others.]

CAESAR.

Go to him, Dolabella, bid him yield;

Being so frustrate, tell him he mocks

The pauses that he makes.

DOLABELLA.

Caesar, I shall.

[Exit.]

[Enter DERCETAS with the sword of ANTONY.]

CAESAR.

Wherefore is that? And what art thou that dar'st

Appear thus to us?

DERCETAS.

I am call'd Dercetas;

Mark Antony I serv'd, who best was worthy

Best to be serv'd: whilst he stood up and spoke,

He was my master, and I wore my life

To spend upon his haters. If thou please

To take me to thee, as I was to him

I'll be to Caesar; if thou pleasest not,

I yield thee up my life.

CAESAR.

What is't thou say'st?

DERCETAS.

I say, O Caesar, Antony is dead.

CAESAR.

The breaking of so great a thing should make

A greater crack: the round world

Should have shook lions into civil streets,

And citizens to their dens. The death of Antony

Is not a single doom; in the name lay

A moiety of the world.

DERCETAS.

He is dead, Caesar;

Not by a public minister of justice,

Nor by a hired knife; but that self hand

Which writ his honour in the acts it did

Hath, with the courage which the heart did lend it,

Splitted the heart.—This is his sword;

I robb'd his wound of it; behold it stain'd

With his most noble blood.

CAESAR.

Look you sad, friends?

The gods rebuke me, but it is tidings

To wash the eyes of kings.

AGRIPPA.

And strange it is

That nature must compel us to lament

Our most persisted deeds.

MAECENAS.

His taints and honours

Weigh'd equal with him.

AGRIPPA.

A rarer spirit never

Did steer humanity. But you, gods, will give us

Some faults to make us men. Caesar is touch'd.

MAECENAS.

When such a spacious mirror's set before him,

He needs must see himself.

CAESAR.

O Antony!

I have follow'd thee to this!—But we do lance

Diseases in our bodies: I must perforce

Have shown to thee such a declining day

Or look on thine; we could not stall together

In the whole world: but yet let me lament,

With tears as sovereign as the blood of hearts,

That thou, my brother, my competitor

In top of all design, my mate in empire,

Friend and companion in the front of war,

The arm of mine own body, and the heart

Where mine his thoughts did kindle,—that our stars,

Unreconciliable, should divide

Our equalness to this.—Hear me, good friends,—

But I will tell you at some meeter season.

[Enter a Messenger.]

The business of this man looks out of him;

We'll hear him what he says.—Whence are you?

MESSENGER.

A poor Egyptian yet. The queen, my mistress,

Confin'd in all she has, her monument,

Of thy intents desires instruction,

That she preparedly may frame herself

To the way she's forc'd to.

CAESAR.

Bid her have good heart:

She soon shall know of us, by some of ours,

How honourable and how kindly we

Determine for her; for Caesar cannot learn

To be ungentle.

MESSENGER.

So the gods preserve thee!

[Exit.]

CAESAR.

Come hither, Proculeius. Go and say

We purpose her no shame: give her what comforts

The quality of her passion shall require

Lest, in her greatness, by some mortal stroke

She do defeat us; for her life in Rome

Would be eternal in our triumph: go,

And with your speediest bring us what she says,

And how you find her.

PROCULEIUS.

Caesar, I shall.

[Exit.]

CAESAR.

Gallus, go you along.—

[Exit GALLUS.]

Where's Dolabella, to second Proculeius?

ALL.

Dolabella!

CAESAR.

Let him alone, for I remember now

How he's employ'd; he shall in time be ready.

Go with me to my tent; where you shall see

How hardly I was drawn into this war;

How calm and gentle I proceeded still

In all my writings: go with me, and see

What I can show in this.

[Exeunt.]

SCENE II. Alexandria. A Room in the Monument.

[Enter CLEOPATRA, CHARMIAN, and IRAS.]

CLEOPATRA.

My desolation does begin to make

A better life. 'Tis paltry to be Caesar;

Not being Fortune, he's but Fortune's knave,

A minister of her will: and it is great

To do that thing that ends all other deeds;

Which shackles accidents and bolts up change;

Which sleeps, and never palates more the dug,

The beggar's nurse and Caesar's.

[Enter, to the gates of the Monument, PROCULEIUS, GALLUS, and Soldiers.]

PROCULEIUS.

Caesar sends greetings to the queen of Egypt;

And bids thee study on what fair demands

Thou mean'st to have him grant thee.

CLEOPATRA.

What's thy name?

PROCULEIUS.

My name is Proculeius.

CLEOPATRA.

Antony

Did tell me of you, bade me trust you; but

I do not greatly care to be deceiv'd,

That have no use for trusting. If your master

Would have a queen his beggar, you must tell him

That majesty, to keep decorum, must

No less beg than a kingdom: if he please

To give me conquer'd Egypt for my son,

He gives me so much of mine own as I

Will kneel to him with thanks.

PROCULEIUS.

Be of good cheer;

You are fallen into a princely hand; fear nothing:

Make your full reference freely to my lord,

Who is so full of grace that it flows over

On all that need: let me report to him

Your sweet dependency; and you shall find

A conqueror that will pray in aid for kindness

Where he for grace is kneel'd to.

CLEOPATRA.

Pray you, tell him

I am his fortune's vassal and I send him

The greatness he has got. I hourly learn

A doctrine of obedience; and would gladly

Look him i' the face.

PROCULEIUS.

This I'll report, dear lady.

Have comfort, for I know your plight is pitied

Of him that caus'd it.

GALLUS.

You see how easily she may be surpris'd:

[Here PROCULEIUS and two of the Guard ascend the Monument by a ladder placed against a window, and, having ascended, come behind CLEOPATRA. Some of the Guard unbar and open the gates.]

[To PROCULEIUS. and the Guear.] Guard her till Caesar come.

[Exit.]

IRAS.

Royal queen!

CHARMIAN.

O Cleopatra! thou art taken, queen!

CLEOPATRA.

Quick, quick, good hands.

[Drawing a dagger.]

PROCULEIUS.

Hold, worthy lady, hold;

[Seizes and disarms her.]

Do not yourself such wrong, who are in this

Reliev'd, but not betray'd.

CLEOPATRA.

What, of death too,

That rids our dogs of languish?

PROCULEIUS.

Cleopatra,

Do not abuse my master's bounty by

Theundoing of yourself: let the world see

His nobleness well acted, which your death

Will never let come forth.

CLEOPATRA.

Where art thou, death?

Come hither, come! Come, come, and take a queen

Worth many babes and beggars!

PROCULEIUS.

O, temperance, lady!

CLEOPATRA.

Sir, I will eat no meat; I'll not drink, sir;

If idle talk will once be accessary,

I'll not sleep neither: this mortal house I'll ruin,

Do Caesar what he can. Know, sir, that I

Will not wait pinion'd at your master's court;

Nor once be chastis'd with the sober eye

Of dull Octavia. Shall they hoist me up,

And show me to the shouting varletry

Of censuring Rome? Rather a ditch in Egypt

Be gentle grave unto me! rather on Nilus' mud

Lay me stark-nak'd, and let the water-flies

Blow me into abhorring! rather make

My country's high pyramides my gibbet,

And hang me up in chains!

PROCULEIUS.

You do extend

These thoughts of horror further than you shall

Find cause in Caesar.

[Enter DOLABELLA.]

DOLABELLA.

Proculeius,

What thou hast done thy master Caesar knows,

And he hath sent for thee: as for the queen,

I'll take her to my guard.

PROCULEIUS.

So, Dolabella,

It shall content me best: be gentle to her.—

[To CLEOPATRA.] To Caesar I will speak what you shall please,

If you'll employ me to him.

CLEOPATRA.

Say I would die.

[Exeunt PROCULEIUS and Soldiers.]

DOLABELLA.

Most noble empress, you have heard of me?

CLEOPATRA.

I cannot tell.

DOLABELLA.

Assuredly you know me.

CLEOPATRA.

No matter, sir, what I have heard or known.

You laugh when boys or women tell their dreams;

Is't not your trick?

DOLABELLA.

I understand not, madam.

CLEOPATRA.

I dream'd there was an Emperor Antony:—

O, such another sleep, that I might see

But such another man!

DOLABELLA.

If it might please you,—

CLEOPATRA.

His face was as the heavens; and therein stuck

A sun and moon, which kept their course, and lighted

The little O, the earth.

DOLABELLA.

Most sovereign creature,—

CLEOPATRA.

His legs bestrid the ocean; his rear'd arm

Crested the world: his voice was propertied

As all the tuned spheres, and that to friends;

But when he meant to quail and shake the orb,

He was as rattling thunder. For his bounty,

There was no winter in't; an autumn 'twas

That grew the more by reaping: his delights

Were dolphin-like; they show'd his back above

The element they liv'd in: in his livery

Walk'd crowns and crownets; realms and islands were

As plates dropp'd from his pocket.

DOLABELLA.

Cleopatra,—

CLEOPATRA.

Think you there was or might be such a man

As this I dream'd of?

DOLABELLA.

Gentle madam, no.

CLEOPATRA.

You lie, up to the hearing of the gods.

But if there be, or ever were, one such,

It's past the size of dreaming: nature wants stuff

To vie strange forms with fancy: yet to imagine

An Antony were nature's piece 'gainst fancy,

Condemning shadows quite.

DOLABELLA.

Hear me, good madam.

Your loss is, as yourself, great; and you bear it

As answering to the weight: would I might never

O'ertake pursu'd success, but I do feel,

By the rebound of yours, a grief that smites

My very heart at root.

CLEOPATRA.

I thank you, sir.

Know you what Caesar means to do with me?

DOLABELLA.

I am loath to tell you what I would you knew.

CLEOPATRA.

Nay, pray you, sir,—

DOLABELLA.

Though he be honourable,—

CLEOPATRA.

He'll lead me, then, in triumph?

DOLABELLA.

Madam, he will;

I know it.

[Flourish within.]

[Within.] Make way there,—Caesar!

[Enter CAESAR, GALLUS, PROCULEIUS, MAECENAS, SELEUCUS, and Attendants.]

CAESAR.

Which is the queen of Egypt?

DOLABELLA.

It is the emperor, madam.

[CLEOPATRA kneels.]

CAESAR.

Arise, you shall not kneel:—

I pray you, rise; rise, Egypt.

CLEOPATRA.

Sir, the gods

Will have it thus; my master and my lord

I must obey.

CAESAR.

Take to you no hard thoughts;

The record of what injuries you did us,

Though written in our flesh, we shall remember

As things but done by chance.

CLEOPATRA.

Sole sir o' the world,

I cannot project mine own cause so well

To make it clear: but do confess I have

Been laden with like frailties which before

Have often sham'd our sex.

CAESAR.

Cleopatra, know

We will extenuate rather than enforce:

If you apply yourself to our intents,—

Which towards you are most gentle,—you shall find

A benefit in this change; but if you seek

To lay on me a cruelty, by taking

Antony's course, you shall bereave yourself

Of my good purposes, and put your children

To that destruction which I'll guard them from,

If thereon you rely. I'll take my leave.

CLEOPATRA.

And may, through all the world: 'tis yours, and we,

Your scutcheons and your signs of conquest, shall

Hang in what place you please. Here, my good lord.

CAESAR.

You shall advise me in all for Cleopatra.

CLEOPATRA.

This is the brief of money, plate, and jewels,

I am possess'd of: 'tis exactly valued;

Not petty things admitted.—Where's Seleucus?

SELEUCUS.

Here, madam.

CLEOPATRA.

This is my treasurer: let him speak, my lord,

Upon his peril, that I have reserv'd

To myself nothing. Speak the truth, Seleucus.

SELEUCUS.

Madam,

I had rather seal my lips than to my peril

Speak that which is not.

CLEOPATRA.

What have I kept back?

SELEUCUS.

Enough to purchase what you have made known.

CAESAR.

Nay, blush not, Cleopatra; I approve

Your wisdom in the deed.

CLEOPATRA.

See, Caesar! O, behold,

How pomp is follow'd! Mine will now be yours;

And, should we shift estates, yours would be mine.

The ingratitude of this Seleucus does

Even make me wild: O slave, of no more trust

Than love that's hir'd!—What, goest thou back? thou shalt

Go back, I warrant thee; but I'll catch thine eyes

Though they had wings; slave, soulless villain, dog!

O rarely base!

CAESAR.

Good queen, let us entreat you.

CLEOPATRA.

O Caesar, what a wounding shame is this,—

That thou vouchsafing here to visit me,

Doing the honour of thy lordliness

To one so meek, that mine own servant should

Parcel the sum of my disgraces by

Addition of his envy! Say, good Caesar,

That I some lady trifles have reserv'd,

Immoment toys, things of such dignity

As we greet modern friends withal; and say,

Some nobler token I have kept apart

For Livia and Octavia, to induce

Their mediation;—must I be unfolded

With one that I have bred? The gods! It smites me

Beneath the fall I have.

[To SELEUCUS.] Pr'ythee go hence;

Or I shall show the cinders of my spirits

Through theashes of my chance.—Wert thou a man,

Thou wouldst have mercy on me.

CAESAR.

Forbear, Seleucus.

[Exit SELEUCUS.]

CLEOPATRA.

Be it known that we, the greatest, are misthought

For things that others do; and when we fall

We answer others' merits in our name,

Are therefore to be pitied.

CAESAR.

Cleopatra,

Not what you have reserv'd, nor what acknowledg'd,

Put we i' the roll of conquest: still be't yours,

Bestow it at your pleasure; and believe

Caesar's no merchant, to make prize with you

Of things that merchants sold. Therefore be cheer'd;

Make not your thoughts your prisons: no, dear queen;

For we intend so to dispose you as

Yourself shall give us counsel. Feed and sleep:

Our care and pity is so much upon you

That we remain your friend; and so, adieu.

CLEOPATRA.

My master and my lord!

CAESAR.

Not so. Adieu.

[Flourish. Exeunt CAESAR and his Train.]

CLEOPATRA.

He words me, girls, he words me, that I should not

Be noble to myself: but hark thee, Charmian!

[Whispers CHARMIAN.]

IRAS.

Finish, good lady; the bright day is done,

And we are for the dark.

CLEOPATRA.

Hie thee again:

I have spoke already, and it is provided;

Go put it to the haste.

CHARMIAN.

Madam, I will.

[Re-enter DOLABELLA.]

DOLABELLA.

Where's the queen?

CHARMIAN.

Behold, sir.

[Exit.]

CLEOPATRA.

Dolabella!

DOLABELLA.

Madam, as thereto sworn by your command,

Which my love makes religion to obey,

I tell you this: Caesar through Syria

Intends his journey; and within three days

You with your children will he send before:

Make your best use of this: I have perform'd

Your pleasure and my promise.

CLEOPATRA.

Dolabella,

I shall remain your debtor.

DOLABELLA.

I your servant.

Adieu, good queen; I must attend on Caesar.

CLEOPATRA.

Farewell, and thanks.

[Exit DOLABELLA.]

Now, Iras, what think'st thou?

Thou, an Egyptian puppet, shall be shown

In Rome as well as I: mechanic slaves,

With greasy aprons, rules, and hammers, shall

Uplift us to the view; in their thick breaths,

Rank of gross diet, shall we be enclouded,

And forc'd to drink their vapour.

IRAS.

The gods forbid!

CLEOPATRA.

Nay, 'tis most certain, Iras:—saucy lictors

Will catch at us like strumpets; and scald rhymers

Ballad us out o' tune: the quick comedians

Extemporally will stage us, and present

Our Alexandrian revels; Antony

Shall be brought drunken forth, and I shall see

Some squeaking Cleopatra boy my greatness

I' the posture of a whore.

IRAS.

O the good gods!

CLEOPATRA.

Nay, that's certain.

IRAS.

I'll never see't; for I am sure mine nails

Are stronger than mine eyes.

CLEOPATRA.

Why, that's the way

To fool their preparation and to conquer

Their most absurd intents.

[Enter CHARMIAN.]

Now, Charmian!—

Show me, my women, like a queen.—Go fetch

My best attires;—I am again for Cydnus,

To meet Mark Antony:—sirrah, Iras, go.—

Now, noble Charmian, we'll despatch indeed;

And when thou hast done this chare, I'll give thee leave

To play till doomsday.—Bring our crown and all.

[Exit IRAS. A noise within.]

Wherefore's this noise?

[Enter one of the Guard.]

GUARD.

Here is a rural fellow

That will not be denied your highness' presence:

He brings you figs.

CLEOPATRA.

Let him come in.

[Exit Guard.]

What poor an instrument

May do a noble deed! he brings me liberty.

My resolution's plac'd, and I have nothing

Of woman in me: now from head to foot

I am marble-constant; now the fleeting moon

No planet is of mine.

[Re-enter Guard, with Clown bringing a basket.]

GUARD.

This is the man.

CLEOPATRA.

Avoid, and leave him.

[Exit Guard.]

Hast thou the pretty worm of Nilus there

That kills and pains not?

CLOWN. Truly, I have him. But I would not be the party that should desire you to touch him, for his biting is immortal; those that do die of it do seldom or never recover.

CLEOPATRA.

Remember'st thou any that have died on't?

CLOWN. Very many, men and women too. I heard of one of them no longer than yesterday: a very honest woman, but something given to lie; as a woman should not do but in the way of honesty: how she died of the biting of it, what pain she felt,—truly she makes a very good report o' the worm; but he that will believe all that they say shall never be saved by half that they do: but this is most falliable, the worm's an odd worm.

CLEOPATRA.

Get thee hence; farewell.

CLOWN.

I wish you all joy of the worm.

[Sets down the basket.]

CLEOPATRA.

Farewell.

CLOWN.

You must think this, look you, that the worm will do his kind.

CLEOPATRA.

Ay, ay; farewell.

CLOWN. Look you, the worm is not to be trusted but in the keeping of wise people; for indeed there is no goodness in the worm.

CLEOPATRA.

Take thou no care; it shall be heeded.

CLOWN. Very good. Give it nothing, I pray you, for it is not worth the feeding.

CLEOPATRA.

Will it eat me?

CLOWN. You must not think I am so simple but I know the devil himself will not eat a woman: I know that a woman is a dish for the gods, if the devil dress her not. But truly, these same whoreson devils do the gods great harm in their women, for in every ten that they make the devils mar five.

CLEOPATRA.

Well, get thee gone; farewell.

CLOWN.

Yes, forsooth. I wish you joy o' the worm.

[Exit.]

[Re-enter IRAS, with a robe, crown, &c.]

CLEOPATRA.

237

Give me my robe, put on my crown; I have

Immortal longings in me: now no more

The juice of Egypt's grape shall moist this lip:—

Yare, yare, good Iras; quick.—Methinks I hear

Antony call; I see him rouse himself

To praise my noble act; I hear him mock

The luck of Caesar, which the gods give men

To excuse their after wrath. Husband, I come:

Now to that name my courage prove my title!

I am fire and air; my other elements

I give to baser life.—So,—have you done?

Come then, and take the last warmth of my lips.

Farewell, kind Charmian;—Iras, long farewell.

[Kisses them. IRAS falls and dies.]

Have I the aspic in my lips? Dost fall?

If thus thou and nature can so gently part,

The stroke of death is as a lover's pinch,

Which hurts and is desir'd. Dost thou lie still?

If thou vanishest, thou tell'st the world

It is not worth leave-taking.

CHARMIAN.

Dissolve, thick cloud, and rain; that I may say

The gods themselves do weep!

CLEOPATRA.

This proves me base:

If she first meet the curled Antony,

He'll make demand of her, and spend that kiss

Which is my heaven to have.—Come, thou mortal wretch,

[To an asp, which she applies to her breast.]

With thy sharp teeth this knot intrinsicate

Of life at once untie: poor venomous fool,

Be angry and despatch. O couldst thou speak,

That I might hear thee call great Caesar ass

Unpolicied!

CHARMIAN.

O eastern star!

CLEOPATRA.

Peace, peace!

Dost thou not see my baby at my breast

That sucks the nurse asleep?

CHARMIAN.

O, break! O, break!

CLEOPATRA.

As sweet as balm, as soft as air, as gentle:—

O Antony! Nay, I will take thee too:—

[Applying another asp to her arm.]

What should I stay,—

[Falls on a bed and dies.]

CHARMIAN.

In this vile world?—So, fare thee well.—

Now boast thee, death, in thy possession lies

A lass unparallel'd.—Downy windows, close;

And golden Phoebus never be beheld

Of eyes again so royal! Your crown's awry;

I'll mend it and then play.

[Enter the guard, rushing in.]

FIRST GUARD.

Where's the queen?

CHARMIAN.

Speak softly, wake her not.

FIRST GUARD.

Caesar hath sent,—

CHARMIAN.

Too slow a messenger.

[Applies an asp.]

O, come apace, despatch: I partly feel thee.

FIRST GUARD.

Approach, ho! all's not well: Caesar's beguil'd.

SECOND GUARD.

There's Dolabella sent from Caesar; call him.

FIRST GUARD.

What work is here!—Charmian, is this well done?

CHARMIAN.

It is well done, and fitting for a princess

Descended of so many royal kings.

Ah, soldier!

[CHARMIAN dies.]

[Re-enter DOLABELLA.]

DOLABELLA.

How goes it here?

SECOND GUARD.

All dead.

DOLABELLA.

Caesar, thy thoughts

Touch their effects in this: thyself art coming

To see perform'd the dreaded act which thou

So sought'st to hinder.

[Within.] A way there, a way for Caesar!

[Re-enter CAESAR and his Train.]

DOLABELLA.

O sir, you are too sure an augurer;

That you did fear is done.

CAESAR.

Bravest at the last,

She levell'd at our purposes, and being royal,

Took her own way.—The manner of their deaths?

I do not see them bleed.

DOLABELLA.

Who was last with them?

FIRST GUARD.

A simple countryman that brought her figs.

This was his basket.

CAESAR.

Poison'd then.

FIRST GUARD.

O Caesar,

This Charmian liv'd but now; she stood and spake:

I found her trimming up the diadem

On her dead mistress; tremblingly she stood,

And on the sudden dropp'd.

CAESAR.

O noble weakness!—

If they had swallow'd poison 'twould appear

By external swelling: but she looks like sleep,—

As she would catch another Antony

In her strong toil of grace.

DOLABELLA.

Here on her breast

There is a vent of blood, and something blown:

The like is on her arm.

FIRST GUARD.

This is an aspic's trail: and these fig-leaves

Have slime upon them, such as the aspic leaves

Upon the caves of Nile.

CAESAR.

Most probable

That so she died; for her physician tells me

She hath pursu'd conclusions infinite

Of easy ways to die. Take up her bed,

And bear her women from the monument:—

She shall be buried by her Antony:

No grave upon the earth shall clip in it

A pair so famous. High events as these

Strike those that make them; and their story is

No less in pity than his glory which

Brought them to be lamented. Our army shall

In solemn show attend this funeral;

And then to Rome.—Come, Dolabella, see

High order in this great solemnity.

[Exeunt.]

CYMBELINE

Dramatis Personæ

CYMBELINE, King of Britain

CLOTEN, son to the Queen by a former husband

POSTHUMUS LEONATUS, a gentleman, husband to Imogen

BELARIUS, a banished lord, disguised under the name of Morgan

GUIDERIUS and ARVIRAGUS, sons to Cymbeline, disguised under the names of POLYDORE and CADWAL, supposed sons to Belarius

PHILARIO, Italian, friend to Posthumus

IACHIMO, Italian, friend to Philario

CAIUS LUCIUS, General of the Roman forces

PISANIO, servant to Posthumus

CORNELIUS, a physician

A SOOTHSAYER

A ROMAN CAPTAIN

TWO BRITISH CAPTAINS

A FRENCH GENTLEMAN, friend to Philario

TWO LORDS of Cymbeline's court

TWO GENTLEMEN of the same

TWO GAOLERS

QUEEN, wife to Cymbeline

IMOGEN, daughter to Cymbeline by a former queen

HELEN, a lady attending on Imogen

APPARITIONS

Lords, Ladies, Roman Senators, Tribunes, a Dutch Gentleman, a Spanish Gentleman, Musicians, Officers, Captains, Soldiers, Messengers, and Attendants

SCENE: Britain; Italy.

ACT I

SCENE I. Britain. The garden of Cymbeline's palace.

Enter two Gentlemen.

FIRST GENTLEMAN.

You do not meet a man but frowns; our bloods

No more obey the heavens than our courtiers

Still seem as does the King's.

SECOND GENTLEMAN.

But what's the matter?

FIRST GENTLEMAN.

His daughter, and the heir of's kingdom, whom

He purpos'd to his wife's sole son—a widow

That late he married—hath referr'd herself

Unto a poor but worthy gentleman. She's wedded;

Her husband banish'd; she imprison'd. All

Is outward sorrow, though I think the King

Be touch'd at very heart.

SECOND GENTLEMAN.

None but the King?

FIRST GENTLEMAN.

He that hath lost her too. So is the Queen,

That most desir'd the match. But not a courtier,

Although they wear their faces to the bent

Of the King's looks, hath a heart that is not

Glad at the thing they scowl at.

SECOND GENTLEMAN.

And why so?

FIRST GENTLEMAN.

He that hath miss'd the Princess is a thing

Too bad for bad report; and he that hath her—

I mean that married her, alack, good man!

And therefore banish'd—is a creature such

As, to seek through the regions of the earth

For one his like, there would be something failing

In him that should compare. I do not think

So fair an outward and such stuff within

Endows a man but he.

SECOND GENTLEMAN.

You speak him far.

FIRST GENTLEMAN.

I do extend him, sir, within himself;

Crush him together rather than unfold

His measure duly.

SECOND GENTLEMAN.

What's his name and birth?

FIRST GENTLEMAN.

I cannot delve him to the root; his father

Was call'd Sicilius, who did join his honour

Against the Romans with Cassibelan,

But had his titles by Tenantius, whom

He serv'd with glory and admir'd success,

So gain'd the sur-addition Leonatus;

And had, besides this gentleman in question,

Two other sons, who, in the wars o' th' time,

Died with their swords in hand; for which their father,

Then old and fond of issue, took such sorrow

That he quit being; and his gentle lady,

Big of this gentleman, our theme, deceas'd

As he was born. The King he takes the babe

To his protection, calls him Posthumus Leonatus,

Breeds him and makes him of his bed-chamber,

Puts to him all the learnings that his time

Could make him the receiver of; which he took,

As we do air, fast as 'twas minist'red,

And in's spring became a harvest, liv'd in court—

Which rare it is to do—most prais'd, most lov'd,

A sample to the youngest; to th' more mature

A glass that feated them; and to the graver

A child that guided dotards. To his mistress,

For whom he now is banish'd, her own price

Proclaims how she esteem'd him and his virtue;

By her election may be truly read

What kind of man he is.

SECOND GENTLEMAN.

I honour him

Even out of your report. But pray you tell me,

Is she sole child to th' King?

FIRST GENTLEMAN.

His only child.

He had two sons—if this be worth your hearing,

Mark it—the eldest of them at three years old,

I' th' swathing clothes the other, from their nursery

Were stol'n; and to this hour no guess in knowledge

Which way they went.

SECOND GENTLEMAN.

How long is this ago?

FIRST GENTLEMAN.

Some twenty years.

SECOND GENTLEMAN.

That a king's children should be so convey'd,

So slackly guarded, and the search so slow

That could not trace them!

FIRST GENTLEMAN.

Howsoe'er 'tis strange,

Or that the negligence may well be laugh'd at,

Yet is it true, sir.

SECOND GENTLEMAN.

I do well believe you.

FIRST GENTLEMAN.

We must forbear; here comes the gentleman,

The Queen, and Princess.

[Exeunt.]

SCENE II. The same.

Enter Queen, Posthumus and Imogen.

QUEEN.

No, be assur'd you shall not find me, daughter,

After the slander of most stepmothers,

Evil-ey'd unto you. You're my prisoner, but

Your gaoler shall deliver you the keys

That lock up your restraint. For you, Posthumus,

So soon as I can win th' offended King,

I will be known your advocate. Marry, yet

The fire of rage is in him, and 'twere good

You lean'd unto his sentence with what patience

Your wisdom may inform you.

POSTHUMUS.

Please your Highness,

I will from hence today.

QUEEN.

You know the peril.

I'll fetch a turn about the garden, pitying

The pangs of barr'd affections, though the King

Hath charg'd you should not speak together.

[Exit.]

IMOGEN.

O dissembling courtesy! How fine this tyrant

Can tickle where she wounds! My dearest husband,

I something fear my father's wrath, but nothing

(Always reserv'd my holy duty) what

His rage can do on me. You must be gone;

And I shall here abide the hourly shot

Of angry eyes, not comforted to live

But that there is this jewel in the world

That I may see again.

POSTHUMUS.

My queen! my mistress!

O lady, weep no more, lest I give cause

To be suspected of more tenderness

Than doth become a man. I will remain

The loyal'st husband that did e'er plight troth;

My residence in Rome at one Philario's,

Who to my father was a friend, to me

Known but by letter; thither write, my queen,

And with mine eyes I'll drink the words you send,

Though ink be made of gall.

Enter Queen.

QUEEN.

Be brief, I pray you.

If the King come, I shall incur I know not

How much of his displeasure. [Aside.] Yet I'll move him

To walk this way. I never do him wrong

But he does buy my injuries, to be friends;

Pays dear for my offences.

[Exit.]

POSTHUMUS.

Should we be taking leave

As long a term as yet we have to live,

The loathness to depart would grow. Adieu!

IMOGEN.

Nay, stay a little.

Were you but riding forth to air yourself,

Such parting were too petty. Look here, love:

This diamond was my mother's; take it, heart;

But keep it till you woo another wife,

When Imogen is dead.

POSTHUMUS.

How, how? Another?

You gentle gods, give me but this I have,

And sear up my embracements from a next

With bonds of death! Remain, remain thou here

[Puts on the ring.]

While sense can keep it on. And, sweetest, fairest,

As I my poor self did exchange for you,

To your so infinite loss, so in our trifles

I still win of you. For my sake wear this;

It is a manacle of love; I'll place it

Upon this fairest prisoner.

[Puts a bracelet on her arm.]

IMOGEN.

O the gods!

When shall we see again?

Enter Cymbeline and Lords.

POSTHUMUS.

Alack, the King!

CYMBELINE.

Thou basest thing, avoid; hence from my sight

If after this command thou fraught the court

With thy unworthiness, thou diest. Away!

Thou'rt poison to my blood.

POSTHUMUS.

The gods protect you,

And bless the good remainders of the court!

I am gone.

[Exit.]

IMOGEN.

There cannot be a pinch in death

255

More sharp than this is.

CYMBELINE.

O disloyal thing,

That shouldst repair my youth, thou heap'st

A year's age on me!

IMOGEN.

I beseech you, sir,

Harm not yourself with your vexation.

I am senseless of your wrath; a touch more rare

Subdues all pangs, all fears.

CYMBELINE.

Past grace? obedience?

IMOGEN.

Past hope, and in despair; that way past grace.

CYMBELINE.

That mightst have had the sole son of my queen!

IMOGEN.

O blessed that I might not! I chose an eagle,

And did avoid a puttock.

CYMBELINE.

Thou took'st a beggar, wouldst have made my throne

A seat for baseness.

IMOGEN.

No; I rather added

A lustre to it.

CYMBELINE.

O thou vile one!

IMOGEN.

Sir,

It is your fault that I have lov'd Posthumus.

You bred him as my playfellow, and he is

A man worth any woman; overbuys me

Almost the sum he pays.

CYMBELINE.

What, art thou mad?

IMOGEN.

Almost, sir. Heaven restore me! Would I were

A neat-herd's daughter, and my Leonatus

Our neighbour shepherd's son!

Enter Queen.

CYMBELINE.

Thou foolish thing!

[To the Queen.] They were again together. You have done

Not after our command. Away with her,

And pen her up.

QUEEN.

Beseech your patience. Peace,

Dear lady daughter, peace!—Sweet sovereign,

Leave us to ourselves, and make yourself some comfort

Out of your best advice.

CYMBELINE.

Nay, let her languish

A drop of blood a day and, being aged,

Die of this folly.

[Exit with Lords.]

Enter Pisanio.

QUEEN.

Fie! you must give way.

Here is your servant. How now, sir! What news?

PISANIO.

My lord your son drew on my master.

QUEEN.

Ha!

No harm, I trust, is done?

PISANIO.

There might have been,

But that my master rather play'd than fought,

And had no help of anger; they were parted

By gentlemen at hand.

QUEEN.

I am very glad on't.

IMOGEN.

Your son's my father's friend; he takes his part

To draw upon an exile! O brave sir!

I would they were in Afric both together;

Myself by with a needle, that I might prick

The goer-back. Why came you from your master?

PISANIO.

On his command. He would not suffer me

To bring him to the haven; left these notes

Of what commands I should be subject to,

When't pleas'd you to employ me.

QUEEN.

This hath been

Your faithful servant. I dare lay mine honour

He will remain so.

PISANIO.

I humbly thank your Highness.

QUEEN.

Pray walk awhile.

IMOGEN.

About some half-hour hence,

Pray you speak with me.

You shall at least go see my lord aboard.

For this time leave me.

[Exeunt.]

SCENE III. Britain. A public place.

Enter Cloten and two Lords.

FIRST LORD.

Sir, I would advise you to shift a shirt; the violence of action hath made you reek as a sacrifice. Where air comes out, air comes in; there's none abroad so wholesome as that you vent.

CLOTEN.

If my shirt were bloody, then to shift it. Have I hurt him?

SECOND LORD.

[Aside.] No, faith; not so much as his patience.

FIRST LORD.

Hurt him! His body's a passable carcass if he be not hurt. It is a throughfare for steel if it be not hurt.

SECOND LORD.

[Aside.] His steel was in debt; it went o' th' backside the town.

CLOTEN.

The villain would not stand me.

SECOND LORD.

[Aside.] No; but he fled forward still, toward your face.

FIRST LORD.

Stand you? You have land enough of your own; but he added to your having, gave you some ground.

SECOND LORD.

[Aside.] As many inches as you have oceans.

Puppies!

CLOTEN.

I would they had not come between us.

SECOND LORD.

[Aside.] So would I, till you had measur'd how long a fool you were upon the ground.

CLOTEN.

And that she should love this fellow, and refuse me!

SECOND LORD.

[Aside.] If it be a sin to make a true election, she is damn'd.

FIRST LORD.

Sir, as I told you always, her beauty and her brain go not together; she's a good sign, but I have seen small reflection of her wit.

SECOND LORD.

[Aside.] She shines not upon fools, lest the reflection should hurt her.

CLOTEN.

Come, I'll to my chamber. Would there had been some hurt done!

SECOND LORD.

[Aside.] I wish not so; unless it had been the fall of an ass, which is no great hurt.

CLOTEN.

You'll go with us?

FIRST LORD.

I'll attend your lordship.

CLOTEN.

Nay, come, let's go together.

SECOND LORD.

Well, my lord.

[Exeunt.]

SCENE IV. Britain. Cymbeline's palace.

Enter Imogen and Pisanio.

IMOGEN.

I would thou grew'st unto the shores o' th' haven,

And questioned'st every sail; if he should write,

And I not have it, 'twere a paper lost,

As offer'd mercy is. What was the last

That he spake to thee?

PISANIO.

It was: his queen, his queen!

IMOGEN.

Then wav'd his handkerchief?

PISANIO.

And kiss'd it, madam.

IMOGEN.

Senseless linen, happier therein than I!

And that was all?

PISANIO.

No, madam; for so long

As he could make me with his eye, or ear

Distinguish him from others, he did keep

The deck, with glove, or hat, or handkerchief,

Still waving, as the fits and stirs of's mind

Could best express how slow his soul sail'd on,

How swift his ship.

IMOGEN.

Thou shouldst have made him

As little as a crow, or less, ere left

To after-eye him.

PISANIO.

Madam, so I did.

IMOGEN.

I would have broke mine eyestrings, crack'd them but

To look upon him, till the diminution

Of space had pointed him sharp as my needle;

Nay, followed him till he had melted from

The smallness of a gnat to air, and then

Have turn'd mine eye and wept. But, good Pisanio,

When shall we hear from him?

PISANIO.

Be assur'd, madam,

With his next vantage.

IMOGEN.

I did not take my leave of him, but had

Most pretty things to say. Ere I could tell him

How I would think on him at certain hours

Such thoughts and such; or I could make him swear

The shes of Italy should not betray

Mine interest and his honour; or have charg'd him,

At the sixth hour of morn, at noon, at midnight,

T' encounter me with orisons, for then

I am in heaven for him; or ere I could

Give him that parting kiss which I had set

Betwixt two charming words, comes in my father,

And like the tyrannous breathing of the north

Shakes all our buds from growing.

Enter a Lady.

LADY.

The Queen, madam,

Desires your Highness' company.

IMOGEN.

Those things I bid you do, get them dispatch'd.

I will attend the Queen.

PISANIO.

Madam, I shall.

[Exeunt.]

SCENE V. Rome. Philario's house.

Enter Philario, Iachimo, a Frenchman, a Dutchman and a Spaniard.

IACHIMO.

Believe it, sir, I have seen him in Britain. He was then of a crescent note, expected to prove so worthy as since he hath been allowed the name of. But I could then have look'd on him without the help of admiration, though the catalogue of his endowments had been tabled by his side, and I to peruse him by items.

PHILARIO.

You speak of him when he was less furnish'd than now he is with that which makes him both without and within.

FRENCHMAN.

I have seen him in France; we had very many there could behold the sun with as firm eyes as he.

IACHIMO.

This matter of marrying his king's daughter, wherein he must be weighed rather by her value than his own, words him, I doubt not, a great deal from the matter.

FRENCHMAN.

And then his banishment.

IACHIMO.

Ay, and the approbation of those that weep this lamentable divorce under her colours are wonderfully to extend him, be it but to fortify her judgement, which else an easy battery might lay flat, for taking a beggar, without less quality. But how comes it he is to sojourn with you? How creeps acquaintance?

PHILARIO.

His father and I were soldiers together, to whom I have been often bound for no less than my life.

Enter Posthumus.

Here comes the Briton. Let him be so entertained amongst you as suits with gentlemen of your knowing to a stranger of his quality. I beseech you all be better known to this gentleman, whom I commend to you as a noble friend of mine. How worthy he is I will leave to appear hereafter, rather than story him in his own hearing.

FRENCHMAN.

Sir, we have known together in Orleans.

POSTHUMUS.

Since when I have been debtor to you for courtesies, which I will be ever to pay and yet pay still.

FRENCHMAN.

Sir, you o'errate my poor kindness. I was glad I did atone my countryman and you; it had been pity you should have been put together with so mortal a purpose as then each bore, upon importance of so slight and trivial a nature.

POSTHUMUS.

By your pardon, sir. I was then a young traveller; rather shunn'd to go even with what I heard than in my every action to be guided by others' experiences; but upon my mended judgement (if I offend not to say it is mended) my quarrel was not altogether slight.

FRENCHMAN.

Faith, yes, to be put to the arbitrement of swords, and by such two that would by all likelihood have confounded one the other or have fall'n both.

IACHIMO.

Can we, with manners, ask what was the difference?

FRENCHMAN.

Safely, I think. 'Twas a contention in public, which may, without contradiction, suffer the report. It was much like an argument that fell out last night, where each of us fell in praise of our country mistresses; this gentleman at that time vouching (and upon warrant of bloody affirmation) his to be more fair, virtuous, wise, chaste, constant, qualified, and less attemptable, than any the rarest of our ladies in France.

IACHIMO.

That lady is not now living, or this gentleman's opinion, by this, worn out.

POSTHUMUS.

She holds her virtue still, and I my mind.

IACHIMO.

You must not so far prefer her 'fore ours of Italy.

POSTHUMUS.

Being so far provok'd as I was in France, I would abate her nothing, though I profess myself her adorer, not her friend.

IACHIMO.

As fair and as good—a kind of hand-in-hand comparison—had been something too fair and too good for any lady in Britain. If she went before others I have seen as that diamond of yours outlustres many I have beheld, I could not but believe she excelled many; but I have not seen the most precious diamond that is, nor you the lady.

POSTHUMUS.

I prais'd her as I rated her. So do I my stone.

IACHIMO.

What do you esteem it at?

POSTHUMUS.

More than the world enjoys.

IACHIMO.

Either your unparagon'd mistress is dead, or she's outpriz'd by a trifle.

POSTHUMUS.

You are mistaken: the one may be sold or given, if there were wealth enough for the purchase or merit for the gift; the other is not a thing for sale, and only the gift of the gods.

IACHIMO.

Which the gods have given you?

POSTHUMUS.

Which by their graces I will keep.

IACHIMO.

You may wear her in title yours; but you know strange fowl light upon neighbouring ponds. Your ring may be stol'n too. So your brace of unprizable estimations, the one is but frail and the other casual; a cunning thief, or a that-way-accomplish'd courtier, would hazard the winning both of first and last.

POSTHUMUS.

Your Italy contains none so accomplish'd a courtier to convince the honour of my mistress, if in the holding or loss of that you term her frail. I do nothing doubt you have store of thieves; notwithstanding, I fear not my ring.

PHILARIO.

Let us leave here, gentlemen.

POSTHUMUS.

Sir, with all my heart. This worthy signior, I thank him, makes no stranger of me; we are familiar at first.

IACHIMO.

With five times so much conversation I should get ground of your fair mistress; make her go back even to the yielding, had I admittance and opportunity to friend.

POSTHUMUS.

No, no.

IACHIMO.

I dare thereupon pawn the moiety of my estate to your ring, which, in my opinion, o'ervalues it something. But I make my wager rather against your confidence than her reputation; and, to bar your offence herein too, I durst attempt it against any lady in the world.

POSTHUMUS.

You are a great deal abus'd in too bold a persuasion, and I doubt not you sustain what y'are worthy of by your attempt.

IACHIMO.

What's that?

POSTHUMUS.

A repulse; though your attempt, as you call it, deserve more; a punishment too.

PHILARIO.

Gentlemen, enough of this. It came in too suddenly; let it die as it was born, and I pray you be better acquainted.

IACHIMO.

Would I had put my estate and my neighbour's on th' approbation of what I have spoke!

POSTHUMUS.

What lady would you choose to assail?

IACHIMO.

Yours, whom in constancy you think stands so safe. I will lay you ten thousand ducats to your ring that, commend me to the court where your lady is, with no more advantage than the opportunity of a second conference, and I will bring from thence that honour of hers which you imagine so reserv'd.

POSTHUMUS.

I will wage against your gold, gold to it. My ring I hold dear as my finger; 'tis part of it.

IACHIMO.

You are a friend, and therein the wiser. If you buy ladies' flesh at a million a dram, you cannot preserve it from tainting. But I see you have some religion in you, that you fear.

POSTHUMUS.

This is but a custom in your tongue; you bear a graver purpose, I hope.

IACHIMO.

I am the master of my speeches, and would undergo what's spoken, I swear.

POSTHUMUS.

Will you? I shall but lend my diamond till your return. Let there be covenants drawn between's. My mistress exceeds in goodness the hugeness of your unworthy thinking. I dare you to this match: here's my ring.

PHILARIO.

I will have it no lay.

IACHIMO.

By the gods, it is one. If I bring you no sufficient testimony that I have enjoy'd the dearest bodily part of your mistress, my ten thousand ducats are yours; so is your diamond too. If I come off, and leave her in such honour as you have trust in, she your jewel, this your jewel, and my gold are yours: provided I have your commendation for my more free entertainment.

POSTHUMUS.

I embrace these conditions; let us have articles betwixt us. Only, thus far you shall answer: if you make your voyage upon her, and give me directly to understand you have prevail'd, I am no further your enemy; she is not worth our debate; if she remain unseduc'd, you not making it appear otherwise, for your ill opinion and th' assault you have made to her chastity you shall answer me with your sword.

IACHIMO.

Your hand, a covenant! We will have these things set down by lawful counsel, and straight away for Britain, lest the bargain should catch cold and starve. I will fetch my gold and have our two wagers recorded.

POSTHUMUS.

Agreed.

[Exeunt Posthumus and Iachimo.]

FRENCHMAN.

Will this hold, think you?

PHILARIO.

Signior Iachimo will not from it. Pray let us follow 'em.

[Exeunt.]

SCENE VI. Britain. Cymbeline's palace.

Enter Queen, Ladies and Cornelius.

QUEEN.

Whiles yet the dew's on ground, gather those flowers;

Make haste; who has the note of them?

LADY.

I, madam.

QUEEN.

Dispatch.

[Exeunt Ladies.]

Now, Master Doctor, have you brought those drugs?

CORNELIUS.

Pleaseth your Highness, ay. Here they are, madam.

[Presenting a box.]

But I beseech your Grace, without offence,

(My conscience bids me ask) wherefore you have

Commanded of me these most poisonous compounds

Which are the movers of a languishing death,

But, though slow, deadly?

QUEEN.

I wonder, Doctor,

Thou ask'st me such a question. Have I not been

Thy pupil long? Hast thou not learn'd me how

To make perfumes? distil? preserve? yea, so

That our great king himself doth woo me oft

For my confections? Having thus far proceeded

(Unless thou think'st me devilish) is't not meet

That I did amplify my judgement in

Other conclusions? I will try the forces

Of these thy compounds on such creatures as

We count not worth the hanging (but none human)

To try the vigour of them, and apply

Allayments to their act, and by them gather

Their several virtues and effects.

CORNELIUS.

Your Highness

Shall from this practice but make hard your heart;

Besides, the seeing these effects will be

Both noisome and infectious.

QUEEN.

O, content thee.

Enter Pisanio.

[Aside.] Here comes a flattering rascal; upon him

Will I first work. He's for his master,

An enemy to my son. How now, Pisanio!

Doctor, your service for this time is ended;

Take your own way.

CORNELIUS.

[Aside.] I do suspect you, madam;

But you shall do no harm.

QUEEN.

[To Pisanio.] Hark thee, a word.

CORNELIUS.

[Aside.] I do not like her. She doth think she has

Strange ling'ring poisons. I do know her spirit,

And will not trust one of her malice with

A drug of such damn'd nature. Those she has

Will stupefy and dull the sense awhile,

Which first perchance she'll prove on cats and dogs,

Then afterward up higher; but there is

No danger in what show of death it makes,

More than the locking up the spirits a time,

To be more fresh, reviving. She is fool'd

With a most false effect; and I the truer

So to be false with her.

QUEEN.

No further service, Doctor,

Until I send for thee.

CORNELIUS.

I humbly take my leave.

[Exit.]

QUEEN.

Weeps she still, say'st thou? Dost thou think in time

She will not quench, and let instructions enter

Where folly now possesses? Do thou work.

When thou shalt bring me word she loves my son,

I'll tell thee on the instant thou art then

As great as is thy master; greater, for

His fortunes all lie speechless, and his name

Is at last gasp. Return he cannot, nor

Continue where he is. To shift his being

Is to exchange one misery with another,

And every day that comes comes to decay

A day's work in him. What shalt thou expect

To be depender on a thing that leans,

Who cannot be new built, nor has no friends

So much as but to prop him?

[The Queen drops the box. Pisanio takes it up.]

Thou tak'st up

Thou know'st not what; but take it for thy labour.

It is a thing I made, which hath the King

Five times redeem'd from death. I do not know

What is more cordial. Nay, I prithee take it;

It is an earnest of a further good

That I mean to thee. Tell thy mistress how

The case stands with her; do't as from thyself.

Think what a chance thou changest on; but think

Thou hast thy mistress still; to boot, my son,

Who shall take notice of thee. I'll move the King

To any shape of thy preferment, such

As thou'lt desire; and then myself, I chiefly,

That set thee on to this desert, am bound

To load thy merit richly. Call my women.

Think on my words.

[Exit Pisanio.]

A sly and constant knave,

Not to be shak'd; the agent for his master,

And the remembrancer of her to hold

The hand-fast to her lord. I have given him that

Which, if he take, shall quite unpeople her

Of liegers for her sweet; and which she after,

Except she bend her humour, shall be assur'd

To taste of too.

Enter Pisanio and Ladies.

So, so. Well done, well done.

The violets, cowslips, and the primroses,

Bear to my closet. Fare thee well, Pisanio;

Think on my words.

[Exeunt Queen and Ladies.]

PISANIO.

And shall do.

But when to my good lord I prove untrue

I'll choke myself: there's all I'll do for you.

[Exit.]

SCENE VII. Britain. The palace.

Enter Imogen alone.

IMOGEN.

A father cruel and a step-dame false;

A foolish suitor to a wedded lady

That hath her husband banish'd. O, that husband!

My supreme crown of grief! and those repeated

Vexations of it! Had I been thief-stol'n,

As my two brothers, happy! but most miserable

Is the desire that's glorious. Blessed be those,

How mean soe'er, that have their honest wills,

Which seasons comfort. Who may this be? Fie!

Enter Pisanio and Iachimo.

PISANIO.

Madam, a noble gentleman of Rome

Comes from my lord with letters.

IACHIMO.

Change you, madam?

The worthy Leonatus is in safety,

And greets your Highness dearly.

[Presents a letter.]

IMOGEN.

Thanks, good sir.

You're kindly welcome.

IACHIMO.

[Aside.] All of her that is out of door most rich!

If she be furnish'd with a mind so rare,

She is alone th' Arabian bird, and I

Have lost the wager. Boldness be my friend!

Arm me, audacity, from head to foot!

Or, like the Parthian, I shall flying fight;

Rather, directly fly.

IMOGEN.

[Reads.] He is one of the noblest note, to whose kindnesses I am most infinitely tied. Reflect upon him accordingly, as you value your trust.

LEONATUS.

So far I read aloud;

But even the very middle of my heart

Is warm'd by th' rest and takes it thankfully.

You are as welcome, worthy sir, as I

Have words to bid you; and shall find it so

In all that I can do.

IACHIMO.

Thanks, fairest lady.

What, are men mad? Hath nature given them eyes

To see this vaulted arch and the rich crop

Of sea and land, which can distinguish 'twixt

The fiery orbs above and the twinn'd stones

Upon the number'd beach, and can we not

Partition make with spectacles so precious

'Twixt fair and foul?

IMOGEN.

What makes your admiration?

IACHIMO.

It cannot be i' th' eye, for apes and monkeys,

'Twixt two such shes, would chatter this way and

Contemn with mows the other; nor i' th' judgement,

For idiots in this case of favour would

Be wisely definite; nor i' th' appetite;

Sluttery, to such neat excellence oppos'd,

Should make desire vomit emptiness,

Not so allur'd to feed.

IMOGEN.

What is the matter, trow?

IACHIMO.

The cloyed will—

That satiate yet unsatisfied desire, that tub

Both fill'd and running—ravening first the lamb,

Longs after for the garbage.

IMOGEN.

What, dear sir,

Thus raps you? Are you well?

IACHIMO.

Thanks, madam; well. Beseech you, sir,

Desire my man's abode where I did leave him.

He's strange and peevish.

PISANIO.

I was going, sir,

To give him welcome.

[Exit.]

IMOGEN.

Continues well my lord? His health beseech you?

IACHIMO.

Well, madam.

IMOGEN.

Is he dispos'd to mirth? I hope he is.

IACHIMO.

Exceeding pleasant; none a stranger there

So merry and so gamesome. He is call'd

The Briton reveller.

IMOGEN.

When he was here

He did incline to sadness, and oft-times

Not knowing why.

IACHIMO.

I never saw him sad.

There is a Frenchman his companion, one

An eminent monsieur that, it seems, much loves

A Gallian girl at home. He furnaces

The thick sighs from him; whiles the jolly Briton

(Your lord, I mean) laughs from's free lungs, cries "O,

Can my sides hold, to think that man, who knows

By history, report, or his own proof,

What woman is, yea, what she cannot choose

But must be, will's free hours languish for

Assured bondage?"

IMOGEN.

Will my lord say so?

IACHIMO.

Ay, madam, with his eyes in flood with laughter.

It is a recreation to be by

And hear him mock the Frenchman. But heavens know

Some men are much to blame.

IMOGEN.

Not he, I hope.

IACHIMO.

Not he; but yet heaven's bounty towards him might

Be us'd more thankfully. In himself, 'tis much;

In you, which I account his, beyond all talents.

Whilst I am bound to wonder, I am bound

To pity too.

IMOGEN.

What do you pity, sir?

IACHIMO.

Two creatures heartily.

IMOGEN.

Am I one, sir?

You look on me: what wreck discern you in me

Deserves your pity?

IACHIMO.

Lamentable! What,

To hide me from the radiant sun and solace

I' th' dungeon by a snuff?

IMOGEN.

I pray you, sir,

Deliver with more openness your answers

To my demands. Why do you pity me?

IACHIMO.

That others do,

I was about to say, enjoy your—But

It is an office of the gods to venge it,

Not mine to speak on't.

IMOGEN.

You do seem to know

Something of me, or what concerns me; pray you,

Since doubting things go ill often hurts more

Than to be sure they do; for certainties

Either are past remedies, or, timely knowing,

The remedy then born—discover to me

What both you spur and stop.

IACHIMO.

Had I this cheek

To bathe my lips upon; this hand, whose touch,

Whose every touch, would force the feeler's soul

To th' oath of loyalty; this object, which

Takes prisoner the wild motion of mine eye,

Fixing it only here; should I, damn'd then,

Slaver with lips as common as the stairs

That mount the Capitol; join gripes with hands

Made hard with hourly falsehood (falsehood as

With labour): then by-peeping in an eye

Base and illustrious as the smoky light

That's fed with stinking tallow: it were fit

That all the plagues of hell should at one time

Encounter such revolt.

IMOGEN.

My lord, I fear,

Has forgot Britain.

IACHIMO.

And himself. Not I

Inclin'd to this intelligence pronounce

The beggary of his change; but 'tis your graces

That from my mutest conscience to my tongue

Charms this report out.

IMOGEN.

Let me hear no more.

IACHIMO.

O dearest soul, your cause doth strike my heart

With pity that doth make me sick! A lady

So fair, and fasten'd to an empery,

Would make the great'st king double, to be partner'd

With tomboys hir'd with that self exhibition

Which your own coffers yield! with diseas'd ventures

That play with all infirmities for gold

Which rottenness can lend nature! Such boil'd stuff

As well might poison poison! Be reveng'd;

Or she that bore you was no queen, and you

Recoil from your great stock.

IMOGEN.

Reveng'd?

How should I be reveng'd? If this be true,

(As I have such a heart that both mine ears

Must not in haste abuse) if it be true,

How should I be reveng'd?

IACHIMO.

Should he make me

Live like Diana's priest betwixt cold sheets,

Whiles he is vaulting variable ramps,

In your despite, upon your purse? Revenge it.

I dedicate myself to your sweet pleasure,

More noble than that runagate to your bed,

And will continue fast to your affection,

Still close as sure.

IMOGEN.

What ho, Pisanio!

IACHIMO.

Let me my service tender on your lips.

IMOGEN.

Away! I do condemn mine ears that have

So long attended thee. If thou wert honourable,

Thou wouldst have told this tale for virtue, not

For such an end thou seek'st, as base as strange.

Thou wrong'st a gentleman who is as far

From thy report as thou from honour; and

Solicits here a lady that disdains

Thee and the devil alike. What ho, Pisanio!

The King my father shall be made acquainted

Of thy assault. If he shall think it fit

A saucy stranger in his court to mart

As in a Romish stew, and to expound

His beastly mind to us, he hath a court

He little cares for, and a daughter who

He not respects at all. What ho, Pisanio!

IACHIMO.

O happy Leonatus! I may say

The credit that thy lady hath of thee

Deserves thy trust, and thy most perfect goodness

Her assur'd credit. Blessed live you long,

A lady to the worthiest sir that ever

Country call'd his! and you his mistress, only

For the most worthiest fit! Give me your pardon.

I have spoke this to know if your affiance

Were deeply rooted, and shall make your lord

That which he is new o'er; and he is one

The truest manner'd, such a holy witch

That he enchants societies into him,

Half all men's hearts are his.

IMOGEN.

You make amends.

IACHIMO.

He sits 'mongst men like a descended god:

He hath a kind of honour sets him off

More than a mortal seeming. Be not angry,

Most mighty Princess, that I have adventur'd

To try your taking of a false report, which hath

Honour'd with confirmation your great judgement

In the election of a sir so rare,

Which you know cannot err. The love I bear him

Made me to fan you thus; but the gods made you,

Unlike all others, chaffless. Pray your pardon.

IMOGEN.

All's well, sir; take my pow'r i' th' court for yours.

IACHIMO.

My humble thanks. I had almost forgot

T' entreat your Grace but in a small request,

And yet of moment too, for it concerns

Your lord; myself and other noble friends

Are partners in the business.

IMOGEN.

Pray what is't?

IACHIMO.

Some dozen Romans of us, and your lord

(The best feather of our wing) have mingled sums

To buy a present for the Emperor;

Which I, the factor for the rest, have done

In France. 'Tis plate of rare device, and jewels

Of rich and exquisite form, their values great;

And I am something curious, being strange,

To have them in safe stowage. May it please you

To take them in protection?

IMOGEN.

Willingly;

And pawn mine honour for their safety. Since

My lord hath interest in them, I will keep them

In my bedchamber.

IACHIMO.

They are in a trunk,

Attended by my men. I will make bold

To send them to you only for this night;

I must aboard tomorrow.

IMOGEN.

O, no, no.

IACHIMO.

Yes, I beseech; or I shall short my word

By length'ning my return. From Gallia

I cross'd the seas on purpose and on promise

To see your Grace.

IMOGEN.

I thank you for your pains.

But not away tomorrow!

IACHIMO.

O, I must, madam.

Therefore I shall beseech you, if you please

To greet your lord with writing, do't tonight.

I have outstood my time, which is material

To th' tender of our present.

IMOGEN.

I will write.

Send your trunk to me; it shall safe be kept

And truly yielded you. You're very welcome.

[Exeunt.]

ACT II

SCENE I. Britain. Before Cymbeline's palace.

Enter Cloten and the two Lords.

CLOTEN.

Was there ever man had such luck! When I kiss'd the jack, upon an upcast to be hit away! I had a hundred pound on't; and then a whoreson jackanapes must take me up for swearing, as if I borrowed mine oaths of him, and might not spend them at my pleasure.

FIRST LORD.

What got he by that? You have broke his pate with your bowl.

SECOND LORD.

[Aside.] If his wit had been like him that broke it, it would have run all out.

CLOTEN.

When a gentleman is dispos'd to swear, it is not for any standers-by to curtail his oaths. Ha?

SECOND LORD.

No, my lord; [Aside.] nor crop the ears of them.

CLOTEN.

Whoreson dog! I gave him satisfaction. Would he had been one of my rank!

SECOND LORD.

[Aside.] To have smell'd like a fool.

CLOTEN.

I am not vex'd more at anything in th' earth. A pox on't! I had rather not be so noble as I am; they dare not fight with me, because of the Queen my mother. Every jackslave hath his bellyful of fighting, and I must go up and down like a cock that nobody can match.

SECOND LORD.

[Aside.] You are cock and capon too; and you crow, cock, with your comb on.

CLOTEN.

Sayest thou?

SECOND LORD.

It is not fit your lordship should undertake every companion that you give offence to.

CLOTEN.

No, I know that; but it is fit I should commit offence to my inferiors.

SECOND LORD.

Ay, it is fit for your lordship only.

CLOTEN.

Why, so I say.

FIRST LORD.

Did you hear of a stranger that's come to court tonight?

CLOTEN.

A stranger, and I not known on't?

SECOND LORD.

[Aside.] He's a strange fellow himself, and knows it not.

FIRST LORD.

There's an Italian come, and, 'tis thought, one of Leonatus' friends.

CLOTEN.

Leonatus? A banish'd rascal; and he's another, whatsoever he be. Who told you of this stranger?

FIRST LORD.

One of your lordship's pages.

CLOTEN.

Is it fit I went to look upon him? Is there no derogation in't?

SECOND LORD.

You cannot derogate, my lord.

CLOTEN.

Not easily, I think.

SECOND LORD.

[Aside.] You are a fool granted; therefore your issues, being foolish, do not derogate.

CLOTEN.

Come, I'll go see this Italian. What I have lost today at bowls I'll win tonight of him. Come, go.

SECOND LORD.

I'll attend your lordship.

> [Exeunt Cloten and First Lord.]

That such a crafty devil as is his mother

Should yield the world this ass! A woman that

294

Bears all down with her brain; and this her son

Cannot take two from twenty, for his heart,

And leave eighteen. Alas, poor princess,

Thou divine Imogen, what thou endur'st,

Betwixt a father by thy step-dame govern'd,

A mother hourly coining plots, a wooer

More hateful than the foul expulsion is

Of thy dear husband, than that horrid act

Of the divorce he'd make! The heavens hold firm

The walls of thy dear honour, keep unshak'd

That temple, thy fair mind, that thou mayst stand

T' enjoy thy banish'd lord and this great land!

[Exit.]

SCENE II. Britain. Imogen's bedchamber in Cymbeline's palace; a trunk in one corner.

Enter Immogen in her bed, and a Lady attending.

IMOGEN.

Who's there? My woman Helen?

LADY.

Please you, madam.

IMOGEN.

What hour is it?

LADY.

Almost midnight, madam.

IMOGEN.

I have read three hours then. Mine eyes are weak;

Fold down the leaf where I have left. To bed.

Take not away the taper, leave it burning;

And if thou canst awake by four o' th' clock,

I prithee call me. Sleep hath seiz'd me wholly.

                                        [Exit Lady.]

To your protection I commend me, gods.

From fairies and the tempters of the night

Guard me, beseech ye!

                    [Sleeps. Iachimo comes from the trunk.]

IACHIMO.

The crickets sing, and man's o'er-labour'd sense

Repairs itself by rest. Our Tarquin thus

Did softly press the rushes ere he waken'd

The chastity he wounded. Cytherea,

How bravely thou becom'st thy bed! fresh lily,

And whiter than the sheets! That I might touch!

But kiss; one kiss! Rubies unparagon'd,

How dearly they do't! 'Tis her breathing that

Perfumes the chamber thus. The flame o' th' taper

Bows toward her and would under-peep her lids

To see th' enclosed lights, now canopied

Under these windows white and azure, lac'd

With blue of heaven's own tinct. But my design

To note the chamber. I will write all down:

Such and such pictures; there the window; such

Th' adornment of her bed; the arras, figures,

Why, such and such; and the contents o' th' story.

Ah, but some natural notes about her body

Above ten thousand meaner movables

Would testify, t' enrich mine inventory.

O sleep, thou ape of death, lie dull upon her!

And be her sense but as a monument,

Thus in a chapel lying! Come off, come off;

[Taking off her bracelet.]

As slippery as the Gordian knot was hard!

'Tis mine; and this will witness outwardly,

As strongly as the conscience does within,

To th' madding of her lord. On her left breast

A mole cinque-spotted, like the crimson drops

I' th' bottom of a cowslip. Here's a voucher

Stronger than ever law could make; this secret

Will force him think I have pick'd the lock and ta'en

The treasure of her honour. No more. To what end?

Why should I write this down that's riveted,

Screw'd to my memory? She hath been reading late

The tale of Tereus; here the leaf's turn'd down

Where Philomel gave up. I have enough.

To th' trunk again, and shut the spring of it.

Swift, swift, you dragons of the night, that dawning

May bare the raven's eye! I lodge in fear;

Though this a heavenly angel, hell is here.

[Clock strikes.]

One, two, three. Time, time!

[Exit into the trunk.]

SCENE III. Cymbeline's palace. An ante-chamber adjoining Imogen's apartments.

Enter Cloten and Lords.

FIRST LORD.

Your lordship is the most patient man in loss, the most coldest that ever turn'd up ace.

CLOTEN.

It would make any man cold to lose.

FIRST LORD.

But not every man patient after the noble temper of your lordship. You are most hot and furious when you win.

CLOTEN.

Winning will put any man into courage. If I could get this foolish Imogen, I should have gold enough. It's almost morning, is't not?

FIRST LORD.

Day, my lord.

CLOTEN.

I would this music would come. I am advised to give her music a mornings; they say it will penetrate.

Enter Musicians.

Come on, tune. If you can penetrate her with your fingering, so. We'll try with tongue too. If none will do, let her remain; but I'll never give o'er. First, a very excellent good-conceited thing; after, a wonderful sweet air, with admirable rich words to it, and then let her consider.

SONG

Hark, hark! the lark at heaven's gate sings,

And Phœbus 'gins arise,

His steeds to water at those springs

On chalic'd flow'rs that lies;

And winking Mary-buds begin

To ope their golden eyes.

With everything that pretty is,

My lady sweet, arise;

Arise, arise!

CLOTEN.

So, get you gone. If this penetrate, I will consider your music the better; if it do not, it is a vice in her ears which horsehairs and calves' guts, nor the voice of unpaved eunuch to boot, can never amend.

[Exeunt Musicians.]

Enter Cymbeline and Queen.

SECOND LORD.

Here comes the King.

CLOTEN.

I am glad I was up so late, for that's the reason I was up so early. He cannot choose but take this service I have done fatherly.—Good morrow to your Majesty and to my gracious mother.

CYMBELINE.

Attend you here the door of our stern daughter?

Will she not forth?

CLOTEN.

I have assail'd her with musics, but she vouchsafes no notice.

CYMBELINE.

The exile of her minion is too new;

She hath not yet forgot him; some more time

Must wear the print of his remembrance on't,

And then she's yours.

QUEEN.

You are most bound to th' King,

Who lets go by no vantages that may

Prefer you to his daughter. Frame yourself

To orderly solicits, and be friended

With aptness of the season; make denials

Increase your services; so seem as if

You were inspir'd to do those duties which

You tender to her; that you in all obey her,

Save when command to your dismission tends,

And therein you are senseless.

CLOTEN.

Senseless? Not so.

Enter a Messenger.

MESSENGER.

So like you, sir, ambassadors from Rome;

The one is Caius Lucius.

CYMBELINE.

A worthy fellow,

Albeit he comes on angry purpose now;

But that's no fault of his. We must receive him

According to the honour of his sender;

And towards himself, his goodness forespent on us,

We must extend our notice. Our dear son,

When you have given good morning to your mistress,

Attend the Queen and us; we shall have need

T' employ you towards this Roman. Come, our queen.

[Exeunt all but Cloten.]

CLOTEN.

If she be up, I'll speak with her; if not,

Let her lie still and dream. By your leave, ho!

[Knocks.]

I know her women are about her; what

If I do line one of their hands? 'Tis gold

Which buys admittance (oft it doth) yea, and makes

Diana's rangers false themselves, yield up

Their deer to th' stand o' th' stealer; and 'tis gold

Which makes the true man kill'd and saves the thief;

Nay, sometime hangs both thief and true man. What

Can it not do and undo? I will make

One of her women lawyer to me, for

I yet not understand the case myself.

By your leave.

[Knocks.]

Enter a Lady.

LADY.

Who's there that knocks?

CLOTEN.

A gentleman.

LADY.

No more?

CLOTEN.

Yes, and a gentlewoman's son.

LADY.

That's more

Than some whose tailors are as dear as yours

Can justly boast of. What's your lordship's pleasure?

CLOTEN.

Your lady's person; is she ready?

LADY.

Ay,

To keep her chamber.

CLOTEN.

There is gold for you; sell me your good report.

LADY.

How? My good name? or to report of you

303

What I shall think is good? The Princess!

Enter Imogen.

CLOTEN.

Good morrow, fairest sister. Your sweet hand.

[Exit Lady.]

IMOGEN.

Good morrow, sir. You lay out too much pains

For purchasing but trouble. The thanks I give

Is telling you that I am poor of thanks,

And scarce can spare them.

CLOTEN.

Still I swear I love you.

IMOGEN.

If you but said so, 'twere as deep with me.

If you swear still, your recompense is still

That I regard it not.

CLOTEN.

This is no answer.

IMOGEN.

But that you shall not say I yield, being silent,

I would not speak. I pray you spare me. Faith,

I shall unfold equal discourtesy

To your best kindness; one of your great knowing

Should learn, being taught, forbearance.

CLOTEN.

To leave you in your madness 'twere my sin;

I will not.

IMOGEN.

Fools are not mad folks.

CLOTEN.

Do you call me fool?

IMOGEN.

As I am mad, I do;

If you'll be patient, I'll no more be mad;

That cures us both. I am much sorry, sir,

You put me to forget a lady's manners

By being so verbal; and learn now, for all,

That I, which know my heart, do here pronounce,

By th' very truth of it, I care not for you,

And am so near the lack of charity

To accuse myself I hate you; which I had rather

You felt than make't my boast.

CLOTEN.

You sin against

Obedience, which you owe your father. For

The contract you pretend with that base wretch,

One bred of alms and foster'd with cold dishes,

With scraps o' th' court, it is no contract, none.

And though it be allowed in meaner parties

(Yet who than he more mean?) to knit their souls

(On whom there is no more dependency

But brats and beggary) in self-figur'd knot,

Yet you are curb'd from that enlargement by

The consequence o' th' crown, and must not foil

The precious note of it with a base slave,

A hilding for a livery, a squire's cloth,

A pantler; not so eminent!

IMOGEN.

Profane fellow!

Wert thou the son of Jupiter, and no more

But what thou art besides, thou wert too base

To be his groom. Thou wert dignified enough,

Even to the point of envy, if 'twere made

Comparative for your virtues to be styl'd

The under-hangman of his kingdom, and hated

For being preferr'd so well.

CLOTEN.

The south fog rot him!

IMOGEN.

He never can meet more mischance than come

To be but nam'd of thee. His mean'st garment

That ever hath but clipp'd his body, is dearer

In my respect, than all the hairs above thee,

Were they all made such men. How now, Pisanio!

Enter Pisanio.

CLOTEN.

'His garment'! Now the devil—

IMOGEN.

To Dorothy my woman hie thee presently.

CLOTEN.

'His garment'!

IMOGEN.

I am sprited with a fool;

Frighted, and ang'red worse. Go bid my woman

Search for a jewel that too casually

Hath left mine arm. It was thy master's; shrew me,

If I would lose it for a revenue

Of any king's in Europe! I do think

I saw't this morning; confident I am

Last night 'twas on mine arm; I kiss'd it.

I hope it be not gone to tell my lord

That I kiss aught but he.

PISANIO.

'Twill not be lost.

IMOGEN.

I hope so. Go and search.

[Exit Pisanio.]

CLOTEN.

You have abus'd me.

'His meanest garment'!

IMOGEN.

Ay, I said so, sir.

If you will make 't an action, call witness to 't.

CLOTEN.

I will inform your father.

IMOGEN.

Your mother too.

She's my good lady and will conceive, I hope,

But the worst of me. So I leave you, sir,

To th' worst of discontent.

[Exit.]

CLOTEN.

I'll be reveng'd.

'His mean'st garment'! Well.

[Exit.]

SCENE IV. Rome. Philario's house.

Enter Posthumus and Philario.

POSTHUMUS.

Fear it not, sir; I would I were so sure

To win the King as I am bold her honour

Will remain hers.

PHILARIO.

What means do you make to him?

POSTHUMUS.

Not any; but abide the change of time,

Quake in the present winter's state, and wish

That warmer days would come. In these fear'd hopes

I barely gratify your love; they failing,

I must die much your debtor.

PHILARIO.

Your very goodness and your company

O'erpays all I can do. By this your king

Hath heard of great Augustus. Caius Lucius

Will do's commission throughly; and I think

He'll grant the tribute, send th' arrearages,

Or look upon our Romans, whose remembrance

Is yet fresh in their grief.

POSTHUMUS.

I do believe

Statist though I am none, nor like to be,

That this will prove a war; and you shall hear

The legions now in Gallia sooner landed

In our not-fearing Britain than have tidings

Of any penny tribute paid. Our countrymen

Are men more order'd than when Julius Cæsar

Smil'd at their lack of skill, but found their courage

Worthy his frowning at. Their discipline,

Now mingled with their courages, will make known

To their approvers they are people such

That mend upon the world.

Enter Iachimo.

PHILARIO.

See! Iachimo!

POSTHUMUS.

The swiftest harts have posted you by land,

And winds of all the corners kiss'd your sails,

To make your vessel nimble.

PHILARIO.

Welcome, sir.

POSTHUMUS.

I hope the briefness of your answer made

The speediness of your return.

IACHIMO.

Your lady

Is one of the fairest that I have look'd upon.

POSTHUMUS.

And therewithal the best; or let her beauty

Look through a casement to allure false hearts,

And be false with them.

IACHIMO.

Here are letters for you.

POSTHUMUS.

Their tenour good, I trust.

IACHIMO.

'Tis very like.

PHILARIO.

Was Caius Lucius in the Britain court

When you were there?

IACHIMO.

He was expected then,

But not approach'd.

POSTHUMUS.

All is well yet.

Sparkles this stone as it was wont, or is't not

Too dull for your good wearing?

IACHIMO.

If I have lost it,

I should have lost the worth of it in gold.

I'll make a journey twice as far t' enjoy

A second night of such sweet shortness which

Was mine in Britain; for the ring is won.

POSTHUMUS.

The stone's too hard to come by.

IACHIMO.

Not a whit,

Your lady being so easy.

POSTHUMUS.

Make not, sir,

Your loss your sport. I hope you know that we

Must not continue friends.

IACHIMO.

Good sir, we must,

If you keep covenant. Had I not brought

The knowledge of your mistress home, I grant

We were to question farther; but I now

Profess myself the winner of her honour,

Together with your ring; and not the wronger

Of her or you, having proceeded but

By both your wills.

POSTHUMUS.

If you can make't apparent

That you have tasted her in bed, my hand

And ring is yours. If not, the foul opinion

You had of her pure honour gains or loses

Your sword or mine, or masterless leaves both

To who shall find them.

IACHIMO.

Sir, my circumstances,

Being so near the truth as I will make them,

Must first induce you to believe; whose strength

I will confirm with oath; which I doubt not

You'll give me leave to spare when you shall find

You need it not.

POSTHUMUS.

Proceed.

IACHIMO.

First, her bedchamber,

(Where I confess I slept not, but profess

Had that was well worth watching) it was hang'd

With tapestry of silk and silver; the story,

Proud Cleopatra when she met her Roman

And Cydnus swell'd above the banks, or for

The press of boats or pride. A piece of work

So bravely done, so rich, that it did strive

In workmanship and value; which I wonder'd

Could be so rarely and exactly wrought,

Since the true life on't was—

POSTHUMUS.

This is true;

And this you might have heard of here, by me

Or by some other.

IACHIMO.

More particulars

Must justify my knowledge.

POSTHUMUS.

So they must,

Or do your honour injury.

IACHIMO.

The chimney

Is south the chamber, and the chimneypiece

Chaste Dian bathing. Never saw I figures

So likely to report themselves. The cutter

Was as another nature, dumb; outwent her,

Motion and breath left out.

POSTHUMUS.

This is a thing

Which you might from relation likewise reap,

Being, as it is, much spoke of.

IACHIMO.

The roof o' th' chamber

With golden cherubins is fretted; her andirons

(I had forgot them) were two winking Cupids

Of silver, each on one foot standing, nicely

Depending on their brands.

POSTHUMUS.

This is her honour!

Let it be granted you have seen all this, and praise

Be given to your remembrance; the description

Of what is in her chamber nothing saves

The wager you have laid.

IACHIMO.

Then, if you can, [Shows the bracelet]

Be pale. I beg but leave to air this jewel. See!

And now 'tis up again. It must be married

To that your diamond; I'll keep them.

POSTHUMUS.

Jove!

Once more let me behold it. Is it that

Which I left with her?

IACHIMO.

Sir (I thank her) that.

She stripp'd it from her arm; I see her yet;

Her pretty action did outsell her gift,

And yet enrich'd it too. She gave it me, and said

She priz'd it once.

POSTHUMUS.

May be she pluck'd it of

To send it me.

IACHIMO.

She writes so to you, doth she?

POSTHUMUS.

O, no, no, no! 'tis true. Here, take this too;

[Gives the ring.]

It is a basilisk unto mine eye,

Kills me to look on't. Let there be no honour

Where there is beauty; truth where semblance; love

Where there's another man. The vows of women

Of no more bondage be to where they are made

Than they are to their virtues, which is nothing.

O, above measure false!

PHILARIO.

Have patience, sir,

And take your ring again; 'tis not yet won.

It may be probable she lost it, or

Who knows if one her women, being corrupted

Hath stol'n it from her?

POSTHUMUS.

Very true;

And so I hope he came by't. Back my ring.

Render to me some corporal sign about her,

More evident than this; for this was stol'n.

IACHIMO.

By Jupiter, I had it from her arm!

POSTHUMUS.

Hark you, he swears; by Jupiter he swears.

'Tis true, nay, keep the ring, 'tis true. I am sure

She would not lose it. Her attendants are

All sworn and honourable:—they induc'd to steal it!

And by a stranger! No, he hath enjoy'd her.

The cognizance of her incontinency

Is this: she hath bought the name of whore thus dearly.

There, take thy hire; and all the fiends of hell

Divide themselves between you!

PHILARIO.

Sir, be patient;

This is not strong enough to be believ'd

Of one persuaded well of.

POSTHUMUS.

Never talk on't;

She hath been colted by him.

IACHIMO.

If you seek

For further satisfying, under her breast

(Worthy the pressing) lies a mole, right proud

Of that most delicate lodging. By my life,

I kiss'd it; and it gave me present hunger

To feed again, though full. You do remember

This stain upon her?

POSTHUMUS.

Ay, and it doth confirm

Another stain, as big as hell can hold,

Were there no more but it.

IACHIMO.

Will you hear more?

POSTHUMUS.

Spare your arithmetic; never count the turns.

Once, and a million!

IACHIMO.

I'll be sworn—

POSTHUMUS.

No swearing.

If you will swear you have not done't, you lie;

And I will kill thee if thou dost deny

Thou'st made me cuckold.

IACHIMO.

I'll deny nothing.

POSTHUMUS.

O that I had her here to tear her limb-meal!

I will go there and do't, i' th' court, before

Her father. I'll do something—

[Exit.]

PHILARIO.

Quite besides

The government of patience! You have won.

Let's follow him and pervert the present wrath

He hath against himself.

IACHIMO.

With all my heart.

[Exeunt.]

SCENE V. Rome. Another room in Philario's house.

Enter Posthumus.

POSTHUMUS.

Is there no way for men to be, but women

Must be half-workers? We are all bastards,

And that most venerable man which I

Did call my father was I know not where

When I was stamp'd. Some coiner with his tools

Made me a counterfeit; yet my mother seem'd

The Dian of that time. So doth my wife

The nonpareil of this. O, vengeance, vengeance!

Me of my lawful pleasure she restrain'd,

And pray'd me oft forbearance; did it with

A pudency so rosy, the sweet view on't

Might well have warm'd old Saturn; that I thought her

As chaste as unsunn'd snow. O, all the devils!

This yellow Iachimo in an hour, was't not?

Or less; at first? Perchance he spoke not, but,

Like a full-acorn'd boar, a German one,

Cried "O!" and mounted; found no opposition

But what he look'd for should oppose and she

Should from encounter guard. Could I find out

The woman's part in me! For there's no motion

That tends to vice in man but I affirm

It is the woman's part. Be it lying, note it,

The woman's; flattering, hers; deceiving, hers;

Lust and rank thoughts, hers, hers; revenges, hers;

Ambitions, covetings, change of prides, disdain,

Nice longing, slanders, mutability,

All faults that man may name, nay, that hell knows,

Why, hers, in part or all; but rather all;

For even to vice

They are not constant, but are changing still

One vice but of a minute old for one

Not half so old as that. I'll write against them,

Detest them, curse them. Yet 'tis greater skill

In a true hate to pray they have their will:

The very devils cannot plague them better.

[Exit.]

ACT III

SCENE I. Britain. A hall in Cymbeline's palace.

Enter in state Cymbeline, Queen, Cloten and Lords at one door, and at another Caius Lucius and Attendants.

CYMBELINE.

Now say, what would Augustus Cæsar with us?

LUCIUS.

When Julius Cæsar, (whose remembrance yet

Lives in men's eyes, and will to ears and tongues

Be theme and hearing ever) was in this Britain,

And conquer'd it, Cassibelan, thine uncle,

Famous in Cæsar's praises no whit less

Than in his feats deserving it, for him

And his succession granted Rome a tribute,

Yearly three thousand pounds, which by thee lately

Is left untender'd.

QUEEN.

And, to kill the marvel,

Shall be so ever.

CLOTEN.

There be many Cæsars ere such another Julius. Britain is a world by itself, and we will nothing pay for wearing our own noses.

QUEEN.

That opportunity,

Which then they had to take from's, to resume

We have again. Remember, sir, my liege,

The kings your ancestors, together with

The natural bravery of your isle, which stands

As Neptune's park, ribb'd and pal'd in

With rocks unscaleable and roaring waters,

With sands that will not bear your enemies' boats

But suck them up to th' top-mast. A kind of conquest

Cæsar made here, but made not here his brag

Of 'Came, and saw, and overcame.' With shame

(The first that ever touch'd him) he was carried

From off our coast, twice beaten; and his shipping

(Poor ignorant baubles!) on our terrible seas,

Like egg-shells mov'd upon their surges, crack'd

As easily 'gainst our rocks; for joy whereof

The fam'd Cassibelan, who was once at point

(O, giglot fortune!) to master Cæsar's sword,

Made Lud's Town with rejoicing fires bright

And Britons strut with courage.

CLOTEN.

Come, there's no more tribute to be paid. Our kingdom is stronger than it was at that time; and, as I said, there is no moe such Cæsars. Other of them may have crook'd noses; but to owe such straight arms, none.

CYMBELINE.

Son, let your mother end.

CLOTEN.

We have yet many among us can gripe as hard as Cassibelan. I do not say I am one; but I have a hand. Why tribute? Why should we pay tribute? If Cæsar can hide the sun from us with a blanket, or put the moon in his pocket, we will pay him tribute for light; else, sir, no more tribute, pray you now.

CYMBELINE.

You must know,

Till the injurious Romans did extort

This tribute from us, we were free. Cæsar's ambition,

Which swell'd so much that it did almost stretch

The sides o' th' world, against all colour here

Did put the yoke upon's; which to shake of

Becomes a warlike people, whom we reckon

Ourselves to be.

CLOTEN.

We do.

CYMBELINE.

Say then to Cæsar,

Our ancestor was that Mulmutius which

Ordain'd our laws, whose use the sword of Cæsar

Hath too much mangled; whose repair and franchise

Shall, by the power we hold, be our good deed,

Though Rome be therefore angry. Mulmutius made our laws,

Who was the first of Britain which did put

His brows within a golden crown, and call'd

Himself a king.

LUCIUS.

I am sorry, Cymbeline,

That I am to pronounce Augustus Cæsar

(Cæsar, that hath moe kings his servants than

Thyself domestic officers) thine enemy.

Receive it from me, then: war and confusion

In Cæsar's name pronounce I 'gainst thee; look

For fury not to be resisted. Thus defied,

I thank thee for myself.

CYMBELINE.

Thou art welcome, Caius.

Thy Cæsar knighted me; my youth I spent

Much under him; of him I gather'd honour,

Which he to seek of me again, perforce,

Behoves me keep at utterance. I am perfect

That the Pannonians and Dalmatians for

Their liberties are now in arms, a precedent

Which not to read would show the Britons cold;

So Cæsar shall not find them.

LUCIUS.

Let proof speak.

CLOTEN.

His majesty bids you welcome. Make pastime with us a day or two, or longer. If you seek us afterwards in other terms, you shall find us in our salt-water girdle. If you beat us out of it, it is yours; if you fall in the adventure, our crows shall fare the better for you; and there's an end.

LUCIUS.

So, sir.

CYMBELINE.

I know your master's pleasure, and he mine;

All the remain is, welcome.

[Exeunt.]

SCENE II. Britain. Another room in Cymbeline's palace.

Enter Pisanio reading of a letter.

PISANIO.

How? of adultery? Wherefore write you not

What monsters her accuse? Leonatus!

O master, what a strange infection

Is fall'n into thy ear! What false Italian

(As poisonous-tongu'd as handed) hath prevail'd

On thy too ready hearing? Disloyal? No.

She's punish'd for her truth, and undergoes,

More goddess-like than wife-like, such assaults

As would take in some virtue. O my master,

Thy mind to her is now as low as were

Thy fortunes. How? that I should murder her?

Upon the love, and truth, and vows, which I

Have made to thy command? I, her? Her blood?

If it be so to do good service, never

Let me be counted serviceable. How look I

That I should seem to lack humanity

So much as this fact comes to?

[Reads.]

'Do't. The letter

That I have sent her, by her own command

Shall give thee opportunity.' O damn'd paper,

Black as the ink that's on thee! Senseless bauble,

Art thou a fedary for this act, and look'st

So virgin-like without? Lo, here she comes.

Enter Imogen.

I am ignorant in what I am commanded.

IMOGEN.

How now, Pisanio?

PISANIO.

Madam, here is a letter from my lord.

IMOGEN.

Who? thy lord? That is my lord, Leonatus?

O, learn'd indeed were that astronomer

That knew the stars as I his characters;

He'd lay the future open. You good gods,

Let what is here contain'd relish of love,

Of my lord's health, of his content; yet not

That we two are asunder; let that grieve him!

Some griefs are med'cinable; that is one of them,

For it doth physic love: of his content,

All but in that. Good wax, thy leave. Blest be

You bees that make these locks of counsel! Lovers

And men in dangerous bonds pray not alike;

Though forfeiters you cast in prison, yet

You clasp young Cupid's tables. Good news, gods!

[Reads.]

Justice and your father's wrath, should he take me in his dominion, could not be so cruel to me as you, O the dearest of creatures, would even renew me with your eyes. Take notice that I am in Cambria, at Milford Haven. What your own love will out of this advise you, follow. So he wishes you all happiness that remains loyal to his vow, and your increasing in love.

LEONATUS POSTHUMUS.

O for a horse with wings! Hear'st thou, Pisanio?

He is at Milford Haven. Read, and tell me

How far 'tis thither. If one of mean affairs

May plod it in a week, why may not I

Glide thither in a day? Then, true Pisanio,

Who long'st like me to see thy lord, who long'st

(O, let me 'bate!) but not like me, yet long'st,

But in a fainter kind. O, not like me,

For mine's beyond beyond: say, and speak thick,

(Love's counsellor should fill the bores of hearing

To th' smothering of the sense) how far it is

To this same blessed Milford. And by th' way

Tell me how Wales was made so happy as

T' inherit such a haven. But first of all,

How we may steal from hence; and for the gap

That we shall make in time from our hence-going

And our return, to excuse. But first, how get hence.

Why should excuse be born or ere begot?

We'll talk of that hereafter. Prithee speak,

How many score of miles may we well rid

'Twixt hour and hour?

PISANIO.

One score 'twixt sun and sun,

Madam, 's enough for you, and too much too.

IMOGEN.

Why, one that rode to's execution, man,

Could never go so slow. I have heard of riding wagers

Where horses have been nimbler than the sands

That run i' th' clock's behalf. But this is fool'ry.

Go bid my woman feign a sickness; say

She'll home to her father; and provide me presently

A riding suit, no costlier than would fit

A franklin's huswife.

PISANIO.

Madam, you're best consider.

IMOGEN.

I see before me, man. Nor here, nor here,

Nor what ensues, but have a fog in them

That I cannot look through. Away, I prithee;

Do as I bid thee. There's no more to say.

Accessible is none but Milford way.

[Exeunt.]

SCENE III. Wales. A mountainous country with a cave.

Enter from the cave Belarius, Guiderius and Arviragus.

BELARIUS.

A goodly day not to keep house with such

Whose roof's as low as ours! Stoop, boys; this gate

Instructs you how t' adore the heavens, and bows you

To a morning's holy office. The gates of monarchs

Are arch'd so high that giants may jet through

And keep their impious turbans on without

Good morrow to the sun. Hail, thou fair heaven!

We house i' th' rock, yet use thee not so hardly

As prouder livers do.

GUIDERIUS.

Hail, heaven!

ARVIRAGUS.

Hail, heaven!

BELARIUS.

Now for our mountain sport. Up to yond hill,

Your legs are young; I'll tread these flats. Consider,

When you above perceive me like a crow,

That it is place which lessens and sets off;

And you may then revolve what tales I have told you

Of courts, of princes, of the tricks in war.

This service is not service so being done,

But being so allow'd. To apprehend thus

Draws us a profit from all things we see,

And often to our comfort shall we find

The sharded beetle in a safer hold

Than is the full-wing'd eagle. O, this life

Is nobler than attending for a check,

Richer than doing nothing for a robe,

Prouder than rustling in unpaid-for silk:

Such gain the cap of him that makes him fine,

Yet keeps his book uncross'd. No life to ours!

GUIDERIUS.

Out of your proof you speak. We, poor unfledg'd,

Have never wing'd from view o' th' nest, nor know not

What air's from home. Haply this life is best,

If quiet life be best; sweeter to you

That have a sharper known; well corresponding

With your stiff age. But unto us it is

A cell of ignorance, travelling abed,

A prison for a debtor that not dares

To stride a limit.

ARVIRAGUS.

What should we speak of

When we are old as you? When we shall hear

The rain and wind beat dark December, how,

In this our pinching cave, shall we discourse.

The freezing hours away? We have seen nothing;

We are beastly: subtle as the fox for prey,

Like warlike as the wolf for what we eat.

Our valour is to chase what flies; our cage

We make a choir, as doth the prison'd bird,

And sing our bondage freely.

BELARIUS.

How you speak!

Did you but know the city's usuries,

And felt them knowingly; the art o' th' court,

As hard to leave as keep, whose top to climb

Is certain falling, or so slipp'ry that

The fear's as bad as falling; the toil o' th' war,

A pain that only seems to seek out danger

I' th' name of fame and honour, which dies i' th' search,

And hath as oft a sland'rous epitaph

As record of fair act; nay, many times,

Doth ill deserve by doing well; what's worse,

Must curtsy at the censure. O, boys, this story

The world may read in me; my body's mark'd

With Roman swords, and my report was once

First with the best of note. Cymbeline lov'd me;

And when a soldier was the theme, my name

Was not far off. Then was I as a tree

Whose boughs did bend with fruit. But in one night

A storm, or robbery, call it what you will,

Shook down my mellow hangings, nay, my leaves,

And left me bare to weather.

GUIDERIUS.

Uncertain favour!

BELARIUS.

My fault being nothing, as I have told you oft,

But that two villains, whose false oaths prevail'd

Before my perfect honour, swore to Cymbeline

I was confederate with the Romans. So

Follow'd my banishment, and this twenty years

This rock and these demesnes have been my world,

Where I have liv'd at honest freedom, paid

More pious debts to heaven than in all

The fore-end of my time. But up to th' mountains!

This is not hunters' language. He that strikes

The venison first shall be the lord o' th' feast;

To him the other two shall minister;

And we will fear no poison, which attends

In place of greater state. I'll meet you in the valleys.

[Exeunt Guiderius and Arviragus.]

How hard it is to hide the sparks of nature!

These boys know little they are sons to th' King,

Nor Cymbeline dreams that they are alive.

They think they are mine; and though train'd up thus meanly

I' th' cave wherein they bow, their thoughts do hit

The roofs of palaces, and nature prompts them

In simple and low things to prince it much

Beyond the trick of others. This Polydore,

The heir of Cymbeline and Britain, who

The King his father call'd Guiderius—Jove!

When on my three-foot stool I sit and tell

The warlike feats I have done, his spirits fly out

Into my story; say 'Thus mine enemy fell,

And thus I set my foot on's neck'; even then

The princely blood flows in his cheek, he sweats,

Strains his young nerves, and puts himself in posture

That acts my words. The younger brother, Cadwal,

Once Arviragus, in as like a figure

Strikes life into my speech, and shows much more

His own conceiving. Hark, the game is rous'd!

O Cymbeline, heaven and my conscience knows

Thou didst unjustly banish me! Whereon,

At three and two years old, I stole these babes,

Thinking to bar thee of succession as

Thou refts me of my lands. Euriphile,

Thou wast their nurse; they took thee for their mother,

And every day do honour to her grave.

Myself, Belarius, that am Morgan call'd,

They take for natural father. The game is up.

[Exit.]

SCENE IV. Wales, near Milford Haven.

Enter Pisanio and Imogen.

IMOGEN.

Thou told'st me, when we came from horse, the place

Was near at hand. Ne'er long'd my mother so

To see me first as I have now. Pisanio! Man!

Where is Posthumus? What is in thy mind

That makes thee stare thus? Wherefore breaks that sigh

From th' inward of thee? One but painted thus

Would be interpreted a thing perplex'd

Beyond self-explication. Put thyself

Into a haviour of less fear, ere wildness

Vanquish my staider senses. What's the matter?

Why tender'st thou that paper to me with

A look untender? If't be summer news,

Smile to't before; if winterly, thou need'st

But keep that count'nance still. My husband's hand?

That drug-damn'd Italy hath out-craftied him,

And he's at some hard point. Speak, man; thy tongue

May take off some extremity, which to read

Would be even mortal to me.

PISANIO.

Please you read,

And you shall find me, wretched man, a thing

The most disdain'd of fortune.

IMOGEN.

[Reads.] Thy mistress, Pisanio, hath play'd the strumpet in my bed, the testimonies whereof lie bleeding in me. I speak not out of weak surmises, but from proof as strong as my grief and as certain as I expect my revenge. That part thou, Pisanio, must act for me, if thy faith be not tainted with the breach of hers. Let thine own hands take away her life; I shall give thee opportunity at Milford Haven; she hath my letter for the purpose; where, if thou fear to strike, and to make me certain it is done, thou art the pandar to her dishonour, and equally to me disloyal.

PISANIO.

What shall I need to draw my sword? The paper

Hath cut her throat already. No, 'tis slander,

Whose edge is sharper than the sword, whose tongue

Outvenoms all the worms of Nile, whose breath

Rides on the posting winds and doth belie

All corners of the world. Kings, queens, and states,

Maids, matrons, nay, the secrets of the grave,

This viperous slander enters. What cheer, madam?

IMOGEN.

False to his bed? What is it to be false?

To lie in watch there, and to think on him?

To weep twixt clock and clock? If sleep charge nature,

To break it with a fearful dream of him,

And cry myself awake? That's false to's bed,

Is it?

PISANIO.

Alas, good lady!

IMOGEN.

I false! Thy conscience witness! Iachimo,

Thou didst accuse him of incontinency;

Thou then look'dst like a villain; now, methinks,

Thy favour's good enough. Some jay of Italy,

Whose mother was her painting, hath betray'd him.

Poor I am stale, a garment out of fashion,

And for I am richer than to hang by th' walls

I must be ripp'd. To pieces with me! O,

Men's vows are women's traitors! All good seeming,

By thy revolt, O husband, shall be thought

Put on for villainy; not born where't grows,

But worn a bait for ladies.

PISANIO.

Good madam, hear me.

IMOGEN.

True honest men being heard, like false Æneas,

Were, in his time, thought false; and Sinon's weeping

Did scandal many a holy tear, took pity

From most true wretchedness. So thou, Posthumus,

Wilt lay the leaven on all proper men:

Goodly and gallant shall be false and perjur'd

From thy great fail. Come, fellow, be thou honest;

Do thou thy master's bidding; when thou seest him,

A little witness my obedience. Look!

I draw the sword myself; take it, and hit

The innocent mansion of my love, my heart.

Fear not; 'tis empty of all things but grief;

Thy master is not there, who was indeed

The riches of it. Do his bidding; strike.

Thou mayst be valiant in a better cause,

But now thou seem'st a coward.

PISANIO.

Hence, vile instrument!

Thou shalt not damn my hand.

IMOGEN.

Why, I must die;

And if I do not by thy hand, thou art

No servant of thy master's. Against self-slaughter

There is a prohibition so divine

That cravens my weak hand. Come, here's my heart:

Something's afore't. Soft, soft! we'll no defence,

Obedient as the scabbard. What is here?

The scriptures of the loyal Leonatus

All turn'd to heresy? Away, away,

Corrupters of my faith, you shall no more

Be stomachers to my heart. Thus may poor fools

Believe false teachers; though those that are betray'd

Do feel the treason sharply, yet the traitor

Stands in worse case of woe. And thou, Posthumus,

That didst set up my disobedience 'gainst the King

My father, and make me put into contempt the suits

Of princely fellows, shalt hereafter find

It is no act of common passage but

A strain of rareness; and I grieve myself

To think, when thou shalt be disedg'd by her

That now thou tirest on, how thy memory

Will then be pang'd by me. Prithee dispatch.

The lamp entreats the butcher. Where's thy knife?

Thou art too slow to do thy master's bidding,

When I desire it too.

PISANIO.

O gracious lady,

Since I receiv'd command to do this busines

I have not slept one wink.

IMOGEN.

Do't, and to bed then.

PISANIO.

I'll wake mine eyeballs first.

IMOGEN.

Wherefore then

Didst undertake it? Why hast thou abus'd

So many miles with a pretence? This place?

Mine action and thine own? our horses' labour?

The time inviting thee? The perturb'd court,

For my being absent? whereunto I never

Purpose return. Why hast thou gone so far

To be unbent when thou hast ta'en thy stand,

Th' elected deer before thee?

PISANIO.

But to win time

To lose so bad employment, in the which

I have consider'd of a course. Good lady,

Hear me with patience.

IMOGEN.

Talk thy tongue weary, speak.

I have heard I am a strumpet, and mine ear,

Therein false struck, can take no greater wound,

Nor tent to bottom that. But speak.

PISANIO.

Then, madam,

I thought you would not back again.

IMOGEN.

Most like,

Bringing me here to kill me.

PISANIO.

Not so, neither;

But if I were as wise as honest, then

My purpose would prove well. It cannot be

But that my master is abus'd. Some villain,

Ay, and singular in his art, hath done you both

This cursed injury.

IMOGEN.

Some Roman courtezan!

PISANIO.

No, on my life!

I'll give but notice you are dead, and send him

Some bloody sign of it, for 'tis commanded

I should do so. You shall be miss'd at court,

And that will well confirm it.

IMOGEN.

Why, good fellow,

What shall I do the while? Where bide? How live?

Or in my life what comfort, when I am

Dead to my husband?

PISANIO.

If you'll back to th' court—

IMOGEN.

No court, no father, nor no more ado

With that harsh, noble, simple nothing,

That Cloten, whose love-suit hath been to me

As fearful as a siege.

PISANIO.

If not at court,

Then not in Britain must you bide.

IMOGEN.

Where then?

Hath Britain all the sun that shines? Day, night,

Are they not but in Britain? I' th' world's volume

Our Britain seems as of it, but not in't;

In a great pool a swan's nest. Prithee think

There's livers out of Britain.

PISANIO.

I am most glad

You think of other place. Th' ambassador,

Lucius the Roman, comes to Milford Haven

Tomorrow. Now, if you could wear a mind

Dark as your fortune is, and but disguise

That which t' appear itself must not yet be

But by self-danger, you should tread a course

Pretty and full of view; yea, happily, near

The residence of Posthumus; so nigh, at least,

That though his actions were not visible, yet

Report should render him hourly to your ear

As truly as he moves.

IMOGEN.

O! for such means,

Though peril to my modesty, not death on't,

I would adventure.

PISANIO.

Well then, here's the point:

You must forget to be a woman; change

Command into obedience; fear and niceness

(The handmaids of all women, or, more truly,

Woman it pretty self) into a waggish courage;

Ready in gibes, quick-answer'd, saucy, and

As quarrelous as the weasel. Nay, you must

Forget that rarest treasure of your cheek,

Exposing it (but, O, the harder heart!

Alack, no remedy) to the greedy touch

Of common-kissing Titan, and forget

Your laboursome and dainty trims wherein

You made great Juno angry.

IMOGEN.

Nay, be brief;

I see into thy end, and am almost

A man already.

PISANIO.

First, make yourself but like one.

Fore-thinking this, I have already fit

('Tis in my cloak-bag) doublet, hat, hose, all

That answer to them. Would you, in their serving,

And with what imitation you can borrow

From youth of such a season, 'fore noble Lucius

Present yourself, desire his service, tell him

Wherein you're happy; which will make him know

If that his head have ear in music; doubtless

With joy he will embrace you; for he's honourable,

And, doubling that, most holy. Your means abroad:

You have me, rich; and I will never fail

Beginning nor supplyment.

IMOGEN.

Thou art all the comfort

The gods will diet me with. Prithee away!

There's more to be consider'd; but we'll even

All that good time will give us. This attempt

I am soldier to, and will abide it with

A prince's courage. Away, I prithee.

PISANIO.

Well, madam, we must take a short farewell,

Lest, being miss'd, I be suspected of

Your carriage from the court. My noble mistress,

Here is a box; I had it from the Queen.

What's in't is precious. If you are sick at sea

Or stomach-qualm'd at land, a dram of this

Will drive away distemper. To some shade,

And fit you to your manhood. May the gods

Direct you to the best!

IMOGEN.

Amen. I thank thee.

[Exeunt severally.]

SCENE V. Britain. Cymbeline's palace.

Enter Cymbeline, Queen, Cloten, Lucius and Lords.

CYMBELINE.

Thus far, and so farewell.

LUCIUS.

Thanks, royal sir.

My emperor hath wrote; I must from hence,

And am right sorry that I must report ye

My master's enemy.

CYMBELINE.

Our subjects, sir,

Will not endure his yoke; and for ourself

To show less sovereignty than they, must needs

Appear unkinglike.

LUCIUS.

So, sir. I desire of you

A conduct overland to Milford Haven.

Madam, all joy befall your Grace, and you!

CYMBELINE.

My lords, you are appointed for that office;

The due of honour in no point omit.

So farewell, noble Lucius.

LUCIUS.

Your hand, my lord.

CLOTEN.

Receive it friendly; but from this time forth

I wear it as your enemy.

LUCIUS.

Sir, the event

Is yet to name the winner. Fare you well.

CYMBELINE.

Leave not the worthy Lucius, good my lords,

Till he have cross'd the Severn. Happiness!

[Exeunt Lucius and Lords.]

QUEEN.

He goes hence frowning; but it honours us

That we have given him cause.

CLOTEN.

'Tis all the better;

Your valiant Britons have their wishes in it.

CYMBELINE.

Lucius hath wrote already to the Emperor

How it goes here. It fits us therefore ripely

Our chariots and our horsemen be in readiness.

The pow'rs that he already hath in Gallia

Will soon be drawn to head, from whence he moves

His war for Britain.

QUEEN.

'Tis not sleepy business,

But must be look'd to speedily and strongly.

CYMBELINE.

Our expectation that it would be thus

Hath made us forward. But, my gentle queen,

Where is our daughter? She hath not appear'd

Before the Roman, nor to us hath tender'd

The duty of the day. She looks us like

A thing more made of malice than of duty;

We have noted it. Call her before us, for

We have been too slight in sufferance.

[Exit an Attendant.]

QUEEN.

Royal sir,

Since the exile of Posthumus, most retir'd

Hath her life been; the cure whereof, my lord,

'Tis time must do. Beseech your Majesty,

Forbear sharp speeches to her; she's a lady

So tender of rebukes that words are strokes,

And strokes death to her.

Enter Attendant.

CYMBELINE.

Where is she, sir? How

Can her contempt be answer'd?

ATTENDANT.

Please you, sir,

Her chambers are all lock'd, and there's no answer

That will be given to th' loud of noise we make.

QUEEN.

My lord, when last I went to visit her,

She pray'd me to excuse her keeping close;

Whereto constrain'd by her infirmity

She should that duty leave unpaid to you

Which daily she was bound to proffer. This

She wish'd me to make known; but our great court

Made me to blame in memory.

CYMBELINE.

Her doors lock'd?

Not seen of late? Grant, heavens, that which I fear

Prove false!

[Exit.]

QUEEN.

Son, I say, follow the King.

CLOTEN.

That man of hers, Pisanio, her old servant,

I have not seen these two days.

QUEEN.

Go, look after.

[Exit Cloten.]

Pisanio, thou that stand'st so for Posthumus!

He hath a drug of mine. I pray his absence

Proceed by swallowing that; for he believes

It is a thing most precious. But for her,

Where is she gone? Haply despair hath seiz'd her;

Or, wing'd with fervour of her love, she's flown

To her desir'd Posthumus. Gone she is

To death or to dishonour, and my end

Can make good use of either. She being down,

I have the placing of the British crown.

Enter Cloten.

How now, my son?

CLOTEN.

'Tis certain she is fled.

Go in and cheer the King. He rages; none

Dare come about him.

QUEEN.

All the better. May

This night forestall him of the coming day!

[Exit.]

CLOTEN.

353

I love and hate her; for she's fair and royal,

And that she hath all courtly parts more exquisite

Than lady, ladies, woman. From every one

The best she hath, and she, of all compounded,

Outsells them all. I love her therefore; but

Disdaining me and throwing favours on

The low Posthumus slanders so her judgement

That what's else rare is chok'd; and in that point

I will conclude to hate her, nay, indeed,

To be reveng'd upon her. For when fools

Shall—

Enter Pisanio.

Who is here? What, are you packing, sirrah?

Come hither. Ah, you precious pandar! Villain,

Where is thy lady? In a word, or else

Thou art straightway with the fiends.

PISANIO.

O good my lord!

CLOTEN.

Where is thy lady? or, by Jupiter—

I will not ask again. Close villain,

I'll have this secret from thy heart, or rip

Thy heart to find it. Is she with Posthumus?

From whose so many weights of baseness cannot

A dram of worth be drawn.

PISANIO.

Alas, my lord,

How can she be with him? When was she miss'd?

He is in Rome.

CLOTEN.

Where is she, sir? Come nearer.

No farther halting! Satisfy me home

What is become of her.

PISANIO.

O my all-worthy lord!

CLOTEN.

All-worthy villain!

Discover where thy mistress is at once,

At the next word. No more of 'worthy lord'!

Speak, or thy silence on the instant is

Thy condemnation and thy death.

PISANIO.

Then, sir,

This paper is the history of my knowledge

Touching her flight.

[Presenting a letter.]

CLOTEN.

Let's see't. I will pursue her

Even to Augustus' throne.

PISANIO.

[Aside.] Or this or perish.

She's far enough; and what he learns by this

May prove his travel, not her danger.

CLOTEN.

Humh!

PISANIO.

[Aside.] I'll write to my lord she's dead. O Imogen,

Safe mayst thou wander, safe return again!

CLOTEN.

Sirrah, is this letter true?

PISANIO.

Sir, as I think.

CLOTEN.

It is Posthumus' hand; I know't. Sirrah, if thou wouldst not be a villain, but do me true service, undergo those employments wherein I should have cause to use thee with a serious industry—that is, what villainy soe'er I bid thee do, to perform it directly and truly—I would think thee an honest man; thou shouldst neither want my means for thy relief nor my voice for thy preferment.

PISANIO.

Well, my good lord.

CLOTEN.

Wilt thou serve me? For since patiently and constantly thou hast stuck to the bare fortune of that beggar Posthumus, thou canst not, in the course of gratitude, but be a diligent follower of mine. Wilt thou serve me?

PISANIO.

Sir, I will.

CLOTEN.

Give me thy hand; here's my purse. Hast any of thy late master's garments in thy possession?

PISANIO.

I have, my lord, at my lodging, the same suit he wore when he took leave of my lady and mistress.

CLOTEN.

The first service thou dost me, fetch that suit hither. Let it be thy first service; go.

PISANIO.

I shall, my lord.

[Exit.]

CLOTEN.

Meet thee at Milford Haven! I forgot to ask him one thing; I'll remember't anon. Even there, thou villain Posthumus, will I kill thee. I would these garments were come. She said upon a time—the bitterness of it I now belch from my heart—that she held the very garment of Posthumus in more respect than my noble and natural person, together with the adornment of my qualities. With that suit upon my back will I ravish her; first kill him, and in her eyes. There shall she see my valour, which will then be a torment to her contempt. He on the ground, my speech of insultment ended on his dead body, and when my lust hath dined—which, as I say, to vex her I will execute in the clothes that she so prais'd—to the court I'll knock her back, foot her home again. She hath despis'd me rejoicingly, and I'll be merry in my revenge.

Enter Pisanio with the clothes.

Be those the garments?

PISANIO.

Ay, my noble lord.

CLOTEN.

How long is't since she went to Milford Haven?

PISANIO.

She can scarce be there yet.

CLOTEN.

Bring this apparel to my chamber; that is the second thing that I have commanded thee. The third is that thou wilt be a voluntary mute to my design. Be but duteous and true, preferment shall tender itself to thee. My revenge is now at Milford, would I had wings to follow it! Come, and be true.

[Exit.]

PISANIO.

Thou bid'st me to my loss; for true to thee

Were to prove false, which I will never be,

To him that is most true. To Milford go,

And find not her whom thou pursuest. Flow, flow,

You heavenly blessings, on her! This fool's speed

Be cross'd with slowness! Labour be his meed!

[Exit.]

SCENE VI. Wales. Before the cave of Belarius.

Enter Imogen alone, in boy's clothes.

IMOGEN.

I see a man's life is a tedious one.

I have tir'd myself, and for two nights together

Have made the ground my bed. I should be sick

But that my resolution helps me. Milford,

When from the mountain-top Pisanio show'd thee,

Thou wast within a ken. O Jove! I think

Foundations fly the wretched; such, I mean,

Where they should be reliev'd. Two beggars told me

I could not miss my way. Will poor folks lie,

That have afflictions on them, knowing 'tis

A punishment or trial? Yes; no wonder,

When rich ones scarce tell true. To lapse in fulness

Is sorer than to lie for need; and falsehood

Is worse in kings than beggars. My dear lord!

Thou art one o' th' false ones. Now I think on thee

My hunger's gone; but even before, I was

At point to sink for food. But what is this?

Here is a path to't; 'tis some savage hold.

I were best not call; I dare not call. Yet famine,

Ere clean it o'erthrow nature, makes it valiant.

Plenty and peace breeds cowards; hardness ever

Of hardiness is mother. Ho! who's here?

If anything that's civil, speak; if savage,

Take or lend. Ho! No answer? Then I'll enter.

Best draw my sword; and if mine enemy

But fear the sword, like me, he'll scarcely look on't.

Such a foe, good heavens!

[Exit into the cave.]

SCENE VII. The same.

Enter Belarius, Guiderius and Arviragus.

BELARIUS.

You, Polydore, have prov'd best woodman and

Are master of the feast. Cadwal and I

Will play the cook and servant; 'tis our match.

The sweat of industry would dry and die

But for the end it works to. Come, our stomachs

Will make what's homely savoury; weariness

Can snore upon the flint, when resty sloth

Finds the down pillow hard. Now, peace be here,

Poor house, that keep'st thyself!

GUIDERIUS.

I am thoroughly weary.

ARVIRAGUS.

I am weak with toil, yet strong in appetite.

GUIDERIUS.

There is cold meat i' th' cave; we'll browse on that

Whilst what we have kill'd be cook'd.

BELARIUS.

[Looking into the cave.] Stay, come not in.

But that it eats our victuals, I should think

Here were a fairy.

GUIDERIUS.

What's the matter, sir?

BELARIUS.

By Jupiter, an angel! or, if not,

An earthly paragon! Behold divineness

No elder than a boy!

Enter Imogen.

IMOGEN.

Good masters, harm me not.

Before I enter'd here I call'd, and thought

To have begg'd or bought what I have took. Good troth,

I have stol'n nought; nor would not though I had found

Gold strew'd i' th' floor. Here's money for my meat.

I would have left it on the board, so soon

As I had made my meal, and parted

With pray'rs for the provider.

GUIDERIUS.

Money, youth?

ARVIRAGUS.

All gold and silver rather turn to dirt,

As 'tis no better reckon'd but of those

Who worship dirty gods.

IMOGEN.

I see you're angry.

Know, if you kill me for my fault, I should

Have died had I not made it.

BELARIUS.

Whither bound?

IMOGEN.

To Milford Haven.

BELARIUS.

What's your name?

IMOGEN.

Fidele, sir. I have a kinsman who

Is bound for Italy; he embark'd at Milford;

To whom being going, almost spent with hunger,

I am fall'n in this offence.

BELARIUS.

Prithee, fair youth,

Think us no churls, nor measure our good minds

By this rude place we live in. Well encounter'd!

'Tis almost night; you shall have better cheer

Ere you depart, and thanks to stay and eat it.

Boys, bid him welcome.

GUIDERIUS.

Were you a woman, youth,

I should woo hard but be your groom. In honesty

I bid for you as I'd buy.

ARVIRAGUS.

I'll make't my comfort

He is a man. I'll love him as my brother;

And such a welcome as I'd give to him

After long absence, such is yours. Most welcome!

Be sprightly, for you fall 'mongst friends.

IMOGEN.

'Mongst friends,

If brothers. [Aside.] Would it had been so that they

Had been my father's sons! Then had my prize

Been less, and so more equal ballasting

To thee, Posthumus.

BELARIUS.

He wrings at some distress.

GUIDERIUS.

Would I could free't!

ARVIRAGUS.

Or I, whate'er it be,

What pain it cost, what danger! Gods!

BELARIUS.

[Whispering.] Hark, boys.

IMOGEN.

[Aside.] Great men,

That had a court no bigger than this cave,

That did attend themselves, and had the virtue

Which their own conscience seal'd them, laying by

That nothing-gift of differing multitudes,

Could not out-peer these twain. Pardon me, gods!

I'd change my sex to be companion with them,

Since Leonatus false.

BELARIUS.

It shall be so.

Boys, we'll go dress our hunt. Fair youth, come in.

Discourse is heavy, fasting; when we have supp'd,

We'll mannerly demand thee of thy story,

So far as thou wilt speak it.

GUIDERIUS.

Pray draw near.

ARVIRAGUS.

The night to th' owl and morn to th' lark less

welcome.

IMOGEN.

Thanks, sir.

ARVIRAGUS.

I pray draw near.

[Exeunt.]

365

SCENE VIII. Rome. A public place.

Enter two Roman Senators and Tribunes.

FIRST SENATOR.

This is the tenour of the Emperor's writ:

That since the common men are now in action

'Gainst the Pannonians and Dalmatians,

And that the legions now in Gallia are

Full weak to undertake our wars against

The fall'n-off Britons, that we do incite

The gentry to this business. He creates

Lucius proconsul; and to you, the tribunes,

For this immediate levy, he commands

His absolute commission. Long live Cæsar!

TRIBUNE.

Is Lucius general of the forces?

SECOND SENATOR.

Ay.

TRIBUNE.

Remaining now in Gallia?

FIRST SENATOR.

With those legions

Which I have spoke of, whereunto your levy

Must be supplyant. The words of your commission

Will tie you to the numbers and the time

Of their dispatch.

TRIBUNE.

We will discharge our duty.

[Exeunt.]

ACT IV

SCENE I. Wales. Near the cave of Belarius.

Enter Cloten alone.

CLOTEN.

I am near to th' place where they should meet, if Pisanio have mapp'd it truly. How fit his garments serve me! Why should his mistress, who was made by him that made the tailor, not be fit too? The rather, saving reverence of the word, for 'tis said a woman's fitness comes by fits. Therein I must play the workman. I dare speak it to myself, for it is not vain-glory for a man and his glass to confer in his own chamber; I mean, the lines of my body are as well drawn as his; no less young, more strong, not beneath him in fortunes, beyond him in the advantage of the time, above him in birth, alike conversant in general services, and more remarkable in single oppositions. Yet this imperceiverant thing loves him in my despite. What mortality is! Posthumus, thy head, which now is growing upon thy shoulders, shall within this hour be off; thy mistress enforced; thy garments cut to pieces before her face; and all this done, spurn her home to her father, who may, haply, be a little angry for my so rough usage; but my mother, having power of his testiness, shall turn all into my commendations. My horse is tied up safe. Out, sword, and to a sore purpose! Fortune, put them into my hand. This is the very description of their meeting-place; and the fellow dares not deceive me.

[Exit.]

SCENE II. Wales. Before the cave of Belarius.

Enter from the cave, Belarius, Guiderius, Arviragus and Imogen.

BELARIUS.

[To Imogen.] You are not well. Remain here in the cave;

We'll come to you after hunting.

ARVIRAGUS.

[To Imogen.] Brother, stay here.

Are we not brothers?

IMOGEN.

So man and man should be;

But clay and clay differs in dignity,

Whose dust is both alike. I am very sick.

GUIDERIUS.

Go you to hunting; I'll abide with him.

IMOGEN.

So sick I am not, yet I am not well;

But not so citizen a wanton as

To seem to die ere sick. So please you, leave me;

Stick to your journal course. The breach of custom

Is breach of all. I am ill, but your being by me

Cannot amend me; society is no comfort

To one not sociable. I am not very sick,

Since I can reason of it. Pray you trust me here.

I'll rob none but myself; and let me die,

Stealing so poorly.

GUIDERIUS.

I love thee; I have spoke it.

How much the quantity, the weight as much

As I do love my father.

BELARIUS.

What? how? how?

ARVIRAGUS.

If it be sin to say so, sir, I yoke me

In my good brother's fault. I know not why

I love this youth, and I have heard you say

Love's reason's without reason. The bier at door,

And a demand who is't shall die, I'd say

'My father, not this youth.'

BELARIUS.

[Aside.] O noble strain!

O worthiness of nature! breed of greatness!

Cowards father cowards and base things sire base.

Nature hath meal and bran, contempt and grace.

I'm not their father; yet who this should be

Doth miracle itself, lov'd before me.—

'Tis the ninth hour o' th' morn.

ARVIRAGUS.

Brother, farewell.

IMOGEN.

I wish ye sport.

ARVIRAGUS.

Your health. [To Belarius.] So please you, sir.

IMOGEN.

[Aside.] These are kind creatures. Gods, what lies I

have heard!

Our courtiers say all's savage but at court.

Experience, O, thou disprov'st report!

Th' imperious seas breed monsters; for the dish,

Poor tributary rivers as sweet fish.

I am sick still; heart-sick. Pisanio,

I'll now taste of thy drug.

[Swallows some.]

GUIDERIUS.

I could not stir him.

He said he was gentle, but unfortunate;

Dishonestly afflicted, but yet honest.

ARVIRAGUS.

Thus did he answer me; yet said hereafter

I might know more.

BELARIUS.

To th' field, to th' field!

We'll leave you for this time. Go in and rest.

ARVIRAGUS.

We'll not be long away.

BELARIUS.

Pray be not sick,

For you must be our huswife.

IMOGEN.

Well, or ill,

I am bound to you.

BELARIUS.

And shalt be ever.

[Exit Imogen into the cave.]

This youth, howe'er distress'd, appears he hath had

Good ancestors.

ARVIRAGUS.

How angel-like he sings!

GUIDERIUS.

But his neat cookery! He cut our roots in characters,

And sauc'd our broths as Juno had been sick,

And he her dieter.

ARVIRAGUS.

Nobly he yokes

A smiling with a sigh, as if the sigh

Was that it was for not being such a smile;

The smile mocking the sigh that it would fly

From so divine a temple to commix

With winds that sailors rail at.

GUIDERIUS.

I do note

That grief and patience, rooted in him both,

Mingle their spurs together.

ARVIRAGUS.

Grow patience!

And let the stinking elder, grief, untwine

His perishing root with the increasing vine!

BELARIUS.

It is great morning. Come, away! Who's there?

Enter Cloten.

CLOTEN.

I cannot find those runagates; that villain

Hath mock'd me. I am faint.

BELARIUS.

Those runagates?

Means he not us? I partly know him; 'tis

Cloten, the son o' th' Queen. I fear some ambush.

I saw him not these many years, and yet

I know 'tis he. We are held as outlaws. Hence!

GUIDERIUS.

He is but one; you and my brother search

What companies are near. Pray you away;

Let me alone with him.

[Exeunt Belarius and Arviragus.]

CLOTEN.

Soft! What are you

That fly me thus? Some villain mountaineers?

I have heard of such. What slave art thou?

GUIDERIUS.

A thing

More slavish did I ne'er than answering

A slave without a knock.

CLOTEN.

Thou art a robber,

A law-breaker, a villain. Yield thee, thief.

GUIDERIUS.

To who? To thee? What art thou? Have not I

An arm as big as thine, a heart as big?

Thy words, I grant, are bigger, for I wear not

My dagger in my mouth. Say what thou art;

Why I should yield to thee.

CLOTEN.

Thou villain base,

Know'st me not by my clothes?

GUIDERIUS.

No, nor thy tailor, rascal,

Who is thy grandfather; he made those clothes,

Which, as it seems, make thee.

CLOTEN.

Thou precious varlet,

My tailor made them not.

GUIDERIUS.

Hence, then, and thank

The man that gave them thee. Thou art some fool;

I am loath to beat thee.

CLOTEN.

Thou injurious thief,

Hear but my name, and tremble.

GUIDERIUS.

What's thy name?

CLOTEN.

Cloten, thou villain.

GUIDERIUS.

Cloten, thou double villain, be thy name,

I cannot tremble at it. Were it Toad, or Adder, Spider,

'Twould move me sooner.

CLOTEN.

To thy further fear,

Nay, to thy mere confusion, thou shalt know

I am son to th' Queen.

GUIDERIUS.

I'm sorry for't; not seeming

So worthy as thy birth.

CLOTEN.

Art not afeard?

GUIDERIUS.

Those that I reverence, those I fear—the wise;

At fools I laugh, not fear them.

CLOTEN.

Die the death.

When I have slain thee with my proper hand,

I'll follow those that even now fled hence,

And on the gates of Lud's Town set your heads.

Yield, rustic mountaineer.

[Exeunt, fighting.]

Enter Belarius and Arviragus.

BELARIUS.

No company's abroad?

ARVIRAGUS.

None in the world; you did mistake him, sure.

BELARIUS.

I cannot tell; long is it since I saw him,

But time hath nothing blurr'd those lines of favour

Which then he wore; the snatches in his voice,

And burst of speaking, were as his. I am absolute

'Twas very Cloten.

ARVIRAGUS.

In this place we left them.

I wish my brother make good time with him,

You say he is so fell.

BELARIUS.

Being scarce made up,

I mean to man, he had not apprehension

Or roaring terrors; for defect of judgement

Is oft the cease of fear.

Enter Guiderius with Cloten's head.

But, see, thy brother.

GUIDERIUS.

This Cloten was a fool, an empty purse;

There was no money in't. Not Hercules

Could have knock'd out his brains, for he had none;

Yet I not doing this, the fool had borne

My head as I do his.

BELARIUS.

What hast thou done?

GUIDERIUS.

I am perfect what: cut off one Cloten's head,

Son to the Queen, after his own report;

Who call'd me traitor, mountaineer, and swore

With his own single hand he'd take us in,

Displace our heads where, thank the gods, they grow,

And set them on Lud's Town.

BELARIUS.

We are all undone.

GUIDERIUS.

Why, worthy father, what have we to lose

But that he swore to take, our lives? The law

Protects not us; then why should we be tender

To let an arrogant piece of flesh threat us,

Play judge and executioner all himself,

For we do fear the law? What company

Discover you abroad?

BELARIUS.

No single soul

Can we set eye on, but in all safe reason

He must have some attendants. Though his humour

Was nothing but mutation, ay, and that

From one bad thing to worse, not frenzy, not

Absolute madness could so far have rav'd,

To bring him here alone. Although perhaps

It may be heard at court that such as we

Cave here, hunt here, are outlaws, and in time

May make some stronger head, the which he hearing,

As it is like him, might break out and swear

He'd fetch us in; yet is't not probable

To come alone, either he so undertaking

Or they so suffering. Then on good ground we fear,

If we do fear this body hath a tail

More perilous than the head.

ARVIRAGUS.

Let ordinance

Come as the gods foresay it. Howsoe'er,

My brother hath done well.

BELARIUS.

I had no mind

To hunt this day; the boy Fidele's sickness

Did make my way long forth.

GUIDERIUS.

With his own sword,

Which he did wave against my throat, I have ta'en

His head from him. I'll throw't into the creek

Behind our rock, and let it to the sea

And tell the fishes he's the Queen's son, Cloten.

That's all I reck.

[Exit.]

BELARIUS.

I fear 'twill be reveng'd.

Would, Polydore, thou hadst not done't! though valour

Becomes thee well enough.

ARVIRAGUS.

Would I had done't,

So the revenge alone pursu'd me! Polydore,

I love thee brotherly, but envy much

Thou hast robb'd me of this deed. I would revenges,

That possible strength might meet, would seek us through,

And put us to our answer.

BELARIUS.

Well, 'tis done.

We'll hunt no more today, nor seek for danger

Where there's no profit. I prithee to our rock.

You and Fidele play the cooks; I'll stay

Till hasty Polydore return, and bring him

To dinner presently.

ARVIRAGUS.

Poor sick Fidele!

I'll willingly to him; to gain his colour

I'd let a parish of such Cloten's blood,

And praise myself for charity.

[Exit.]

BELARIUS.

O thou goddess,

Thou divine Nature, thou thyself thou blazon'st

In these two princely boys! They are as gentle

As zephyrs blowing below the violet,

Not wagging his sweet head; and yet as rough,

Their royal blood enchaf'd, as the rud'st wind

That by the top doth take the mountain pine

And make him stoop to th' vale. 'Tis wonder

That an invisible instinct should frame them

To royalty unlearn'd, honour untaught,

Civility not seen from other, valour

That wildly grows in them, but yields a crop

As if it had been sow'd. Yet still it's strange

What Cloten's being here to us portends,

Or what his death will bring us.

Enter Guiderius.

GUIDERIUS.

Where's my brother?

I have sent Cloten's clotpoll down the stream,

In embassy to his mother; his body's hostage

For his return.

[Solemn music.]

BELARIUS.

My ingenious instrument!

Hark, Polydore, it sounds. But what occasion

Hath Cadwal now to give it motion? Hark!

GUIDERIUS.

Is he at home?

BELARIUS.

He went hence even now.

GUIDERIUS.

What does he mean? Since death of my dear'st mother

It did not speak before. All solemn things

Should answer solemn accidents. The matter?

Triumphs for nothing and lamenting toys

Is jollity for apes and grief for boys.

Is Cadwal mad?

Enter Arviragus with Imogen as dead, bearing her in his arms.

BELARIUS.

Look, here he comes,

And brings the dire occasion in his arms

Of what we blame him for!

ARVIRAGUS.

The bird is dead

That we have made so much on. I had rather

Have skipp'd from sixteen years of age to sixty,

To have turn'd my leaping time into a crutch,

Than have seen this.

GUIDERIUS.

O sweetest, fairest lily!

My brother wears thee not the one half so well

As when thou grew'st thyself.

BELARIUS.

O melancholy!

Who ever yet could sound thy bottom? find

The ooze to show what coast thy sluggish crare

Might'st easiliest harbour in? Thou blessed thing!

Jove knows what man thou mightst have made; but I,

Thou diedst, a most rare boy, of melancholy.

How found you him?

ARVIRAGUS.

Stark, as you see;

Thus smiling, as some fly had tickled slumber,

Not as death's dart, being laugh'd at; his right cheek

Reposing on a cushion.

GUIDERIUS.

Where?

ARVIRAGUS.

O' th' floor;

His arms thus leagu'd. I thought he slept, and put

My clouted brogues from off my feet, whose rudeness

Answer'd my steps too loud.

GUIDERIUS.

Why, he but sleeps.

If he be gone he'll make his grave a bed;

With female fairies will his tomb be haunted,

And worms will not come to thee.

ARVIRAGUS.

With fairest flowers,

Whilst summer lasts and I live here, Fidele,

I'll sweeten thy sad grave. Thou shalt not lack

The flower that's like thy face, pale primrose; nor

The azur'd hare-bell, like thy veins; no, nor

The leaf of eglantine, whom not to slander,

Out-sweet'ned not thy breath. The ruddock would,

With charitable bill (O bill, sore shaming

Those rich-left heirs that let their fathers lie

Without a monument!) bring thee all this;

Yea, and furr'd moss besides, when flow'rs are none,

To winter-ground thy corse—

GUIDERIUS.

Prithee have done,

And do not play in wench-like words with that

Which is so serious. Let us bury him,

And not protract with admiration what

Is now due debt. To th' grave.

ARVIRAGUS.

Say, where shall's lay him?

GUIDERIUS.

By good Euriphile, our mother.

ARVIRAGUS.

Be't so;

And let us, Polydore, though now our voices

Have got the mannish crack, sing him to th' ground,

As once to our mother; use like note and words,

Save that Euriphile must be Fidele.

GUIDERIUS.

Cadwal,

I cannot sing. I'll weep, and word it with thee;

For notes of sorrow out of tune are worse

Than priests and fanes that lie.

ARVIRAGUS.

We'll speak it, then.

BELARIUS.

Great griefs, I see, med'cine the less, for Cloten

Is quite forgot. He was a queen's son, boys;

And though he came our enemy, remember

He was paid for that. Though mean and mighty rotting

Together have one dust, yet reverence,

That angel of the world, doth make distinction

Of place 'tween high and low. Our foe was princely;

And though you took his life, as being our foe,

Yet bury him as a prince.

GUIDERIUS.

Pray you fetch him hither.

Thersites' body is as good as Ajax',

When neither are alive.

ARVIRAGUS.

If you'll go fetch him,

We'll say our song the whilst. Brother, begin.

[Exit Belarius.]

GUIDERIUS.

Nay, Cadwal, we must lay his head to th' East;

My father hath a reason for't.

ARVIRAGUS.

'Tis true.

GUIDERIUS.

Come on, then, and remove him.

ARVIRAGUS.

So. Begin.

SONG

GUIDERIUS.

Fear no more the heat o' th' sun,

   Nor the furious winter's rages;

Thou thy worldly task hast done,

   Home art gone, and ta'en thy wages.

Golden lads and girls all must,

As chimney-sweepers, come to dust.

ARVIRAGUS.

Fear no more the frown o' th' great;

   Thou art past the tyrant's stroke.

Care no more to clothe and eat;

   To thee the reed is as the oak.

The sceptre, learning, physic, must

All follow this and come to dust.

GUIDERIUS.

Fear no more the lightning flash.

ARVIRAGUS.

Nor th' all-dreaded thunder-stone.

GUIDERIUS.

Fear not slander, censure rash;

ARVIRAGUS.

Thou hast finish'd joy and moan.

BOTH.

All lovers young, all lovers must

Consign to thee and come to dust.

GUIDERIUS.

No exorciser harm thee!

ARVIRAGUS.

Nor no witchcraft charm thee!

GUIDERIUS.

Ghost unlaid forbear thee!

ARVIRAGUS.

Nothing ill come near thee!

BOTH.

Quiet consummation have,

And renowned be thy grave!

Enter Belarius with the body of Cloten.

GUIDERIUS.

We have done our obsequies. Come, lay him down.

BELARIUS.

Here's a few flowers; but 'bout midnight, more.

The herbs that have on them cold dew o' th' night

Are strewings fit'st for graves. Upon their faces.

You were as flow'rs, now wither'd. Even so

These herblets shall which we upon you strew.

Come on, away. Apart upon our knees.

The ground that gave them first has them again.

Their pleasures here are past, so is their pain.

[Exeunt all but Imogen.]

IMOGEN.

[Awaking.] Yes, sir, to Milford Haven. Which is the way?

I thank you. By yond bush? Pray, how far thither?

'Ods pittikins! can it be six mile yet?

I have gone all night. Faith, I'll lie down and sleep.

But, soft! no bedfellow. O gods and goddesses!

[Seeing the body.]

These flow'rs are like the pleasures of the world;

This bloody man, the care on't. I hope I dream;

For so I thought I was a cave-keeper,

And cook to honest creatures. But 'tis not so;

'Twas but a bolt of nothing, shot at nothing,

Which the brain makes of fumes. Our very eyes

Are sometimes, like our judgements, blind. Good faith,

I tremble still with fear; but if there be

Yet left in heaven as small a drop of pity

As a wren's eye, fear'd gods, a part of it!

The dream's here still. Even when I wake it is

Without me, as within me; not imagin'd, felt.

A headless man? The garments of Posthumus?

I know the shape of's leg; this is his hand,

His foot Mercurial, his Martial thigh,

The brawns of Hercules; but his Jovial face—

Murder in heaven! How! 'Tis gone. Pisanio,

All curses madded Hecuba gave the Greeks,

And mine to boot, be darted on thee! Thou,

Conspir'd with that irregulous devil, Cloten,

Hath here cut off my lord. To write and read

Be henceforth treacherous! Damn'd Pisanio

Hath with his forged letters (damn'd Pisanio)

From this most bravest vessel of the world

Struck the main-top. O Posthumus! alas,

Where is thy head? Where's that? Ay me! where's that?

Pisanio might have kill'd thee at the heart,

And left this head on. How should this be? Pisanio?

'Tis he and Cloten; malice and lucre in them

Have laid this woe here. O, 'tis pregnant, pregnant!

The drug he gave me, which he said was precious

And cordial to me, have I not found it

Murd'rous to th' senses? That confirms it home.

This is Pisanio's deed, and Cloten. O!

Give colour to my pale cheek with thy blood,

That we the horrider may seem to those

Which chance to find us. O, my lord, my lord!

[Falls fainting on the body.]

Enter Lucius, Captains and a Soothsayer.

CAPTAIN.

To them the legions garrison'd in Gallia,

After your will, have cross'd the sea, attending

You here at Milford Haven; with your ships,

They are in readiness.

LUCIUS.

But what from Rome?

CAPTAIN.

The Senate hath stirr'd up the confiners

And gentlemen of Italy, most willing spirits,

That promise noble service; and they come

Under the conduct of bold Iachimo,

Sienna's brother.

LUCIUS.

When expect you them?

CAPTAIN.

With the next benefit o' th' wind.

LUCIUS.

This forwardness

Makes our hopes fair. Command our present numbers

Be muster'd; bid the captains look to't. Now, sir,

What have you dream'd of late of this war's purpose?

SOOTHSAYER.

Last night the very gods show'd me a vision

(I fast and pray'd for their intelligence) thus:

I saw Jove's bird, the Roman eagle, wing'd

From the spongy south to this part of the west,

There vanish'd in the sunbeams; which portends,

Unless my sins abuse my divination,

Success to th' Roman host.

LUCIUS.

Dream often so,

And never false. Soft, ho! what trunk is here

Without his top? The ruin speaks that sometime

It was a worthy building. How? a page?

Or dead or sleeping on him? But dead, rather;

For nature doth abhor to make his bed

With the defunct, or sleep upon the dead.

Let's see the boy's face.

CAPTAIN.

He's alive, my lord.

LUCIUS.

He'll then instruct us of this body. Young one,

Inform us of thy fortunes; for it seems

They crave to be demanded. Who is this

Thou mak'st thy bloody pillow? Or who was he

That, otherwise than noble nature did,

Hath alter'd that good picture? What's thy interest

In this sad wreck? How came't? Who is't?

What art thou?

IMOGEN.

I am nothing; or if not,

Nothing to be were better. This was my master,

A very valiant Briton and a good,

That here by mountaineers lies slain. Alas!

There is no more such masters. I may wander

From east to occident; cry out for service;

Try many, all good; serve truly; never

Find such another master.

LUCIUS.

'Lack, good youth!

Thou mov'st no less with thy complaining than

Thy master in bleeding. Say his name, good friend.

IMOGEN.

Richard du Champ. [Aside.] If I do lie, and do

No harm by it, though the gods hear, I hope

They'll pardon it.—Say you, sir?

LUCIUS.

Thy name?

IMOGEN.

Fidele, sir.

LUCIUS.

Thou dost approve thyself the very same;

Thy name well fits thy faith, thy faith thy name.

Wilt take thy chance with me? I will not say

Thou shalt be so well master'd; but, be sure,

No less belov'd. The Roman Emperor's letters,

Sent by a consul to me, should not sooner

Than thine own worth prefer thee. Go with me.

IMOGEN.

I'll follow, sir. But first, an't please the gods,

I'll hide my master from the flies, as deep

As these poor pickaxes can dig; and when

With wild wood-leaves and weeds I ha' strew'd his grave,

And on it said a century of prayers,

Such as I can, twice o'er, I'll weep and sigh;

And leaving so his service, follow you,

So please you entertain me.

LUCIUS.

Ay, good youth;

And rather father thee than master thee.

My friends,

The boy hath taught us manly duties; let us

Find out the prettiest daisied plot we can,

And make him with our pikes and partisans

A grave. Come, arm him. Boy, he is preferr'd

By thee to us; and he shall be interr'd

As soldiers can. Be cheerful; wipe thine eyes.

Some falls are means the happier to arise.

[Exeunt.]

SCENE III. Britain. Cymbeline's palace.

Enter Cymbeline, Lords, Pisanio and Attendants.

CYMBELINE.

Again! and bring me word how 'tis with her.

[Exit an Attendant.]

A fever with the absence of her son;

A madness, of which her life's in danger. Heavens,

How deeply you at once do touch me! Imogen,

The great part of my comfort, gone; my queen

Upon a desperate bed, and in a time

When fearful wars point at me; her son gone,

So needful for this present. It strikes me past

The hope of comfort. But for thee, fellow,

Who needs must know of her departure and

Dost seem so ignorant, we'll enforce it from thee

By a sharp torture.

PISANIO.

Sir, my life is yours;

I humbly set it at your will; but for my mistress,

I nothing know where she remains, why gone,

Nor when she purposes return. Beseech your Highness,

Hold me your loyal servant.

LORD.

Good my liege,

The day that she was missing he was here.

I dare be bound he's true and shall perform

All parts of his subjection loyally. For Cloten,

There wants no diligence in seeking him,

And will no doubt be found.

CYMBELINE.

The time is troublesome.

[To Pisanio.] We'll slip you for a season; but our jealousy

Does yet depend.

LORD.

So please your Majesty,

The Roman legions, all from Gallia drawn,

Are landed on your coast, with a supply

Of Roman gentlemen by the Senate sent.

CYMBELINE.

Now for the counsel of my son and queen!

I am amaz'd with matter.

LORD.

Good my liege,

Your preparation can affront no less

Than what you hear of. Come more, for more you're ready.

The want is but to put those pow'rs in motion

That long to move.

CYMBELINE.

I thank you. Let's withdraw,

And meet the time as it seeks us. We fear not

What can from Italy annoy us; but

We grieve at chances here. Away!

[Exeunt all but Pisanio.]

PISANIO.

I heard no letter from my master since

I wrote him Imogen was slain. 'Tis strange.

Nor hear I from my mistress, who did promise

To yield me often tidings. Neither know I

What is betid to Cloten, but remain

Perplex'd in all. The heavens still must work.

Wherein I am false I am honest; not true, to be true.

These present wars shall find I love my country,

Even to the note o' th' King, or I'll fall in them.

All other doubts, by time let them be clear'd:

Fortune brings in some boats that are not steer'd.

[Exit.]

SCENE IV. Wales. Before the cave of Belarius.

Enter Belarius, Guiderius and Arviragus.

GUIDERIUS.

The noise is round about us.

BELARIUS.

Let us from it.

ARVIRAGUS.

What pleasure, sir, find we in life, to lock it

From action and adventure?

GUIDERIUS.

Nay, what hope

Have we in hiding us? This way the Romans

Must or for Britons slay us, or receive us

For barbarous and unnatural revolts

During their use, and slay us after.

BELARIUS.

Sons,

We'll higher to the mountains; there secure us.

To the King's party there's no going. Newness

Of Cloten's death (we being not known, not muster'd

Among the bands) may drive us to a render

Where we have liv'd, and so extort from's that

Which we have done, whose answer would be death,

Drawn on with torture.

GUIDERIUS.

This is, sir, a doubt

In such a time nothing becoming you

Nor satisfying us.

ARVIRAGUS.

It is not likely

That when they hear the Roman horses neigh,

Behold their quarter'd fires, have both their eyes

And ears so cloy'd importantly as now,

That they will waste their time upon our note,

To know from whence we are.

BELARIUS.

O, I am known

Of many in the army. Many years,

Though Cloten then but young, you see, not wore him

From my remembrance. And, besides, the King

Hath not deserv'd my service nor your loves,

Who find in my exile the want of breeding,

The certainty of this hard life; aye hopeless

To have the courtesy your cradle promis'd,

But to be still hot summer's tanlings and

The shrinking slaves of winter.

GUIDERIUS.

Than be so,

Better to cease to be. Pray, sir, to th' army.

I and my brother are not known; yourself

So out of thought, and thereto so o'ergrown,

Cannot be questioned.

ARVIRAGUS.

By this sun that shines,

I'll thither. What thing is't that I never

Did see man die! scarce ever look'd on blood

But that of coward hares, hot goats, and venison!

Never bestrid a horse, save one that had

A rider like myself, who ne'er wore rowel

Nor iron on his heel! I am asham'd

To look upon the holy sun, to have

The benefit of his blest beams, remaining

So long a poor unknown.

GUIDERIUS.

By heavens, I'll go!

If you will bless me, sir, and give me leave,

I'll take the better care; but if you will not,

The hazard therefore due fall on me by

The hands of Romans!

ARVIRAGUS.

So say I. Amen.

BELARIUS.

No reason I, since of your lives you set

So slight a valuation, should reserve

My crack'd one to more care. Have with you, boys!

If in your country wars you chance to die,

That is my bed too, lads, and there I'll lie.

Lead, lead. [Aside.] The time seems long; their blood thinks scorn

Till it fly out and show them princes born.

[Exeunt.]

ACT V

SCENE I. Britain. The Roman camp.

Enter Posthumus alone, with a bloody handkerchief.

POSTHUMUS.

Yea, bloody cloth, I'll keep thee; for I wish'd

Thou shouldst be colour'd thus. You married ones,

If each of you should take this course, how many

Must murder wives much better than themselves

For wrying but a little! O Pisanio!

Every good servant does not all commands;

No bond but to do just ones. Gods! if you

Should have ta'en vengeance on my faults, I never

Had liv'd to put on this; so had you saved

The noble Imogen to repent, and struck

Me, wretch more worth your vengeance. But alack,

You snatch some hence for little faults; that's love,

To have them fall no more. You some permit

To second ills with ills, each elder worse,

And make them dread it, to the doers' thrift.

But Imogen is your own. Do your best wills,

And make me blest to obey. I am brought hither

Among th' Italian gentry, and to fight

Against my lady's kingdom. 'Tis enough

That, Britain, I have kill'd thy mistress; peace!

I'll give no wound to thee. Therefore, good heavens,

Hear patiently my purpose. I'll disrobe me

Of these Italian weeds, and suit myself

As does a Britain peasant. So I'll fight

Against the part I come with; so I'll die

For thee, O Imogen, even for whom my life

Is every breath a death. And thus unknown,

Pitied nor hated, to the face of peril

Myself I'll dedicate. Let me make men know

More valour in me than my habits show.

Gods, put the strength o' th' Leonati in me!

To shame the guise o' th' world, I will begin

The fashion less without and more within.

[Exit.]

SCENE II. Britain. A field of battle between the British and Roman camps.

Enter Lucius, Iachimo and the Roman army at one door, and the British army at another, Leonatus Posthumus following like a poor soldier. They march over and go out. Alarums. Then enter again, in skirmish, Iachimo and Posthumus. He vanquisheth and disarmeth Iachimo and then leaves him.

IACHIMO.

The heaviness and guilt within my bosom

Takes off my manhood. I have belied a lady,

The Princess of this country, and the air on't

Revengingly enfeebles me; or could this carl,

A very drudge of nature's, have subdu'd me

In my profession? Knighthoods and honours borne

As I wear mine are titles but of scorn.

If that thy gentry, Britain, go before

This lout as he exceeds our lords, the odds

Is that we scarce are men, and you are gods.

[Exit.]

The battle continues; the Britons fly; Cymbeline is taken. Then enter to his rescue Belarius, Guiderius and Arviragus.

BELARIUS.

Stand, stand! We have th' advantage of the ground;

The lane is guarded; nothing routs us but

The villainy of our fears.

GUIDERIUS and ARVIRAGUS.

Stand, stand, and fight!

Enter Posthumus and seconds the Britons; they rescue Cymbeline and exeunt. Then re-enter Lucius and Iachimo with Imogen.

LUCIUS.

Away, boy, from the troops, and save thyself;

For friends kill friends, and the disorder's such

As war were hoodwink'd.

IACHIMO.

'Tis their fresh supplies.

LUCIUS.

It is a day turn'd strangely. Or betimes

Let's reinforce or fly.

[Exeunt.]

SCENE III. Another part of the field.

Enter Posthumus and a Briton Lord.

LORD.

Cam'st thou from where they made the stand?

POSTHUMUS.

I did:

Though you, it seems, come from the fliers.

LORD.

I did.

POSTHUMUS.

No blame be to you, sir, for all was lost,

But that the heavens fought. The King himself

Of his wings destitute, the army broken,

And but the backs of Britons seen, all flying,

Through a strait lane; the enemy, full-hearted,

Lolling the tongue with slaught'ring, having work

More plentiful than tools to do't, struck down

Some mortally, some slightly touch'd, some falling

Merely through fear, that the strait pass was damm'd

With dead men hurt behind, and cowards living

To die with length'ned shame.

LORD.

Where was this lane?

POSTHUMUS.

Close by the battle, ditch'd, and wall'd with turf,

Which gave advantage to an ancient soldier,

An honest one, I warrant, who deserv'd

So long a breeding as his white beard came to,

In doing this for's country. Athwart the lane

He, with two striplings (lads more like to run

The country base than to commit such slaughter;

With faces fit for masks, or rather fairer

Than those for preservation cas'd or shame)

Made good the passage, cried to those that fled

'Our Britain's harts die flying, not our men.

To darkness fleet souls that fly backwards! Stand;

Or we are Romans and will give you that,

Like beasts, which you shun beastly, and may save

But to look back in frown. Stand, stand!' These three,

Three thousand confident, in act as many—

For three performers are the file when all

The rest do nothing—with this word 'Stand, stand!'

Accommodated by the place, more charming

With their own nobleness, which could have turn'd

A distaff to a lance, gilded pale looks,

Part shame, part spirit renew'd; that some turn'd coward

But by example (O, a sin in war

Damn'd in the first beginners) 'gan to look

The way that they did and to grin like lions

Upon the pikes o' th' hunters. Then began

A stop i' th' chaser, a retire; anon

A rout, confusion thick. Forthwith they fly,

Chickens, the way which they stoop'd eagles; slaves,

The strides they victors made; and now our cowards,

Like fragments in hard voyages, became

The life o' th' need. Having found the back-door open

Of the unguarded hearts, heavens, how they wound!

Some slain before, some dying, some their friends

O'erborne i' th' former wave. Ten chas'd by one

Are now each one the slaughterman of twenty.

Those that would die or ere resist are grown

The mortal bugs o' th' field.

LORD.

This was strange chance:

A narrow lane, an old man, and two boys.

POSTHUMUS.

Nay, do not wonder at it; you are made

Rather to wonder at the things you hear

Than to work any. Will you rhyme upon't,

And vent it for a mock'ry? Here is one:

> 'Two boys, an old man (twice a boy), a lane,
>
> Preserv'd the Britons, was the Romans' bane.'

LORD.

Nay, be not angry, sir.

POSTHUMUS.

'Lack, to what end?

Who dares not stand his foe I'll be his friend;

For if he'll do as he is made to do,

I know he'll quickly fly my friendship too.

You have put me into rhyme.

LORD.

Farewell; you're angry.

[Exit.]

POSTHUMUS.

Still going? This is a lord! O noble misery,

To be i' th' field and ask 'What news?' of me!

Today how many would have given their honours

To have sav'd their carcasses! took heel to do't,

And yet died too! I, in mine own woe charm'd,

Could not find death where I did hear him groan,

Nor feel him where he struck. Being an ugly monster,

'Tis strange he hides him in fresh cups, soft beds,

Sweet words; or hath moe ministers than we

That draw his knives i' th' war. Well, I will find him;

For being now a favourer to the Briton,

No more a Briton, I have resum'd again

The part I came in. Fight I will no more,

But yield me to the veriest hind that shall

Once touch my shoulder. Great the slaughter is

Here made by th' Roman; great the answer be

Britons must take. For me, my ransom's death;

On either side I come to spend my breath,

Which neither here I'll keep nor bear again,

But end it by some means for Imogen.

Enter two British Captains and soldiers.

FIRST CAPTAIN.

Great Jupiter be prais'd! Lucius is taken.

'Tis thought the old man and his sons were angels.

SECOND CAPTAIN.

There was a fourth man, in a silly habit,

That gave th' affront with them.

FIRST CAPTAIN.

So 'tis reported;

But none of 'em can be found. Stand! who's there?

POSTHUMUS.

A Roman,

Who had not now been drooping here if seconds

Had answer'd him.

SECOND CAPTAIN.

Lay hands on him; a dog!

A leg of Rome shall not return to tell

What crows have peck'd them here. He brags his service,

As if he were of note. Bring him to th' King.

Enter Cymbeline, Belarius, Guiderius, Arviragus, Pisanio and Roman captives. The Captains present Posthumus to Cymbeline, who delivers him over to a gaoler.

[Exeunt omnes.]

SCENE IV. Britain. A prison.

Enter Posthumus and two Gaolers.

FIRST GAOLER. You shall not now be stol'n, you have locks upon you;

So graze as you find pasture.

SECOND GAOLER.

Ay, or a stomach.

[Exeunt Gaolers.]

POSTHUMUS.

Most welcome, bondage! for thou art a way,

I think, to liberty. Yet am I better

Than one that's sick o' th' gout, since he had rather

Groan so in perpetuity than be cur'd

By th' sure physician death, who is the key

T' unbar these locks. My conscience, thou art fetter'd

More than my shanks and wrists; you good gods, give me

The penitent instrument to pick that bolt,

Then, free for ever! Is't enough I am sorry?

So children temporal fathers do appease;

Gods are more full of mercy. Must I repent,

I cannot do it better than in gyves,

Desir'd more than constrain'd. To satisfy,

If of my freedom 'tis the main part, take

No stricter render of me than my all.

I know you are more clement than vile men,

Who of their broken debtors take a third,

A sixth, a tenth, letting them thrive again

On their abatement; that's not my desire.

For Imogen's dear life take mine; and though

'Tis not so dear, yet 'tis a life; you coin'd it.

'Tween man and man they weigh not every stamp;

Though light, take pieces for the figure's sake;

You rather mine, being yours. And so, great pow'rs,

If you will take this audit, take this life,

And cancel these cold bonds. O Imogen!

I'll speak to thee in silence.

[Sleeps.]

Solemn music. Enter, as in an apparition, Sicilius Leonatus, father to Posthumus, an old man attired like a warrior; leading in his hand an ancient matron, his wife and Mother to Posthumus, with music before them. Then, after other music, follows the two young Leonati, brothers to Posthumus, with wounds, as they died in the wars. They circle Posthumus round as he lies sleeping.

SICILIUS.

No more, thou thunder-master, show

Thy spite on mortal flies.

With Mars fall out, with Juno chide,

That thy adulteries

Rates and revenges.

Hath my poor boy done aught but well,

Whose face I never saw?

I died whilst in the womb he stay'd

Attending nature's law;

Whose father then, as men report

Thou orphans' father art,

Thou shouldst have been, and shielded him

From this earth-vexing smart.

MOTHER.

Lucina lent not me her aid,

But took me in my throes,

That from me was Posthumus ripp'd,

Came crying 'mongst his foes,

A thing of pity.

SICILIUS.

Great Nature like his ancestry

Moulded the stuff so fair

That he deserv'd the praise o' th' world

As great Sicilius' heir.

FIRST BROTHER.

When once he was mature for man,

In Britain where was he

That could stand up his parallel,

Or fruitful object be

In eye of Imogen, that best

Could deem his dignity?

MOTHER.

With marriage wherefore was he mock'd,

To be exil'd and thrown

From Leonati seat and cast

From her his dearest one,

Sweet Imogen?

SICILIUS.

Why did you suffer Iachimo,

Slight thing of Italy,

To taint his nobler heart and brain

With needless jealousy,

And to become the geck and scorn

O' th' other's villainy?

SECOND BROTHER.

For this from stiller seats we came,

Our parents and us twain,

That, striking in our country's cause,

Fell bravely and were slain,

Our fealty and Tenantius' right

With honour to maintain.

FIRST BROTHER.

Like hardiment Posthumus hath

To Cymbeline perform'd.

Then, Jupiter, thou king of gods,

Why hast thou thus adjourn'd

The graces for his merits due,

Being all to dolours turn'd?

SICILIUS.

Thy crystal window ope; look out;

No longer exercise

Upon a valiant race thy harsh

And potent injuries.

MOTHER.

Since, Jupiter, our son is good,

Take off his miseries.

SICILIUS.

Peep through thy marble mansion. Help!

Or we poor ghosts will cry

To th' shining synod of the rest

Against thy deity.

BROTHERS.

Help, Jupiter! or we appeal,

And from thy justice fly.

Jupiter descends in thunder and lightning, sitting upon an eagle. He throws a thunderbolt. The Ghosts fall on their knees.

JUPITER.

No more, you petty spirits of region low,

Offend our hearing; hush! How dare you ghosts

Accuse the Thunderer whose bolt, you know,

Sky-planted, batters all rebelling coasts?

Poor shadows of Elysium, hence and rest

Upon your never-withering banks of flow'rs.

Be not with mortal accidents opprest:

No care of yours it is; you know 'tis ours.

Whom best I love I cross; to make my gift,

The more delay'd, delighted. Be content;

Your low-laid son our godhead will uplift;

His comforts thrive, his trials well are spent.

Our Jovial star reign'd at his birth, and in

Our temple was he married. Rise and fade!

He shall be lord of Lady Imogen,

And happier much by his affliction made.

This tablet lay upon his breast, wherein

Our pleasure his full fortune doth confine;

And so, away; no farther with your din

Express impatience, lest you stir up mine.

Mount, eagle, to my palace crystalline.

[Ascends.]

SICILIUS.

He came in thunder; his celestial breath

Was sulphurous to smell; the holy eagle

Stoop'd as to foot us. His ascension is

More sweet than our blest fields. His royal bird

Prunes the immortal wing, and cloys his beak,

As when his god is pleas'd.

ALL.

Thanks, Jupiter!

SICILIUS.

The marble pavement closes, he is enter'd

His radiant roof. Away! and, to be blest,

Let us with care perform his great behest.

[Ghosts vanish.]

POSTHUMUS.

[Waking.] Sleep, thou has been a grandsire and begot

A father to me; and thou hast created

A mother and two brothers. But, O scorn,

Gone! They went hence so soon as they were born.

And so I am awake. Poor wretches, that depend

On greatness' favour, dream as I have done;

Wake and find nothing. But, alas, I swerve;

Many dream not to find, neither deserve,

And yet are steep'd in favours; so am I,

That have this golden chance, and know not why.

What fairies haunt this ground? A book? O rare one!

Be not, as is our fangled world, a garment

Nobler than that it covers. Let thy effects

So follow to be most unlike our courtiers,

As good as promise.

[Reads.] When as a lion's whelp shall, to himself unknown, without seeking find, and be embrac'd by a piece of tender air; and when from a stately cedar shall be lopp'd branches which, being dead many years, shall after revive, be jointed to the old stock, and freshly grow; then shall Posthumus end his miseries, Britain be fortunate and flourish in peace and plenty.

'Tis still a dream, or else such stuff as madmen

Tongue, and brain not; either both or nothing,

Or senseless speaking, or a speaking such

As sense cannot untie. Be what it is,

The action of my life is like it, which

I'll keep, if but for sympathy.

Enter Gaoler.

GAOLER.

Come, sir, are you ready for death?

POSTHUMUS.

Over-roasted rather; ready long ago.

GAOLER.

Hanging is the word, sir; if you be ready for that, you are well cook'd.

POSTHUMUS.

So, if I prove a good repast to the spectators, the dish pays the shot.

GAOLER.

A heavy reckoning for you, sir. But the comfort is, you shall be called to no more payments, fear no more tavern bills, which are often the sadness of parting, as the procuring of mirth. You come in faint for want of meat, depart reeling with too much drink; sorry that you have paid too much, and sorry that you are paid too much; purse and brain both empty; the brain the heavier for being too light, the purse too light, being drawn of heaviness. O, of this contradiction you shall now be quit. O, the charity of a penny cord! It sums up thousands in a trice. You have no true debitor and creditor but it; of what's past, is, and to come, the discharge. Your neck, sir, is pen, book, and counters; so the acquittance follows.

POSTHUMUS.

I am merrier to die than thou art to live.

GAOLER.

Indeed, sir, he that sleeps feels not the toothache. But a man that were to sleep your sleep, and a hangman to help him to bed, I think he would change places with his officer; for look you, sir, you know not which way you shall go.

POSTHUMUS.

Yes indeed do I, fellow.

GAOLER.

Your death has eyes in's head, then; I have not seen him so pictur'd. You must either be directed by some that take upon them to know, or to take upon yourself that which I am sure you do not know, or jump the after-inquiry on your own peril. And how you shall speed in your journey's end, I think you'll never return to tell one.

POSTHUMUS.

I tell thee, fellow, there are none want eyes to direct them the way I am going, but such as wink and will not use them.

GAOLER.

What an infinite mock is this, that a man should have the best use of eyes to see the way of blindness! I am sure hanging's the way of winking.

Enter a Messenger.

MESSENGER.

Knock off his manacles; bring your prisoner to the King.

POSTHUMUS.

Thou bring'st good news: I am call'd to be made free.

GAOLER.

I'll be hang'd then.

POSTHUMUS.

Thou shalt be then freer than a gaoler; no bolts for the dead.

[Exeunt Posthumus and Messenger.]

GAOLER.

Unless a man would marry a gallows and beget young gibbets, I never saw one so prone. Yet, on my conscience, there are verier knaves desire to live, for all he be a Roman; and there be some of them too that die against their wills; so should I, if I were one. I would we were all of one mind, and one mind good. O, there were desolation of gaolers and gallowses! I speak against my present profit, but my wish hath a preferment in't.

[Exit.]

SCENE V. Britain. Cymbeline's tent.

Enter Cymbeline, Belarius, Guiderius, Arviragus, Pisanio, Lords, Officers and Attendants.

CYMBELINE.

Stand by my side, you whom the gods have made

Preservers of my throne. Woe is my heart

That the poor soldier that so richly fought,

Whose rags sham'd gilded arms, whose naked breast

Stepp'd before targes of proof, cannot be found.

He shall be happy that can find him, if

Our grace can make him so.

BELARIUS.

I never saw

Such noble fury in so poor a thing;

Such precious deeds in one that promis'd nought

But beggary and poor looks.

CYMBELINE.

No tidings of him?

PISANIO.

He hath been search'd among the dead and living,

But no trace of him.

CYMBELINE.

To my grief, I am

The heir of his reward, [To Belarius, Guiderius, and Arviragus] which I will add

To you, the liver, heart, and brain of Britain,

By whom I grant she lives. 'Tis now the time

To ask of whence you are. Report it.

BELARIUS.

Sir,

In Cambria are we born, and gentlemen;

Further to boast were neither true nor modest,

Unless I add we are honest.

CYMBELINE.

Bow your knees.

Arise my knights o' th' battle; I create you

Companions to our person, and will fit you

With dignities becoming your estates.

Enter Cornelius and Ladies.

There's business in these faces. Why so sadly

Greet you our victory? You look like Romans,

And not o' th' court of Britain.

CORNELIUS.

Hail, great King!

To sour your happiness I must report

The Queen is dead.

CYMBELINE.

Who worse than a physician

Would this report become? But I consider

By med'cine life may be prolong'd, yet death

Will seize the doctor too. How ended she?

CORNELIUS.

With horror, madly dying, like her life;

Which, being cruel to the world, concluded

Most cruel to herself. What she confess'd

I will report, so please you; these her women

Can trip me if I err, who with wet cheeks

Were present when she finish'd.

CYMBELINE.

Prithee say.

CORNELIUS.

First, she confess'd she never lov'd you; only

Affected greatness got by you, not you;

Married your royalty, was wife to your place;

Abhorr'd your person.

CYMBELINE.

She alone knew this;

And but she spoke it dying, I would not

Believe her lips in opening it. Proceed.

CORNELIUS.

Your daughter, whom she bore in hand to love

With such integrity, she did confess

Was as a scorpion to her sight; whose life,

But that her flight prevented it, she had

Ta'en off by poison.

CYMBELINE.

O most delicate fiend!

Who is't can read a woman? Is there more?

CORNELIUS.

More, sir, and worse. She did confess she had

For you a mortal mineral, which, being took,

Should by the minute feed on life, and ling'ring,

By inches waste you. In which time she purpos'd,

By watching, weeping, tendance, kissing, to

O'ercome you with her show; and in time,

When she had fitted you with her craft, to work

Her son into th' adoption of the crown;

But failing of her end by his strange absence,

Grew shameless-desperate, open'd, in despite

Of heaven and men, her purposes, repented

The evils she hatch'd were not effected; so,

Despairing, died.

CYMBELINE.

Heard you all this, her women?

LADIES.

We did, so please your Highness.

CYMBELINE.

Mine eyes

Were not in fault, for she was beautiful;

Mine ears, that heard her flattery; nor my heart

That thought her like her seeming. It had been vicious

To have mistrusted her; yet, O my daughter!

That it was folly in me thou mayst say,

And prove it in thy feeling. Heaven mend all!

Enter Lucius, Iachimo, the Soothsayer and other Roman prisoners, guarded; Posthumus behind, and Imogen.

Thou com'st not, Caius, now for tribute; that

The Britons have raz'd out, though with the loss

Of many a bold one, whose kinsmen have made suit

That their good souls may be appeas'd with slaughter

Of you their captives, which ourself have granted;

So think of your estate.

LUCIUS.

Consider, sir, the chance of war. The day

Was yours by accident; had it gone with us,

We should not, when the blood was cool, have threaten'd

Our prisoners with the sword. But since the gods

Will have it thus, that nothing but our lives

May be call'd ransom, let it come. Sufficeth

A Roman with a Roman's heart can suffer.

Augustus lives to think on't; and so much

For my peculiar care. This one thing only

I will entreat: my boy, a Briton born,

Let him be ransom'd. Never master had

A page so kind, so duteous, diligent,

So tender over his occasions, true,

So feat, so nurse-like; let his virtue join

With my request, which I'll make bold your Highness

Cannot deny; he hath done no Briton harm

Though he have serv'd a Roman. Save him, sir,

And spare no blood beside.

CYMBELINE.

I have surely seen him;

His favour is familiar to me. Boy,

Thou hast look'd thyself into my grace,

And art mine own. I know not why, wherefore

To say "Live, boy." Ne'er thank thy master. Live;

And ask of Cymbeline what boon thou wilt,

Fitting my bounty and thy state, I'll give it;

Yea, though thou do demand a prisoner,

The noblest ta'en.

IMOGEN.

I humbly thank your Highness.

LUCIUS.

I do not bid thee beg my life, good lad,

And yet I know thou wilt.

IMOGEN.

No, no! Alack,

There's other work in hand. I see a thing

Bitter to me as death; your life, good master,

Must shuffle for itself.

LUCIUS.

The boy disdains me,

He leaves me, scorns me. Briefly die their joys

That place them on the truth of girls and boys.

Why stands he so perplex'd?

CYMBELINE.

What wouldst thou, boy?

I love thee more and more; think more and more

What's best to ask. Know'st him thou look'st on? Speak,

Wilt have him live? Is he thy kin? thy friend?

IMOGEN.

He is a Roman, no more kin to me

Than I to your Highness; who, being born your vassal,

Am something nearer.

CYMBELINE.

Wherefore ey'st him so?

IMOGEN.

I'll tell you, sir, in private, if you please

To give me hearing.

CYMBELINE.

Ay, with all my heart,

And lend my best attention. What's thy name?

IMOGEN.

Fidele, sir.

CYMBELINE.

Thou'rt my good youth, my page;

I'll be thy master. Walk with me; speak freely.

[Cymbeline and Imogen converse apart.]

BELARIUS.

Is not this boy reviv'd from death?

ARVIRAGUS.

One sand another

Not more resembles that sweet rosy lad

Who died and was Fidele. What think you?

GUIDERIUS.

The same dead thing alive.

BELARIUS.

Peace, peace! see further. He eyes us not; forbear.

Creatures may be alike; were't he, I am sure

He would have spoke to us.

GUIDERIUS.

But we see him dead.

BELARIUS.

Be silent; let's see further.

PISANIO.

[Aside.] It is my mistress.

Since she is living, let the time run on

To good or bad.

                                   [Cymbeline and Imogen advance.]

CYMBELINE.

Come, stand thou by our side;

Make thy demand aloud. [To Iachimo.] Sir, step you forth;

Give answer to this boy, and do it freely,

Or, by our greatness and the grace of it,

Which is our honour, bitter torture shall

Winnow the truth from falsehood. On, speak to him.

IMOGEN.

My boon is that this gentleman may render

Of whom he had this ring.

POSTHUMUS.

[Aside.] What's that to him?

CYMBELINE.

That diamond upon your finger, say

How came it yours?

IACHIMO.

Thou'lt torture me to leave unspoken that

Which to be spoke would torture thee.

CYMBELINE.

How? me?

IACHIMO.

I am glad to be constrain'd to utter that

Which torments me to conceal. By villainy

I got this ring; 'twas Leonatus' jewel,

Whom thou didst banish; and—which more may grieve thee,

As it doth me—a nobler sir ne'er liv'd

'Twixt sky and ground. Wilt thou hear more, my lord?

CYMBELINE.

All that belongs to this.

IACHIMO.

That paragon, thy daughter,

For whom my heart drops blood and my false spirits

Quail to remember—Give me leave, I faint.

CYMBELINE.

My daughter? What of her? Renew thy strength;

I had rather thou shouldst live while nature will

Than die ere I hear more. Strive, man, and speak.

IACHIMO.

Upon a time, unhappy was the clock

That struck the hour: was in Rome, accurs'd

The mansion where: 'twas at a feast, O, would

Our viands had been poison'd (or at least

Those which I heav'd to head) the good Posthumus

(What should I say? he was too good to be

Where ill men were, and was the best of all

Amongst the rar'st of good ones) sitting sadly

Hearing us praise our loves of Italy

For beauty that made barren the swell'd boast

Of him that best could speak; for feature, laming

The shrine of Venus or straight-pight Minerva,

Postures beyond brief nature; for condition,

A shop of all the qualities that man

Loves woman for; besides that hook of wiving,

Fairness which strikes the eye.

CYMBELINE.

I stand on fire.

Come to the matter.

IACHIMO.

All too soon I shall,

Unless thou wouldst grieve quickly. This Posthumus,

Most like a noble lord in love and one

That had a royal lover, took his hint;

And (not dispraising whom we prais'd, therein

He was as calm as virtue) he began

His mistress' picture; which by his tongue being made,

And then a mind put in't, either our brags

Were crack'd of kitchen trulls, or his description

Prov'd us unspeaking sots.

CYMBELINE.

Nay, nay, to th' purpose.

IACHIMO.

Your daughter's chastity (there it begins)

He spake of her as Dian had hot dreams

And she alone were cold; whereat I, wretch,

Made scruple of his praise, and wager'd with him

Pieces of gold 'gainst this which then he wore

Upon his honour'd finger, to attain

In suit the place of's bed, and win this ring

By hers and mine adultery. He, true knight,

No lesser of her honour confident

Than I did truly find her, stakes this ring;

And would so, had it been a carbuncle

Of Phoebus' wheel; and might so safely, had it

Been all the worth of's car. Away to Britain

Post I in this design. Well may you, sir,

Remember me at court, where I was taught

Of your chaste daughter the wide difference

'Twixt amorous and villainous. Being thus quench'd

Of hope, not longing, mine Italian brain

Gan in your duller Britain operate

Most vilely; for my vantage, excellent;

And, to be brief, my practice so prevail'd

That I return'd with simular proof enough

To make the noble Leonatus mad,

By wounding his belief in her renown

With tokens thus and thus; averring notes

Of chamber-hanging, pictures, this her bracelet

(O cunning, how I got it!) nay, some marks

Of secret on her person, that he could not

But think her bond of chastity quite crack'd,

I having ta'en the forfeit. Whereupon

Methinks I see him now—

POSTHUMUS.

[Coming forward.] Ay, so thou dost,

Italian fiend! Ay me, most credulous fool,

Egregious murderer, thief, anything

That's due to all the villains past, in being,

To come! O, give me cord, or knife, or poison,

Some upright justicer! Thou, King, send out

For torturers ingenious. It is I

That all th' abhorred things o' th' earth amend

By being worse than they. I am Posthumus,

That kill'd thy daughter; villain-like, I lie;

That caus'd a lesser villain than myself,

A sacrilegious thief, to do't. The temple

Of virtue was she; yea, and she herself.

Spit, and throw stones, cast mire upon me, set

The dogs o' th' street to bay me. Every villain

Be call'd Posthumus Leonatus, and

Be villainy less than 'twas! O Imogen!

My queen, my life, my wife! O Imogen,

Imogen, Imogen!

IMOGEN.

Peace, my lord. Hear, hear!

POSTHUMUS.

Shall's have a play of this? Thou scornful page,

There lies thy part.

[Strikes her. She falls.]

PISANIO.

O gentlemen, help!

Mine and your mistress! O, my lord Posthumus!

You ne'er kill'd Imogen till now. Help, help!

Mine honour'd lady!

CYMBELINE.

Does the world go round?

POSTHUMUS.

How comes these staggers on me?

PISANIO.

Wake, my mistress!

CYMBELINE.

If this be so, the gods do mean to strike me

To death with mortal joy.

PISANIO.

How fares my mistress?

IMOGEN.

O, get thee from my sight;

Thou gav'st me poison. Dangerous fellow, hence!

Breathe not where princes are.

CYMBELINE.

The tune of Imogen!

PISANIO.

Lady,

The gods throw stones of sulphur on me, if

That box I gave you was not thought by me

A precious thing! I had it from the Queen.

CYMBELINE.

New matter still?

IMOGEN.

It poison'd me.

CORNELIUS.

O gods!

I left out one thing which the Queen confess'd,

Which must approve thee honest. 'If Pisanio

Have' said she 'given his mistress that confection

Which I gave him for cordial, she is serv'd

As I would serve a rat.'

CYMBELINE.

What's this, Cornelius?

CORNELIUS.

The Queen, sir, very oft importun'd me

To temper poisons for her; still pretending

The satisfaction of her knowledge only

In killing creatures vile, as cats and dogs,

Of no esteem. I, dreading that her purpose

Was of more danger, did compound for her

A certain stuff, which, being ta'en would cease

The present pow'r of life, but in short time

All offices of nature should again

Do their due functions. Have you ta'en of it?

IMOGEN.

Most like I did, for I was dead.

BELARIUS.

My boys,

There was our error.

GUIDERIUS.

This is sure Fidele.

IMOGEN.

Why did you throw your wedded lady from you?

Think that you are upon a rock, and now

Throw me again.

> [Embracing him.]

POSTHUMUS.

Hang there like fruit, my soul,

Till the tree die!

CYMBELINE.

How now, my flesh? my child?

What, mak'st thou me a dullard in this act?

Wilt thou not speak to me?

IMOGEN.

[Kneeling.] Your blessing, sir.

BELARIUS.

[To Guiderius and Arviragus.] Though you did love this youth, I blame ye not;

You had a motive for't.

CYMBELINE.

My tears that fall

Prove holy water on thee! Imogen,

Thy mother's dead.

IMOGEN.

I am sorry for't, my lord.

CYMBELINE.

O, she was naught, and long of her it was

That we meet here so strangely; but her son

Is gone, we know not how nor where.

PISANIO.

My lord,

Now fear is from me, I'll speak troth. Lord Cloten,

Upon my lady's missing, came to me

With his sword drawn, foam'd at the mouth, and swore,

If I discover'd not which way she was gone,

It was my instant death. By accident

I had a feigned letter of my master's

Then in my pocket, which directed him

To seek her on the mountains near to Milford;

Where, in a frenzy, in my master's garments,

Which he enforc'd from me, away he posts

With unchaste purpose, and with oath to violate

My lady's honour. What became of him

I further know not.

GUIDERIUS.

Let me end the story:

I slew him there.

CYMBELINE.

Marry, the gods forfend!

I would not thy good deeds should from my lips

Pluck a hard sentence. Prithee, valiant youth,

Deny't again.

GUIDERIUS.

I have spoke it, and I did it.

CYMBELINE.

He was a prince.

GUIDERIUS.

A most incivil one. The wrongs he did me

Were nothing prince-like; for he did provoke me

With language that would make me spurn the sea,

If it could so roar to me. I cut off's head,

And am right glad he is not standing here

To tell this tale of mine.

CYMBELINE.

I am sorry for thee.

By thine own tongue thou art condemn'd, and must

Endure our law. Thou'rt dead.

IMOGEN.

That headless man

I thought had been my lord.

CYMBELINE.

Bind the offender,

And take him from our presence.

BELARIUS.

Stay, sir King.

This man is better than the man he slew,

As well descended as thyself, and hath

More of thee merited than a band of Clotens

Had ever scar for. [To the guard.] Let his arms alone;

They were not born for bondage.

CYMBELINE.

Why, old soldier,

Wilt thou undo the worth thou art unpaid for

By tasting of our wrath? How of descent

As good as we?

ARVIRAGUS.

In that he spake too far.

CYMBELINE.

And thou shalt die for't.

BELARIUS.

We will die all three;

But I will prove that two on's are as good

As I have given out him. My sons, I must

For mine own part unfold a dangerous speech,

Though haply well for you.

ARVIRAGUS.

Your danger's ours.

GUIDERIUS.

And our good his.

BELARIUS.

Have at it then by leave!

Thou hadst, great King, a subject who

Was call'd Belarius.

CYMBELINE.

What of him? He is

A banish'd traitor.

BELARIUS.

He it is that hath

Assum'd this age; indeed a banish'd man;

I know not how a traitor.

CYMBELINE.

Take him hence,

The whole world shall not save him.

BELARIUS.

Not too hot.

First pay me for the nursing of thy sons,

And let it be confiscate all, so soon

As I have receiv'd it.

CYMBELINE.

Nursing of my sons?

BELARIUS.

I am too blunt and saucy: here's my knee.

Ere I arise I will prefer my sons;

Then spare not the old father. Mighty sir,

These two young gentlemen that call me father,

And think they are my sons, are none of mine;

They are the issue of your loins, my liege,

And blood of your begetting.

CYMBELINE.

How? my issue?

BELARIUS.

So sure as you your father's. I, old Morgan,

Am that Belarius whom you sometime banish'd.

Your pleasure was my mere offence, my punishment

Itself, and all my treason; that I suffer'd

Was all the harm I did. These gentle princes

(For such and so they are) these twenty years

Have I train'd up; those arts they have as I

Could put into them. My breeding was, sir, as

Your Highness knows. Their nurse, Euriphile,

Whom for the theft I wedded, stole these children

Upon my banishment; I mov'd her to't,

Having receiv'd the punishment before

For that which I did then. Beaten for loyalty

Excited me to treason. Their dear loss,

The more of you 'twas felt, the more it shap'd

Unto my end of stealing them. But, gracious sir,

Here are your sons again, and I must lose

Two of the sweet'st companions in the world.

The benediction of these covering heavens

Fall on their heads like dew! for they are worthy

To inlay heaven with stars.

CYMBELINE.

Thou weep'st and speak'st.

The service that you three have done is more

Unlike than this thou tell'st. I lost my children.

If these be they, I know not how to wish

A pair of worthier sons.

BELARIUS.

Be pleas'd awhile.

This gentleman, whom I call Polydore,

Most worthy prince, as yours, is true Guiderius;

This gentleman, my Cadwal, Arviragus,

Your younger princely son; he, sir, was lapp'd

In a most curious mantle, wrought by th' hand

Of his queen mother, which for more probation

I can with ease produce.

CYMBELINE.

Guiderius had

Upon his neck a mole, a sanguine star;

It was a mark of wonder.

BELARIUS.

This is he,

446

Who hath upon him still that natural stamp.

It was wise nature's end in the donation,

To be his evidence now.

CYMBELINE.

O, what am I?

A mother to the birth of three? Ne'er mother

Rejoic'd deliverance more. Blest pray you be,

That, after this strange starting from your orbs,

You may reign in them now! O Imogen,

Thou hast lost by this a kingdom.

IMOGEN.

No, my lord;

I have got two worlds by't. O my gentle brothers,

Have we thus met? O, never say hereafter

But I am truest speaker! You call'd me brother,

When I was but your sister: I you brothers,

When we were so indeed.

CYMBELINE.

Did you e'er meet?

ARVIRAGUS.

Ay, my good lord.

GUIDERIUS.

And at first meeting lov'd,

Continu'd so until we thought he died.

CORNELIUS.

By the Queen's dram she swallow'd.

CYMBELINE.

O rare instinct!

When shall I hear all through? This fierce abridgement

Hath to it circumstantial branches, which

Distinction should be rich in. Where? how liv'd you?

And when came you to serve our Roman captive?

How parted with your brothers? how first met them?

Why fled you from the court? and whither? These,

And your three motives to the battle, with

I know not how much more, should be demanded,

And all the other by-dependances,

From chance to chance; but nor the time nor place

Will serve our long interrogatories. See,

Posthumus anchors upon Imogen;

And she, like harmless lightning, throws her eye

On him, her brothers, me, her master, hitting

Each object with a joy; the counterchange

Is severally in all. Let's quit this ground,

And smoke the temple with our sacrifices.

[To Belarius.] Thou art my brother; so we'll hold thee ever.

IMOGEN.

You are my father too, and did relieve me

To see this gracious season.

CYMBELINE.

All o'erjoy'd

Save these in bonds. Let them be joyful too,

For they shall taste our comfort.

IMOGEN.

My good master,

I will yet do you service.

LUCIUS.

Happy be you!

CYMBELINE.

The forlorn soldier, that so nobly fought,

He would have well becom'd this place and grac'd

The thankings of a king.

POSTHUMUS.

I am, sir,

The soldier that did company these three

In poor beseeming; 'twas a fitment for

The purpose I then follow'd. That I was he,

Speak, Iachimo. I had you down, and might

Have made you finish.

IACHIMO.

[Kneeling.] I am down again;

But now my heavy conscience sinks my knee,

As then your force did. Take that life, beseech you,

Which I so often owe; but your ring first,

And here the bracelet of the truest princess

That ever swore her faith.

POSTHUMUS.

Kneel not to me.

The pow'r that I have on you is to spare you;

The malice towards you to forgive you. Live,

And deal with others better.

CYMBELINE.

Nobly doom'd!

We'll learn our freeness of a son-in-law;

Pardon's the word to all.

ARVIRAGUS.

You holp us, sir,

As you did mean indeed to be our brother;

Joy'd are we that you are.

POSTHUMUS.

Your servant, Princes. Good my lord of Rome,

Call forth your soothsayer. As I slept, methought

Great Jupiter, upon his eagle back'd,

Appear'd to me, with other spritely shows

Of mine own kindred. When I wak'd, I found

This label on my bosom; whose containing

Is so from sense in hardness that I can

Make no collection of it. Let him show

His skill in the construction.

LUCIUS.

Philarmonus!

SOOTHSAYER.

Here, my good lord.

LUCIUS.

Read, and declare the meaning.

SOOTHSAYER.

[Reads.] When as a lion's whelp shall, to himself unknown, without seeking find, and be embrac'd by a piece of tender air; and when from a stately cedar shall be lopp'd branches which, being dead many years, shall after revive, be jointed to the old stock, and freshly grow; then shall Posthumus end his miseries, Britain be fortunate and flourish in peace and plenty.

Thou, Leonatus, art the lion's whelp;

The fit and apt construction of thy name,

Being Leo-natus, doth import so much.

[To Cymbeline] The piece of tender air, thy virtuous daughter,

Which we call mollis aer, and mollis aer

We term it mulier; which mulier I divine

Is this most constant wife, who even now

Answering the letter of the oracle,

Unknown to you, unsought, were clipp'd about

With this most tender air.

CYMBELINE.

This hath some seeming.

SOOTHSAYER.

The lofty cedar, royal Cymbeline,

Personates thee; and thy lopp'd branches point

Thy two sons forth, who, by Belarius stol'n,

For many years thought dead, are now reviv'd,

To the majestic cedar join'd, whose issue

Promises Britain peace and plenty.

CYMBELINE.

Well,

My peace we will begin. And, Caius Lucius,

Although the victor, we submit to Cæsar

And to the Roman empire, promising

To pay our wonted tribute, from the which

We were dissuaded by our wicked queen,

Whom heavens in justice, both on her and hers,

Have laid most heavy hand.

SOOTHSAYER.

The fingers of the pow'rs above do tune

The harmony of this peace. The vision

Which I made known to Lucius ere the stroke

Of yet this scarce-cold battle, at this instant

Is full accomplish'd; for the Roman eagle,

From south to west on wing soaring aloft,

Lessen'd herself and in the beams o' th' sun

So vanish'd; which foreshow'd our princely eagle,

Th' imperial Cæsar, Cæsar, should again unite

His favour with the radiant Cymbeline,

Which shines here in the west.

CYMBELINE.

Laud we the gods;

And let our crooked smokes climb to their nostrils

From our bless'd altars. Publish we this peace

To all our subjects. Set we forward; let

A Roman and a British ensign wave

Friendly together. So through Lud's Town march;

And in the temple of great Jupiter

Our peace we'll ratify; seal it with feasts.

Set on there! Never was a war did cease,

Ere bloody hands were wash'd, with such a peace.

[Exeunt.]

453

About Author

Shakespeare produced most of his known works between 1589 and 1613. His early plays were primarily comedies and histories and are regarded as some of the best work produced in these genres. Until about 1608, he wrote mainly tragedies, among them Hamlet, Othello, King Lear, and Macbeth, all considered to be among the finest works in the English language. In the last phase of his life, he wrote tragicomedies (also known as romances) and collaborated with other playwrights.

Many of Shakespeare's plays were published in editions of varying quality and accuracy in his lifetime. However, in 1623, two fellow actors and friends of Shakespeare's, John Heminges and Henry Condell, published a more definitive text known as the First Folio, a posthumous collected edition of Shakespeare's dramatic works that included all but two of his plays. The volume was prefaced with a poem by Ben Jonson, in which Jonson presciently hails Shakespeare in a now-famous quote as "not of an age, but for all time".

Throughout the 20th and 21st centuries, Shakespeare's works have been continually adapted and rediscovered by new movements in scholarship and performance. His plays remain popular and are studied, performed, and reinterpreted through various cultural and political contexts around the world.

Early life

William Shakespeare was the son of John Shakespeare, an alderman and a successful glover (glove-maker) originally from Snitterfield, and Mary Arden, the daughter of an affluent landowning farmer. He was born in Stratford-upon-Avon and baptised there on 26 April 1564. His actual date of birth remains unknown, but is traditionally observed on 23 April, Saint George's Day. This date, which can be traced to a mistake made by an 18th-century scholar, has proved appealing to biographers because Shakespeare died on the same date in 1616. He was the third of eight children, and the eldest surviving son.

Although no attendance records for the period survive, most biographers agree that Shakespeare was probably educated at the King's New School in Stratford, a free school chartered in 1553, about a quarter-mile (400 m) from his home. Grammar schools varied in quality during the Elizabethan era, but grammar school curricula were largely similar: the basic Latin text was standardised by royal decree, and the school would have provided an intensive education in grammar based upon Latin classical authors.

At the age of 18, Shakespeare married 26-year-old Anne Hathaway. The consistory court of the Diocese of Worcester issued a marriage licence on 27 November 1582. The next day, two of Hathaway's neighbours posted bonds guaranteeing that no lawful claims impeded the marriage. The ceremony may have been arranged in some haste since the Worcester chancellor allowed the marriage banns to be read once instead of the usual three times, and six months after the marriage Anne gave birth to a daughter, Susanna, baptised 26 May 1583. Twins, son Hamnet and daughter Judith, followed almost two years later and were baptised 2 February 1585. Hamnet died of unknown causes at the age of 11 and was buried 11 August 1596.

After the birth of the twins, Shakespeare left few historical traces until he is mentioned as part of the London theatre scene in 1592. The exception is the appearance of his name in the "complaints bill" of a law case before the Queen's Bench court at Westminster dated Michaelmas Term 1588 and 9 October 1589. Scholars refer to the years between 1585 and 1592 as Shakespeare's "lost years". Biographers attempting to account for this period have reported many apocryphal stories. Nicholas Rowe, Shakespeare's first biographer, recounted a Stratford legend that Shakespeare fled the town for London to escape prosecution for deer poaching in the estate of local squire Thomas Lucy. Shakespeare is also supposed to have taken his revenge on Lucy by writing a scurrilous ballad about him. Another 18th-century story has Shakespeare starting his theatrical career minding the horses of theatre patrons in London. John Aubrey reported that Shakespeare had been a country schoolmaster. Some 20th-century scholars have suggested that Shakespeare may have been employed as a schoolmaster by Alexander

Hoghton of Lancashire, a Catholic landowner who named a certain "William Shakeshafte" in his will. Little evidence substantiates such stories other than hearsay collected after his death, and Shakeshafte was a common name in the Lancashire area.

London and theatrical career

It is not known definitively when Shakespeare began writing, but contemporary allusions and records of performances show that several of his plays were on the London stage by 1592. By then, he was sufficiently known in London to be attacked in print by the playwright Robert Greene in his Groats-Worth of Wit:

... there is an upstart Crow, beautified with our feathers, that with his Tiger's heart wrapped in a Player's hide, supposes he is as well able to bombast out a blank verse as the best of you: and being an absolute Johannes factotum, is in his own conceit the only Shake-scene in a country.

Scholars differ on the exact meaning of Greene's words, but most agree that Greene was accusing Shakespeare of reaching above his rank in trying to match such university-educated writers as Christopher Marlowe, Thomas Nashe, and Greene himself (the so-called "University Wits"). The italicised phrase parodying the line "Oh, tiger's heart wrapped in a woman's hide" from Shakespeare's Henry VI, Part 3, along with the pun "Shake-scene", clearly identify Shakespeare as Greene's target. As used here, Johannes Factotum ("Jack of all trades") refers to a second-rate tinkerer with the work of others, rather than the more common "universal genius".

Greene's attack is the earliest surviving mention of Shakespeare's work in the theatre. Biographers suggest that his career may have begun any time from the mid-1580s to just before Greene's remarks. After 1594, Shakespeare's plays were performed only by the Lord Chamberlain's Men, a company owned by a group of players, including Shakespeare, that soon became the leading playing company in London. After the death of Queen Elizabeth in 1603, the company was awarded a royal patent by the new King James I, and changed its name to the King's Men.

"All the world's a stage,

and all the men and women merely players:

they have their exits and their entrances;

and one man in his time plays many parts ..."

—As You Like It, Act II, Scene 7, 139–142

In 1599, a partnership of members of the company built their own theatre on the south bank of the River Thames, which they named the Globe. In 1608, the partnership also took over the Blackfriars indoor theatre. Extant records of Shakespeare's property purchases and investments indicate that his association with the company made him a wealthy man, and in 1597, he bought the second-largest house in Stratford, New Place, and in 1605, invested in a share of the parish tithes in Stratford.

Some of Shakespeare's plays were published in quarto editions, beginning in 1594, and by 1598, his name had become a selling point and began to appear on the title pages. Shakespeare continued to act in his own and other plays after his success as a playwright. The 1616 edition of Ben Jonson's Works names him on the cast lists for Every Man in His Humour (1598) and Sejanus His Fall (1603). The absence of his name from the 1605 cast list for Jonson's Volpone is taken by some scholars as a sign that his acting career was nearing its end. The First Folio of 1623, however, lists Shakespeare as one of "the Principal Actors in all these Plays", some of which were first staged after Volpone, although we cannot know for certain which roles he played. In 1610, John Davies of Hereford wrote that "good Will" played "kingly" roles. In 1709, Rowe passed down a tradition that Shakespeare played the ghost of Hamlet's father. Later traditions maintain that he also played Adam in As You Like It, and the Chorus in Henry V, though scholars doubt the sources of that information.

Throughout his career, Shakespeare divided his time between London and Stratford. In 1596, the year before he bought New Place as his family home in Stratford, Shakespeare was living in the parish of St. Helen's, Bishopsgate, north of the River Thames. He moved across the river to Southwark by 1599, the same year his company constructed the Globe Theatre there. By 1604, he had moved north of the river again, to an area north of St Paul's Cathedral with many fine houses. There, he rented rooms from a French Huguenot named Christopher Mountjoy, a maker of ladies' wigs and other headgear.

Later years and death

Rowe was the first biographer to record the tradition, repeated by Johnson, that Shakespeare retired to Stratford "some years before his death". He was still working as an actor in London in 1608; in an answer to the sharers' petition in 1635, Cuthbert Burbage stated that after purchasing the lease of the Blackfriars Theatre in 1608 from Henry Evans, the King's Men "placed men players" there, "which were Heminges, Condell, Shakespeare, etc.". However, it is perhaps relevant that the bubonic plague raged in London throughout 1609. The London public playhouses were repeatedly closed during extended outbreaks of the plague (a total of over 60 months closure between May 1603 and February 1610), which meant there was often no acting work. Retirement from all work was uncommon at that time. Shakespeare continued to visit London during the years 1611–1614. In 1612, he was called as a witness in Bellott v. Mountjoy, a court case concerning the marriage settlement of Mountjoy's daughter, Mary. In March 1613, he bought a gatehouse in the former Blackfriars priory; and from November 1614, he was in London for several weeks with his son-in-law, John Hall. After 1610, Shakespeare wrote fewer plays, and none are attributed to him after 1613. His last three plays were collaborations, probably with John Fletcher, who succeeded him as the house playwright of the King's Men.

Shakespeare died on 23 April 1616, at the age of 52. He died within a month of signing his will, a document which he begins by describing himself as being in "perfect health". No extant contemporary source explains how or why he died. Half a century later, John Ward, the vicar of Stratford, wrote in his notebook: "Shakespeare, Drayton, and Ben Jonson had a merry meeting and, it seems, drank too hard, for Shakespeare died of a fever there contracted", not an impossible scenario since Shakespeare knew Jonson and Drayton. Of the tributes from fellow authors, one refers to his relatively sudden death: "We wondered, Shakespeare, that thou went'st so soon / From the world's stage to the grave's tiring room."

He was survived by his wife and two daughters. Susanna had married a physician, John Hall, in 1607, and Judith had married Thomas Quiney, a vintner, two months before Shakespeare's death. Shakespeare signed his last will and testament on 25 March 1616; the following day, his new son-in-law, Thomas Quiney was found guilty of fathering an illegitimate son by Margaret Wheeler, who had died during childbirth. Thomas was ordered by the church court to do public penance, which would have caused much shame and embarrassment for the Shakespeare family.

Shakespeare bequeathed the bulk of his large estate to his elder daughter Susanna under stipulations that she pass it down intact to "the first son of her body". The Quineys had three children, all of whom died without marrying. The Halls had one child, Elizabeth, who married twice but died without children in 1670, ending Shakespeare's direct line. Shakespeare's will scarcely mentions his wife, Anne, who was probably entitled to one-third of his estate automatically. He did make a point, however, of leaving her "my second best bed", a bequest that has led to much speculation. Some scholars see the bequest as an insult to Anne, whereas others believe that the second-best bed would have been the matrimonial bed and therefore rich in significance.

Shakespeare was buried in the chancel of the Holy Trinity Church two days after his death. The epitaph carved into the stone slab covering his grave includes a curse against moving his bones, which was carefully avoided during restoration of the church in 2008:

Good frend for Iesvs sake forbeare,

To digg the dvst encloased heare.

Bleste be Middle English the.svg man Middle English that.svg spares thes stones,

And cvrst be he Middle English that.svg moves my bones.

(Modern spelling: Good friend, for Jesus' sake forbear, / To dig the dust enclosed here. / Blessed be the man that spares these stones, / And cursed be he that moves my bones.)

Some time before 1623, a funerary monument was erected in his memory on the north wall, with a half-effigy of him in the act of writing. Its plaque compares him to Nestor, Socrates, and Virgil. In 1623, in conjunction with the publication of the First Folio, the Droeshout engraving was published.

Shakespeare has been commemorated in many statues and memorials around the world, including funeral monuments in Southwark Cathedral and Poets' Corner in Westminster Abbey.

Plays

Most playwrights of the period typically collaborated with others at some point, and critics agree that Shakespeare did the same, mostly early and late in his career. Some attributions, such as Titus Andronicus and the early history plays, remain controversial while The Two Noble Kinsmen and the lost Cardenio have well-attested contemporary documentation. Textual evidence also supports the view that several of the plays were revised by other writers after their original composition.

The first recorded works of Shakespeare are Richard III and the three parts of Henry VI, written in the early 1590s during a vogue for historical drama. Shakespeare's plays are difficult to date precisely, however, and studies of the texts suggest that Titus Andronicus, The Comedy of Errors, The Taming of the Shrew, and The Two Gentlemen of Verona may also belong to Shakespeare's earliest period. His first histories, which draw heavily on the 1587 edition of Raphael Holinshed's Chronicles of England, Scotland, and Ireland, dramatise the destructive results of weak or corrupt rule and have been interpreted as a justification for the origins of the Tudor dynasty. The early plays were influenced by the works of other Elizabethan dramatists, especially Thomas Kyd and Christopher Marlowe, by the traditions of medieval drama, and by the plays of Seneca. The Comedy of Errors was also based on classical models, but no source for The Taming of the Shrew has been found, though it is related to a separate play of the same name and may have derived from a folk story. Like The Two Gentlemen of Verona, in which two friends appear to approve of rape, the Shrew's story of the taming of a woman's independent spirit by a man sometimes troubles modern critics, directors, and audiences.

Shakespeare's early classical and Italianate comedies, containing tight double plots and precise comic sequences, give way in the mid-1590s to the romantic atmosphere of his most acclaimed comedies. A Midsummer Night's Dream is a witty mixture of romance, fairy magic, and comic lowlife scenes. Shakespeare's next comedy, the equally romantic Merchant of Venice, contains a portrayal of the vengeful Jewish moneylender Shylock, which reflects Elizabethan views but may appear derogatory to modern audiences. The wit and wordplay of Much Ado About Nothing, the charming rural setting of As You Like It, and the lively merrymaking of Twelfth Night complete Shakespeare's sequence of great comedies. After the lyrical Richard II, written almost entirely in verse, Shakespeare introduced prose comedy into the histories of the late 1590s, Henry IV, parts 1 and 2, and Henry V. His characters become more complex and tender as he switches deftly between comic and serious scenes, prose and poetry, and achieves the narrative variety of his mature work. This period begins and ends with two tragedies: Romeo and Juliet, the famous romantic tragedy of sexually charged adolescence, love, and death; and Julius Caesar—based on Sir Thomas North's 1579 translation of Plutarch's Parallel Lives—which introduced a new kind of drama. According to Shakespearean scholar James Shapiro, in Julius Caesar, "the various strands of politics, character, inwardness, contemporary events, even Shakespeare's own reflections on the act of writing, began to infuse each other".

In the early 17th century, Shakespeare wrote the so-called "problem plays" Measure for Measure, Troilus and Cressida, and All's Well That Ends Well and a number of his best known tragedies. Many critics believe that Shakespeare's greatest tragedies represent the peak of his art. The titular hero of one of Shakespeare's greatest tragedies, Hamlet, has probably been discussed more than any other Shakespearean character, especially for his famous soliloquy which begins "To be or not to be; that is the question". Unlike the introverted Hamlet, whose fatal flaw is hesitation, the heroes of the tragedies that followed, Othello and King Lear, are undone by hasty errors of judgement. The plots of Shakespeare's tragedies often hinge on such fatal errors or flaws, which overturn order and destroy the hero and those he loves. In Othello, the villain Iago stokes Othello's sexual jealousy to the point where he murders the innocent wife who loves him. In King Lear, the old king commits the tragic error of giving up his powers, initiating the events which lead to the torture and blinding of the Earl of Gloucester and the murder of Lear's youngest daughter Cordelia. According to the critic Frank Kermode, "the play-offers neither its good characters nor its audience any relief from its cruelty". In Macbeth, the shortest and most compressed of Shakespeare's tragedies, uncontrollable ambition incites Macbeth and his wife, Lady Macbeth, to murder the rightful king and usurp the throne until their own guilt destroys them in turn. In this play, Shakespeare adds a supernatural element to the tragic structure. His last major tragedies, Antony and Cleopatra and Coriolanus, contain some of Shakespeare's finest poetry and were considered his most successful tragedies by the poet and critic T.S. Eliot.

In his final period, Shakespeare turned to romance or tragicomedy and completed three more major plays: Cymbeline, The Winter's Tale, and The Tempest, as well as the collaboration, Pericles, Prince of Tyre. Less bleak than the tragedies, these four plays are graver in tone than the comedies of the 1590s, but they end with reconciliation and the forgiveness of potentially tragic errors. Some commentators have seen this change in mood as evidence of a more serene view of life on Shakespeare's part, but it may merely reflect the theatrical fashion of the day. Shakespeare collaborated on two further surviving plays, Henry VIII and The Two Noble Kinsmen, probably with John Fletcher.

Performances

It is not clear for which companies Shakespeare wrote his early plays. The title page of the 1594 edition of Titus Andronicus reveals that the play had been acted by three different troupes. After the plagues of 1592–3, Shakespeare's plays were performed by his own company at The Theatre and the Curtain in Shoreditch, north of the Thames. Londoners flocked there to see the first part of Henry IV, Leonard Digges recording, "Let but Falstaff come, Hal, Poins, the rest ... and you scarce shall have a room". When the company found themselves in dispute with their landlord, they pulled The

Theatre down and used the timbers to construct the Globe Theatre, the first playhouse built by actors for actors, on the south bank of the Thames at Southwark. The Globe opened in autumn 1599, with Julius Caesar one of the first plays staged. Most of Shakespeare's greatest post-1599 plays were written for the Globe, including Hamlet, Othello, and King Lear.

After the Lord Chamberlain's Men were renamed the King's Men in 1603, they entered a special relationship with the new King James. Although the performance records are patchy, the King's Men performed seven of Shakespeare's plays at court between 1 November 1604, and 31 October 1605, including two performances of The Merchant of Venice. After 1608, they performed at the indoor Blackfriars Theatre during the winter and the Globe during the summer. The indoor setting, combined with the Jacobean fashion for lavishly staged masques, allowed Shakespeare to introduce more elaborate stage devices. In Cymbeline, for example, Jupiter descends "in thunder and lightning, sitting upon an eagle: he throws a thunderbolt. The ghosts fall on their knees."

The actors in Shakespeare's company included the famous Richard Burbage, William Kempe, Henry Condell and John Heminges. Burbage played the leading role in the first performances of many of Shakespeare's plays, including Richard III, Hamlet, Othello, and King Lear. The popular comic actor Will Kempe played the servant Peter in Romeo and Juliet and Dogberry in Much Ado About Nothing, among other characters. He was replaced around 1600 by Robert Armin, who played roles such as Touchstone in As You Like It and the fool in King Lear. In 1613, Sir Henry Wotton recorded that Henry VIII "was set forth with many extraordinary circumstances of pomp and ceremony". On 29 June, however, a cannon set fire to the thatch of the Globe and burned the theatre to the ground, an event which pinpoints the date of a Shakespeare play with rare precision.

Textual sources

In 1623, John Heminges and Henry Condell, two of Shakespeare's friends from the King's Men, published the First Folio, a collected edition of Shakespeare's plays. It contained 36 texts, including 18 printed for the first time. Many of the plays had already appeared in quarto versions—flimsy books made from sheets of paper folded twice to make four leaves. No evidence suggests that Shakespeare approved these editions, which the First Folio describes as "stol'n and surreptitious copies". Nor did Shakespeare plan or expect his works to survive in any form at all; those works likely would have faded into oblivion but for his friends' spontaneous idea, after his death, to create and publish the First Folio.

Alfred Pollard termed some of the pre-1623 versions as "bad quartos" because of their adapted, paraphrased or garbled texts, which may in places have been reconstructed from memory. Where several versions of a play survive, each differs from the other. The differences may stem from copying or printing errors, from notes by actors or audience members, or from Shakespeare's own papers. In some cases, for example, Hamlet, Troilus and Cressida, and Othello, Shakespeare could have revised the texts between the quarto and folio editions. In the case of King Lear, however, while most modern editions do conflate them, the 1623 folio version is so different from the 1608 quarto that the Oxford Shakespeare prints them both, arguing that they cannot be conflated without confusion.

Influence from neighbours in London

Ten years of research by Geoffrey Marsh (museum director) of the Victoria and Albert Museum in London may have shown that Shakespeare got many of the ideas and information for his plays, from his neighbours that he lived near in London in the late 1590s.

Geoffrey Marsh found the site of Shakespeare's house in St Helen's Church, Bishopsgate parish, at the corner of St.Helen's churchyard and Bishopsgate Street, north of the churchyard, from the records of the Leathersellers Company. Many wealthy and notable people (including Sir John Spencer and Dr. Edward Jorden and Dr. Peter Turner), with connections across Europe, lived near Shakespeare.

Poems

In 1593 and 1594, when the theatres were closed because of plague,

Shakespeare published two narrative poems on sexual themes, Venus and Adonis and The Rape of Lucrece. He dedicated them to Henry Wriothesley, Earl of Southampton. In Venus and Adonis, an innocent Adonis rejects the sexual advances of Venus; while in The Rape of Lucrece, the virtuous wife Lucrece is raped by the lustful Tarquin. Influenced by Ovid's Metamorphoses, the poems show the guilt and moral confusion that result from uncontrolled lust. Both proved popular and were often reprinted during Shakespeare's lifetime. A third narrative poem, A Lover's Complaint, in which a young woman laments her seduction by a persuasive suitor, was printed in the first edition of the Sonnets in 1609. Most scholars now accept that Shakespeare wrote A Lover's Complaint. Critics consider that its fine qualities are marred by leaden effects. The Phoenix and the Turtle, printed in Robert Chester's 1601 Love's Martyr, mourns the deaths of the legendary phoenix and his lover, the faithful turtle dove. In 1599, two early drafts of sonnets 138 and 144 appeared in The Passionate Pilgrim, published under Shakespeare's name but without his permission.

Sonnets

Published in 1609, the Sonnets were the last of Shakespeare's non-dramatic works to be printed. Scholars are not certain when each of the 154 sonnets was composed, but evidence suggests that Shakespeare wrote sonnets throughout his career for a private readership. Even before the two unauthorised sonnets appeared in The Passionate Pilgrim in 1599, Francis Meres had referred in 1598 to Shakespeare's "sugred Sonnets among his private friends". Few analysts believe that the published collection follows Shakespeare's intended sequence. He seems to have planned two contrasting series: one about uncontrollable lust for a married woman of dark complexion (the "dark lady"), and one about conflicted love for a fair young man (the "fair youth"). It remains unclear if these figures represent real individuals, or if the authorial "I" who addresses them represents Shakespeare himself, though Wordsworth believed that with the sonnets "Shakespeare unlocked his heart".

"Shall I compare thee to a summer's day?

Thou art more lovely and more temperate ..."

466

—Lines from Shakespeare's Sonnet 18.

The 1609 edition was dedicated to a "Mr. W.H.", credited as "the only begetter" of the poems. It is not known whether this was written by Shakespeare himself or by the publisher, Thomas Thorpe, whose initials appear at the foot of the dedication page; nor is it known who Mr. W.H. was, despite numerous theories, or whether Shakespeare even authorised the publication. Critics praise the Sonnets as a profound meditation on the nature of love, sexual passion, procreation, death, and time.

Style

Shakespeare's first plays were written in the conventional style of the day. He wrote them in a stylised language that does not always spring naturally from the needs of the characters or the drama. The poetry depends on extended, sometimes elaborate metaphors and conceits, and the language is often rhetorical—written for actors to declaim rather than speak. The grand speeches in Titus Andronicus, in the view of some critics, often hold up the action, for example; and the verse in The Two Gentlemen of Verona has been described as stilted.

However, Shakespeare soon began to adapt the traditional styles to his own purposes. The opening soliloquy of Richard III has its roots in the self-declaration of Vice in medieval drama. At the same time, Richard's vivid self-awareness looks forward to the soliloquies of Shakespeare's mature plays. No single play marks a change from the traditional to the freer style. Shakespeare combined the two throughout his career, with Romeo and Juliet perhaps the best example of the mixing of the styles. By the time of Romeo and Juliet, Richard II, and A Midsummer Night's Dream in the mid-1590s, Shakespeare had begun to write a more natural poetry. He increasingly tuned his metaphors and images to the needs of the drama itself.

Shakespeare's standard poetic form was blank verse, composed in iambic pentameter. In practice, this meant that his verse was usually unrhymed and consisted of ten syllables to a line, spoken with a stress on every second syllable. The blank verse of his early plays is quite different from that of his later ones. It is often beautiful, but its sentences tend to start, pause, and finish at the end of lines, with the risk of monotony. Once Shakespeare mastered traditional blank verse, he began to interrupt and vary its flow. This technique releases the new power and flexibility of the poetry in plays such as Julius Caesar and Hamlet. Shakespeare uses it, for example, to convey the turmoil in Hamlet's mind:

> Sir, in my heart there was a kind of fighting
>
> That would not let me sleep. Methought I lay
>
> Worse than the mutines in the bilboes. Rashly—
>
> And prais'd be rashness for it—let us know
>
> Our indiscretion sometimes serves us well ...
>
> —Hamlet, Act 5, Scene 2, 4–8

After Hamlet, Shakespeare varied his poetic style further, particularly in the more emotional passages of the late tragedies. The literary critic A. C. Bradley described this style as "more concentrated, rapid, varied, and, in construction, less regular, not seldom twisted or elliptical". In the last phase of his career, Shakespeare adopted many techniques to achieve these effects. These included run-on lines, irregular pauses and stops, and extreme variations in sentence structure and length. In Macbeth, for example, the language darts from one unrelated metaphor or simile to another: "was the hope drunk/ Wherein you dressed yourself?" (1.7.35–38); "... pity, like a naked new-born babe/ Striding the blast, or heaven's cherubim, hors'd/ Upon the sightless couriers of the air ..." (1.7.21–25). The listener is challenged to complete the sense. The late romances, with their shifts in time and surprising turns of plot, inspired a last poetic style in which long and short sentences are set against one another, clauses are piled up, subject and object are reversed, and words are omitted, creating an effect of spontaneity.

Shakespeare combined poetic genius with a practical sense of the theatre. Like all playwrights of the time, he dramatised stories from sources such as Plutarch and Holinshed. He reshaped each plot to create several centres of interest and to show as many sides of a narrative to the audience as possible. This strength of design ensures that a Shakespeare play can survive translation, cutting and wide interpretation without loss to its core drama. As Shakespeare's mastery grew, he gave his characters clearer and more varied motivations and distinctive patterns of speech. He preserved aspects of his earlier style in the later plays, however. In Shakespeare's late romances, he deliberately returned to a more artificial style, which emphasised the illusion of theatre.

Influence

Shakespeare's work has made a lasting impression on later theatre and literature. In particular, he expanded the dramatic potential of characterisation, plot, language, and genre. Until Romeo and Juliet, for example, romance had not been viewed as a worthy topic for tragedy. Soliloquies had been used mainly to convey information about characters or events, but Shakespeare used them to explore characters' minds. His work heavily influenced later poetry. The Romantic poets attempted to revive Shakespearean verse drama, though with little success. Critic George Steiner described all English verse dramas from Coleridge to Tennyson as "feeble variations on Shakespearean themes."

Shakespeare influenced novelists such as Thomas Hardy, William Faulkner, and Charles Dickens. The American novelist Herman Melville's soliloquies owe much to Shakespeare; his Captain Ahab in Moby-Dick is a classic tragic hero, inspired by King Lear. Scholars have identified 20,000 pieces of music linked to Shakespeare's works. These include three operas by Giuseppe Verdi, Macbeth, Otello and Falstaff, whose critical standing compares with that of the source plays. Shakespeare has also inspired many painters, including the Romantics and the Pre-Raphaelites. The Swiss Romantic artist Henry Fuseli, a friend of William Blake, even translated Macbeth into German. The psychoanalyst Sigmund Freud drew on Shakespearean psychology, in particular, that of Hamlet, for his theories of human nature.

In Shakespeare's day, English grammar, spelling, and pronunciation were less standardised than they are now, and his use of language helped shape modern English. Samuel Johnson quoted him more often than any other author in his A Dictionary of the English Language, the first serious work of its type. Expressions such as "with bated breath" (Merchant of Venice) and "a foregone conclusion" (Othello) have found their way into everyday English speech.

Works

Classification of the plays

Shakespeare's works include the 36 plays printed in the First Folio of 1623, listed according to their folio classification as comedies, histories, and tragedies. Two plays not included in the First Folio, The Two Noble Kinsmen and Pericles, Prince of Tyre, are now accepted as part of the canon, with today's scholars agreeing that Shakespeare made major contributions to the writing of both. No Shakespearean poems were included in the First Folio.

In the late 19th century, Edward Dowden classified four of the late comedies as romances, and though many scholars prefer to call them tragicomedies, Dowden's term is often used. In 1896, Frederick S. Boas coined the term "problem plays" to describe four plays: All's Well That Ends Well, Measure for Measure, Troilus and Cressida, and Hamlet. "Dramas as singular in theme and temper cannot be strictly called comedies or tragedies", he wrote. "We may, therefore, borrow a convenient phrase from the theatre of today and class them together as Shakespeare's problem plays." The term, much debated and sometimes applied to other plays, remains in use, though Hamlet is definitively classed as a tragedy. (Source: Wikipedia)

CPSIA information can be obtained
at www.ICGtesting.com
Printed in the USA
BVHW071924160919
558564BV00003B/657/P

9 789353 835620